T0183894

# Lecture Notes of the Institute for Computer Sciences, Social Informatics and Telecommunications Engineering 266

## Editorial Board

Ozgur Akan
*Middle East Technical University, Ankara, Turkey*

Paolo Bellavista
*University of Bologna, Bologna, Italy*

Jiannong Cao
*Hong Kong Polytechnic University, Hong Kong, Hong Kong*

Geoffrey Coulson
*Lancaster University, Lancaster, UK*

Falko Dressler
*University of Erlangen, Erlangen, Germany*

Domenico Ferrari
*Università Cattolica Piacenza, Piacenza, Italy*

Mario Gerla
*UCLA, Los Angeles, USA*

Hisashi Kobayashi
*Princeton University, Princeton, USA*

Sergio Palazzo
*University of Catania, Catania, Italy*

Sartaj Sahni
*University of Florida, Florida, USA*

Xuemin Sherman Shen
*University of Waterloo, Waterloo, Canada*

Mircea Stan
*University of Virginia, Charlottesville, USA*

Jia Xiaohua
*City University of Hong Kong, Kowloon, Hong Kong*

Albert Y. Zomaya
*University of Sydney, Sydney, Australia*

More information about this series at http://www.springer.com/series/8197

Phan Cong Vinh · Vangalur Alagar (Eds.)

# Context-Aware Systems and Applications, and Nature of Computation and Communication

7th EAI International Conference, ICCASA 2018
and 4th EAI International Conference, ICTCC 2018
Viet Tri City, Vietnam, November 22–23, 2018
Proceedings

Springer

*Editors*
Phan Cong Vinh
Nguyen Tat Thanh University
Ho Chi Minh City, Vietnam

Vangalur Alagar
Concordia University
Montreal, QC, Canada

ISSN 1867-8211 ISSN 1867-822X (electronic)
Lecture Notes of the Institute for Computer Sciences, Social Informatics
and Telecommunications Engineering
ISBN 978-3-030-06151-7 ISBN 978-3-030-06152-4 (eBook)
https://doi.org/10.1007/978-3-030-06152-4

Library of Congress Control Number: 2018964611

© ICST Institute for Computer Sciences, Social Informatics and Telecommunications Engineering 2019
This work is subject to copyright. All rights are reserved by the Publisher, whether the whole or part of the material is concerned, specifically the rights of translation, reprinting, reuse of illustrations, recitation, broadcasting, reproduction on microfilms or in any other physical way, and transmission or information storage and retrieval, electronic adaptation, computer software, or by similar or dissimilar methodology now known or hereafter developed.
The use of general descriptive names, registered names, trademarks, service marks, etc. in this publication does not imply, even in the absence of a specific statement, that such names are exempt from the relevant protective laws and regulations and therefore free for general use.
The publisher, the authors, and the editors are safe to assume that the advice and information in this book are believed to be true and accurate at the date of publication. Neither the publisher nor the authors or the editors give a warranty, express or implied, with respect to the material contained herein or for any errors or omissions that may have been made. The publisher remains neutral with regard to jurisdictional claims in published maps and institutional affiliations.

This Springer imprint is published by the registered company Springer Nature Switzerland AG
The registered company address is: Gewerbestrasse 11, 6330 Cham, Switzerland

# Preface

ICCASA and ICTCC 2018, the international scientific conferences for research in the field of smart computing and communication, were held during November 22–23, 2018, in Viet Tri City, Vietnam. The aim of the conferences is to provide an internationally respected forum for scientific research in the technologies and applications of smart computing and communication. These conferences provide an excellent opportunity for researchers to discuss modern approaches and techniques for smart computing systems and their applications. The proceedings of ICCASA and ICTCC 2018 are published by Springer in the series *Lecture Notes of the Institute for Computer Sciences, Social Informatics and Telecommunications Engineering* (LNICST; indexed by DBLP, EI, Google Scholar, Scopus, Thomson ISI).

For this seventh edition of ICCASA and fourth edition of ICTCC, repeating the success of the previous year, the Program Committee received submissions from 11 countries and each paper was reviewed by at least three expert reviewers. We chose 20 papers after intensive discussions held among the Program Committee members. We really appreciate the excellent reviews and lively discussions of the Program Committee members and external reviewers in the review process. This year we had four prominent invited speakers, Prof. Zuriati Ahmad Zukarnain from Universiti Putra Malaysia in Malaysia, Prof. Manik Sharma from DAV University Jalandhar in India, Prof. Akhilesh K. Sharma from Manipal University Jaipur in India, and Prof. Waralak V. Siricharoen from Silpakorn University in Thailand.

ICCASA and ICTCC 2018 were jointly organized by The European Alliance for Innovation (EAI), Hung Vuong University in Phu Tho Province (HVU), and Nguyen Tat Thanh University (NTTU). These conferences could not have been organized without the strong support from the staff members of the three organizations. We would especially like to thank Prof. Imrich Chlamtac (University of Trento and Create-NET), Kristina Lappyova (EAI), and Martin Karbovanec (EAI) for their great help in organizing the conferences. We also appreciate the gentle guidance and help from Prof. Nguyen Manh Hung, Chairman and Rector of NTTU, and Dr. Trinh The Truyen, Rector of HVU.

November 2018

Phan Cong Vinh
Vangalur Alagar

# Organization

## Steering Committee

Imrich Chlamtac (Chair)    University of Trento, Italy
Phan Cong Vinh             Nguyen Tat Thanh University, Vietnam
Thanos Vasilakos           Kuwait University, Kuwait

## Organizing Committee

### Honorary General Chairs

Trinh The Truyen           Hung Vuong University, Vietnam
Nguyen Manh Hung           Nguyen Tat Thanh University, Vietnam

### General Chair

Phan Cong Vinh             Nguyen Tat Thanh University, Vietnam

### Program Chairs

Vangalur Alagar            Concordia University, Canada
Emil Vassev                Lero at University of Limerick, Ireland
Hamid Mcheick              University of Quebec at Chicoutimi, Canada

### Publications Chair

Phan Cong Vinh             Nguyen Tat Thanh University, Vietnam

### Publicity and Social Media Chair

Do Tung                    Hung Vuong University, Vietnam

### Workshop Chair

Emil Vassev                University of Limerick, Ireland

### Sponsorship and Exhibits Chairs

Nguyen Tai Nang            Hung Vuong University, Vietnam
Bach Long Giang            Nguyen Tat Thanh University, Vietnam

### Local Chairs

Nguyen Hung Cuong          Hung Vuong University, Vietnam
Do Nguyen Anh Thu          Nguyen Tat Thanh University, Vietnam

**Web Chair**

Thai Thi Thanh Thao            Nguyen Tat Thanh University, Vietnam

## Technical Program Committee

| | |
|---|---|
| Abayomi-Alli Adebayo | Federal University of Agriculture, Nigeria |
| Abdur Rakib | The University of the West of England, UK |
| Akhilesh Sharma | Manipal University, India |
| Amol Patwardhan | Louisiana State University, USA |
| Aniruddha Bhattacharjya | Narasaraopeta Engineering College, India |
| Areerat Songsakulwattana | Rangsit University, Thailand |
| Asad Masood Khattak | Zayed University, UAE |
| Charu Gandhi | Jaypee Institute of Information Technology, India |
| Chernyi Sergei | Admiral Makarov State University of Maritime and Inland Shipping, Russia |
| Chia-Hung Hung | Missouri University of Science and Technology, USA |
| Chien-Chih Yu | National ChengChi University, Taiwan |
| Chintan Bhatt | Charotar University of Science and Technology, India |
| David Sundaram | The University of Auckland, New Zealand |
| Do Trang | Institute for High Performance Computing, A*STAR, Singapore |
| Doan Van Thang | Ho Chi Minh City University of Industry, Vietnam |
| François Siewe | De Montfort University, UK |
| Gabrielle Peko | The University of Auckland, New Zealand |
| Giacomo Cabri | University of Modena and Reggio Emilia, Italy |
| Govardhan Aliseri | Jawaharlal Nehru Technological University Hyderabad, India |
| Hafiz Mahfooz Ul Haque | University of Lahore, Pakistan |
| Hamid Mcheick | University of Quebec at Chicoutimi, Canada |
| Huynh Trung Hieu | Ho Chi Minh City University of Industry, Vietnam |
| Huynh Xuan Hiep | Can Tho University, Vietnam |
| Issam Damaj | The American University of Kuwait, Kuwait |
| Jamus Collier | University of Bremen, Germany |
| Jeonghwan Gwak | Seoul National University Hospital, South Korea |
| Krishna Asawa | Jaypee Institute of Information Technology, India |
| Krishna Kambhampaty | North Dakota State University, USA |
| Kurt Geihs | University of Kassel, Germany |
| Le Hong Anh | University of Mining and Geology, Vietnam |
| Le Tuan Anh | Thu Dau Mot University, Vietnam |
| Le Xuan Khoa | Ulster University, UK |
| Manik Sharma | DAV University, India |
| Manmeet Mahinderjit Singh | Universiti Sains Malaysia, Malaysia |
| Moeiz Miraoui | University of Quebec, Canada |
| Mohamed Fayad | San Jose State University, USA |

| Muhammad Athar Javed Sethi | University of Engineering and Technology Peshawar, Pakistan |
| Muhammad Fahad Khan | Federal Urdu University of Arts, Science and Technology, Pakistan |
| Nguyen Ha Huy Cuong | Quang Nam University, Vietnam |
| Nguyen Hung Cuong | Hung Vuong University, Vietnam |
| Nguyen Kim Quoc | Nguyen Tat Thanh University, Vietnam |
| Nguyen Phu Binh | Victoria University of Wellington, New Zealand |
| Nguyen Phuoc Loc | Sunflower Soft Co., Vietnam |
| Nguyen Quoc Huy | Saigon University, Vietnam |
| Ondrej Krejcar | University of Hradec Kralove, Czech Republic |
| Pham Quoc Cuong | Ho Chi Minh City University of Technology, Vietnam |
| Phan Tan Quoc | Saigon University, Vietnam |
| Phan Ngoc Hoang | Ba Ria-Vung Tau University, Vietnam |
| Phayung Meesad | King Mongkut's University of Technology North Bangkok, Thailand |
| Prasanalakshmi Balaji | Professional Group of Institutions, India |
| Prashant Vats | Career Point University, India |
| Rohin Mittal | State University of New York at Buffalo, USA |
| S. Balakrishnan | Anna University, India |
| S. Satyanarayana | KL University, India |
| Shahed Mohammadi Dehnavi | Ragheb Isfahani Higher Education Institute, Iran |
| Shanmugam BalaMurugan | Mindnotix Technologies, India |
| Tran Huu Tam | University of Kassel, Germany |
| Tran Vinh Phuoc | Thu Dau Mot University, Vietnam |
| Van The Thanh | Ho Chi Minh City University of Food Industry, Vietnam |
| Vijayakumar Ponnusamy | SRM Institute of Science and Technology, Chennai, India |
| Vijender Kumar Solanki | Institute of Technology and Science, Ghaziabad, India |
| Vinh Truong Hoang | Ho Chi Minh City Open University, Vietnam |
| Waralak V. Siricharoen | Silpakorn University, Thailand |
| WenBin Li | Missouri University of Science and Technology, USA |
| Zhu Huibiao | East China Normal University, China |

# · Contents

## ICTCC 2018

ICCASA 2018

# Formal Context Representation and Calculus for Context-Aware Computing

Ammar Alsaig$^{(\boxtimes)}$ ⓘD, Vangalur Alagar, and Nematollaah Shiri

Concordia University, Montreal, QC, Canada
{a_alsaig,alagar,shiri}@encs.concordia.ca

**Abstract.** Context is a rich concept that is mostly understood and used with different representations and interpretations in many different fields. This variety of usage adds both richness and vagueness, thus creating more complexity to comprehension, interpretation, and reasoning with contexts. As pervasive computing technology becomes more and more intrusive there is a need to construct formally verifiable context-aware computing environment, in which human dignity is preserved through safety, security, and privacy. These features cannot be ensured unless context notion is formalized, both in representation and reasoning. Motivated by this concern this paper introduces a formal context representation and a context calculus which can be used to build context models for many applications.

**Keywords:** Context modeling · Context-awareness
Formal representation · Reasoning

## 1  Introduction

The term "context" has been around for centuries, and consists of the ancient Greek words "con" (meaning "together") and "texere" (meaning "to weave"). Context provides the circumstances where an event, statement, or idea occurs, and help to understand and evaluate the occurrence. Context has been the subject of numerous studies by philosophers, psychologists [7], and linguists [6]. Since early 1980s, the importance of context has been recognized in different research areas including information retrieval, knowledge representation and expert systems, mechanized formal reasoning in AI, and analysis of computer programs, most notably by Weyhrauch [27], McCarthy [19], Akman and Surav [1], and Giunchiglia [14]. Dowley et al. [10] was the first one to propose the notion of *dimensions* for contexts after recognizing that "hidden contexts" add *dimensions*

This work was supported in part by grants from the Natural Sciences and Engineering Research Council (NSERC) of Canada. The first author is supported by a scholarship from the Saudi Arabian Government.

© ICST Institute for Computer Sciences, Social Informatics and Telecommunications Engineering 2019
Published by Springer Nature Switzerland AG 2019. All Rights Reserved

P. Cong Vinh and V. Alagar (Eds.): ICCASA 2018/ICTCC 2018, LNICST 266, pp. 3–13, 2019.
https://doi.org/10.1007/978-3-030-06152-4_1

to expressions. Much later in 1994, Schilit et al. [22] mentioned the necessity of "dimensions" for "context-aware computing" in system development. However, they neither proposed a "dimension-based" representation nor developed a reasoning framework. Almost 10 years later, Wan [25] proposed a context representation using dimensions and tags and used them to introduce context as a first class citizen in Lucid programming language extended with intensional semantics. The formal semantics of intentional programming and architectures for context-aware computing were also discussed by Wan [3,24].

In this paper, we pick up these notions, formalize, generalize and enrich them in three tiers. In Tier 1 we define *Context Schema*, in Tier 2 we derive *Typed Context Schemas*, and in Tier 3 we formalize *Contexts* as a set of families of *Context Instances* generated from Typed Schemas. For all the three tiers a uniform representation is used, under set theoretical setting. We defined operations in Tier 1 and show they are inherited in successive tiers, and in particular how it can be enriched in Tier 3. Our approach, because of its generality and simplicity, has the potential for generating different families of contexts for different applications within an application domain.

## 2   Related Work

The literature on context is vast and diverse and a comprehensive survey of the topic is beyond the scope of this paper. In what follows we review research most relevant to our work on context modeling and formalism. We group the current work on context into six categories detailed as follows:

1. *Interdisciplinary Emphasis:* The nature of diversity and interdisciplinary research can be seen in LNAI publication series "Modeling and Using Context", proceedings of CONTEXT International conference being held from 1997 [18]. More recent collection of papers in [4] only reinforces the practice of a variety of mostly informal notations and views in this interdisciplinary research on context.
2. *Human Computer Interface Group (HCI):*  Early in 2001 the works of Dey et al. [8] and Winograd [28] in HCI are based on intuitive ad-hoc notations, bordering on vagueness and informality. These papers bring out also the disagreement within this group in conceptualizing and modeling contexts.
3. *Languages:* The works of Dowley et al. [10], Sato et al. [21], and Alagar et al. [3] use contexts at different levels of abstraction in intensional and functional programming languages. Sato et al. uses a formal context representation based on relational semantics while Sato et al. uses $\lambda$ calculus notation.
4. *AI and Reasoning:* The works of Weyhrauch [27], McCarthy [19,20], Guha [16], Akman and Surav [1], Shoham [23], and Giunchiglia [14] are some of the early ground-breaking works on logic of contexts and context-based reasoning. None of them use any formal method to represent contexts.

5. *Pervasive Computing:* Based on the survey papers [9,11], it is evident that the notion of context in pervasive computing is still mostly ad-hoc. The formalisms attempted by a few are non-rigorous, either domain-specific or application dependent [5]. Besides, there is no consensus on what a context should be and how it should be represented for pervasive computing application domain. While formal representation and reasoning procedures are quite important to reason about pervasive computing applications that involve human safety and privacy, they are not emphasized in these works.

6. *Context-aware Computing:* The introduction of dimensions by Dowley et al. [10] to deal with hidden contexts in intensional programming languages perhaps influenced Schilit et al. [22] to incorporate it in developing context-aware systems, although there is no report such an attempt was made. Later on, the context representation was formalized by Wan [25] and subsequently used in building context-aware systems [3,24]. They also developed a context calculus, and showed how to reuse their context toolkit in different applications such as privacy and security enforcement [2].

Against this background we claim our contribution in this paper is both novel and new. In a computerized system context must capture both *internal* and *external* settings. Since, the external world (environment) is composed of several dimensions and the knowledge to execute different operations within the system will come different "worlds", context is "multi-dimensional". The work of Wan [25], which conceptualized this notion of context through an aggregation of *<dimension, tag>* pairs had the restriction that each dimension occurs once in the aggregation, and with each dimension only one atomic value is associated. In our theory discussed below, context schemas, not just context instances, are defined, thereby the restrictions in [25] are removed.

## 3  Tier 1: Context Schema Representation and Calculus

Context schema (CS) is abstract, and its generality gives flexibility for a practical system designer to choose attributes to be associated with a dimension. Once we fix the (non-empty) set of dimensions $\mathbb{D}$ and the (non-empty) set of attributes $\mathbb{A}$, the set $S_{\mathscr{C}}(\mathbb{D}, \mathbb{A})$ of all CSs is fixed. Formally, a CS over the pair $(\mathbb{D}, \mathbb{A})$ is the set of pairs $\mathscr{C} = \{d : A_d \mid d \in \mathbb{D} \wedge A_d \subseteq \mathbb{A}\}$.

*Example 1.* To define a conference context schema we first define the dimension set $\mathbb{D} = \{Date, Time, Location\}$, and attribute set $\mathbb{A} = \{a_1, a_2, a_3, a_4\}$. Next the conference context schema can be defined as $\mathscr{C}_{\mathrm{conf}} = \{Date : \{a_1, a_2\}, Time : \{a_3\}, Location : \{a_4\}\}$.

In order to access information of an already constructed context schema, two functions are defined. The "DIM" function extracts the set of dimensions in a context schema, and the "ATT" function extracts the set of attributes associated with a dimension in a context schema. Formally, $DIM : S_{\mathscr{C}} \rightarrow \mathbb{P}(\mathbb{D})$, $ATT : \mathbb{D} \times S_{\mathscr{C}} \rightarrow \mathbb{P}(\mathbb{A})$, such that $DIM(\mathscr{C}) = \{d \mid < d, A_d > \in \mathscr{C}\}$, and $ATT(d, \mathscr{C}) = A_d$.

*Example 2.* For the "conference context schema" introduced in Example 1 $DIM(\mathscr{C}_{\text{conf}}) = \{Date, Time, Location\}$, $ATT(Date, \mathscr{C}_{\text{conf}}) = \{a_1, a_2\}$, $ATT(Time, \mathscr{C}_{\text{conf}}) = \{a_3\}$, and $ATT(Location, \mathscr{C}_{\text{conf}}) = \{a_4\}$.

For the sake of completeness we include "Null Context Schema" and "Full Context Schema" in out theory. If $DIM(\mathscr{C}) = \phi$, $A_d = \phi$ we get the Null Context Schema $\mathscr{C}_\phi$. If $DIM(\mathscr{C}) = \mathbb{D}$, $A_d = \mathbb{A}$ we get "Full Context Schema". McCarthy [19] postulated that "every context is contained in an outer context". In general, a context can contain many inner contexts. However, no formal definition for "containment relationship" exists because of lack of formal representation. Using our formalism we can formally define containment relationship ($\sqsubseteq$) over the set $S_\mathscr{C}(\mathbb{D}, \mathbb{A})$. If $\mathscr{C} = \{< d, A_d > \,|\, d \in \mathbb{D} \,\wedge\, A_d \subseteq \mathbb{A}\}$ and $\mathscr{C}' = \{< d', A_d' > \,|\, d' \in \mathbb{D} \,\wedge\, A_d' \subseteq \mathbb{A}\}$ are two Context Schemas in $S_\mathscr{C}(\mathbb{D}, \mathbb{A})$, we say that $\mathscr{C}' \sqsubseteq \mathscr{C}$ if $DIM(\mathscr{C}') \subseteq DIM(\mathscr{C})$, and $\forall\, d' \in \mathscr{C}' \bullet ATT(d', \mathscr{C}') \subseteq ATT(d', \mathscr{C})$. The relation $\sqsubseteq$ on the set $S_\mathscr{C}(\mathbb{D}, \mathbb{A})$ is a *partial order* because it is *reflexive*, *anti-symmetric*, and *transitive*. Hence, $\langle S_\mathscr{C}(\mathbb{D}, \mathbb{A}), \sqsubseteq \rangle$ is a *partially ordered set* (poset).

*Example 3.* Consider the context schema $\mathscr{C}'_{conf} = \{Date : \{a_1\}, Time : \{a3\}\}$ defined on the same set of dimensions and attributes as in Example 1. Because $DIM(\mathscr{C}'_{conf}) \subseteq DIM(\mathscr{C}_{conf})$, and $ATT(d', \mathscr{C}'_{conf})) \subseteq ATT(d', \mathscr{C}_{conf}))$, for all $d' \in DIM(\mathscr{C}'_{conf})$ it follows that $\mathscr{C}'_{conf} \sqsubseteq \mathscr{C}_{conf}$.

## 3.1   Operations and Calculus

Based on containment relation $\sqsubseteq$ we define equality ($=$). For two context schemas $\mathscr{C}$ and $\mathscr{C}'$, if $\mathscr{C} \sqsubseteq \mathscr{C}'$, and $\mathscr{C}' \sqsubseteq \mathscr{C}$, then $\mathscr{C} = \mathscr{C}'$. In order to relate and deal with every pair of schemas in the poset $\langle S_\mathscr{C}(D, A), \sqsubseteq \rangle$ we introduce the two operators "join" ($\oplus$) and "meet" ($\odot$). The "join" of two context schemas produces the "smallest" context schema that contains those two context schemas. The "meet" of two schemas produces the "largest" context schema that is contained in those two schemas. These operations, when implemented as part of context tool kit in an application will enable "exporting knowledge and reasoning" across contexts. Formally,

$$\oplus : S_\mathscr{C}(\mathbb{D}, \mathbb{A}) \times S_\mathscr{C}(\mathbb{D}, \mathbb{A}) \to S_\mathscr{C}(\mathbb{D}, \mathbb{A})$$

$$\mathscr{C} \oplus \mathscr{C}' = \{< d'', A_{d''} > \,|\, d'' \in DIM(\mathscr{C}) \cup DIM(\mathscr{C}') \,\wedge$$
$$A_{d''} = \{ATT(d'', \mathscr{C}) \cup ATT(d'', \mathscr{C}')\}\} \quad \blacksquare$$

$$\odot : S_\mathscr{C}(\mathbb{D}, \mathbb{A}) \times S_\mathscr{C}(\mathbb{D}, \mathbb{A}) \to S_\mathscr{C}(\mathbb{D}, \mathbb{A})$$

$$\mathscr{C} \odot \mathscr{C}' = \{< d'', A_{d''} > \,|\, d'' \in DIM(\mathscr{C}) \cap DIM(\mathscr{C}') \,\wedge$$
$$A_{d''} = \{ATT(d'', \mathscr{C}) \cap ATT(d'', \mathscr{C}')\}\} \quad \blacksquare$$

It is easy to observe that for any three schemas $\mathscr{C}_1, \mathscr{C}_2, \mathscr{C}_3$ in $\{S_\mathscr{C}(D, A), \sqsubseteq\}$, $\oplus$ and $\odot$ operators satisfy *absorption, commutative, associative*, and *distributive* properties. In particular, $\oplus$ is distributive over $\odot$ and vise versa:

- $\mathscr{C}_1 \oplus (\mathscr{C}_2 \odot \mathscr{C}_3) = (\mathscr{C}_1 \oplus \mathscr{C}_2) \odot (\mathscr{C}_1 \oplus \mathscr{C}_3)$
- $\mathscr{C}_1 \odot (\mathscr{C}_2 \oplus \mathscr{C}_3) = (\mathscr{C}_1 \odot \mathscr{C}_2) \oplus (\mathscr{C}_1 \odot \mathscr{C}_3)$

*Example 4.* Applying the join and meet operations on the two conference context schemas $\mathscr{C}_{conf}$ and $\mathscr{C}'_{conf}$ in Examples 1 and 3 we get two new context schemas:

$$\mathscr{C}_{conf} \oplus \mathscr{C}'_{conf} = \{Date : \{a_1, a_2\}, Time : \{a_3\}, Location : \{a_4\}\}$$
$$\mathscr{C}_{conf} \odot \mathscr{C}'_{conf} = \{Date : \{a_1\}, Time : \{a_3\}\}$$

## 3.2 Context Schema Lattice

With the join and meet operations on the poset $\langle S_\mathscr{C}, \sqsubseteq \rangle$ the set $\mathscr{L} = (S_\mathscr{C}, \sqsubseteq, \oplus, \odot)$ is a lattice [15]. In particular, the lattice $\mathscr{L}$ is also *closed* and *distributive*. It is closed because its minimum element is the null context schema and the maximum element is the context schema composed with all dimensions in set $\mathbb{D}$ and all attributes of $\mathbb{A}$ associated across the dimensions. It is distributive because for $x, y, z \in \mathscr{L}$, we can verify the two properties: (1) $(x \odot y) \oplus (x \odot z) = x \odot (y \oplus z)$, and (2) $(x \oplus y) \odot (x \oplus z) = x \oplus (y \odot z)$. Hence $\mathscr{L}(\mathbb{D}, \mathbb{A}) = (S_\mathscr{C}(\mathbb{D}, \mathbb{A}), \oplus, \odot, \sqsubseteq)$ is a complete lattice. These properties have enormous consequence on the system level. First, when the set $(\mathbb{D}, \mathbb{A})$ is fixed, the set of all context schemas in the lattice structure is closed with respect to the join and meet operations. Consequently, no typed context and thus context instances (defined in the later sections) are "left unaccountable". That means, we have a "closed world" of families of context instances and the knowledge they enclose. This closed world property fulfills the requirement of "sufficient completeness of actions in contexts" for ensuring safety and privacy properties at system execution stage. The distributive property enables "simplification" of expressions that involve context instances and hence the evaluation of "predicates" that need to be evaluated at context instances. In the rest of the discussion we agree that $\mathbb{D}, \mathbb{A}$ is fixed and simply use the notation $S_\mathscr{C}$ for context schema and $\mathscr{L}$ for the complete lattice.

# 4 Tier 2: Typed Context Schema Representation and Calculus

Typed Context Schema (TCS) is a context schema in which attributes are associated with types. Each attribute is typed in the sense that it has a domain of values with respect to the type associated with it. Representation and calculus of schemas in TCS are inherited from the un-typed schemas defined in Tier 1.

## 4.1   Typed Context Schema Representation

Let $\mathbb{T} = \{T_1, T_2, ..., T_n\}$ denote a finite set of types such that for each type $T_x \in \mathbb{T}$ there exists a pair $<V_x, OP_x>$, where $V_x$ is a "maximal" set of values, and $OP_x$ denotes a set of operations allowed on the set $V_x$. By "maximal" we mean (1) $V_x$ does not overlap with the set $V_y$ of values of any other type $T_y \in \mathbb{T}$, and (2) if $V'_x$ is any other set containing the values of $T_x$ then $V'_x \subset V_x$. A type assignment to attributes in $\mathbb{A}$ is a mapping (a finite function) $M : \mathbb{A} \to \mathbb{T}$ that associates a unique type for every attribute in $\mathbb{A}$. We denote the set of all such type assignments by $\mathbb{A}^\mathbb{T}$. Two mappings $M_1, M_2 \in \mathbb{A}^\mathbb{T}$ are *equal* only if $M_1(a) = M_2(a)$ for every $a \in \mathbb{A}$. It is possible that two mappings $M_1$ and $M_2$ are different while they could have some common attributes. Formally, with respect to $M \in \mathbb{A}^\mathbb{T}$, the typed version of context schema $\mathscr{C}$, denoted as $\mathscr{C}^M$, is $\mathscr{C}^M = \{<d, A_d^M>|d \in DIM(\mathscr{C}), A_d^M = \{a^{M(a)}|a \in A_d\}\}$.

*Example 5.* Let $\mathbb{D} = \{d_1, d_2\}$, and $\mathbb{A} = \{a_1, a_2, a_3\}$. A context schema $\mathscr{C}_1$ over $\mathbb{D}$ and $\mathbb{A}$ is $\mathscr{C}_1 = \{d_1 : \{a_1, a_2\}, d_2 : \{a_2, a_3\}\}$. We emphasize that any standard or abstract data type may be associated to an attribute, and more than one attribute may have the same type. As an illustration, consider the set of types such that $\mathbb{T} = \{Int, Char, Range\}$ where $Int$ and $Char$ are the standard Integer and Character types. Assume that $Range$ type has the set of operations $\{=, After, Before, Lowest, Highest\}$, and has the domain of values $[1 \cdots 10]$. Let $M_1 = \{a_1 \to Int, a_2 \to Char, a_3 \to Range\}$ and $M_2 = \{a_1 \to Int, a_2 \to Int, a_3 \to Char\}$ be two mappings. The typed attribute sets corresponding to these mappings are $\{a_1^{Int}, a_2^{Char}, a_3^{Range}\}$, and $\{a_1^{Int}, a_2^{Int}, a_3^{Char}\}$. Thus, the two distinct typed schemas are

$$\mathscr{C}_1^{M_1} = \{d_1 : \{a_1^{Int}, a_2^{Char}\}, d_2 : \{a_2^{Char}, a_3^{Range}\}\}$$

$$\mathscr{C}_1^{M_2} = \{d_1 : \{a_1^{Int}, a_2^{Int}\}, d_2 : \{a_2^{Int}, a_3^{Char}\}\}$$

Notice that $\mathscr{C}_1^{M_1} \neq \mathscr{C}_1^{M_2}$ because of the different type assignment $M_1$ and $M_2$.

Both schema calculus and lattice definition are extended to $S_{\mathscr{C}M}$, the family of schemas that have the same type. Schema operations that are defined earlier are well-defined only within each family. That is, operations are not extended across families of typed schemas. Thus, the operations $\mathscr{C}_1^{M_1} \oplus \mathscr{C}_1^{M_2}$, $\mathscr{C}_1^{M_1} \odot \mathscr{C}_1^{M_2}$ are not defined since $M_1 \neq M_2$. However, for typed context $\mathscr{C}_3^{M_1} = \{d_2 : \{a_1^{Int}\}\}$ we can define $\mathscr{C}_1^{M_1} \oplus \mathscr{C}_3^{M_1}$ and $\mathscr{C}_1^{M_1} \odot \mathscr{C}_3^{M_1}$. The family of context schema $S_{\mathscr{C}M}(\mathbb{D}, \mathbb{A})$ with join and meet operators is a complete typed lattice $\mathscr{L}(\mathbb{D}, \mathbb{A})^M$. This lattice includes all possible context schemas of type $M$. In addition to the schema operations it may be possible to define additional operations induced by the operators associated with type $T$ induced by mapping $M$. We emphasize that if $\alpha = |\mathbb{A}^\mathbb{T}|$ then there are potentially $\alpha$ mappings, each associating every attribute of $\mathbb{A}$ to a type in $\mathbb{T}$. Consequently, from one schema $\mathscr{C} \in S_{\mathscr{C}}(\mathbb{D}, \mathbb{A})$ we can generate $\alpha$ different typed schemas. Thus, for a fixed set of dimensions/attributes set $(D, A)$ we can generate $\alpha \times \beta$ typed schemas where $\beta = |S_{\mathscr{C}}(\mathbb{D}, \mathbb{A})|$. As an illustration, for a set of dimensions $\mathbb{D} = \{d_1, d_2\}$ and a set of attributes

$\mathbb{A} = \{a_1, a_2\}$, let $\mathscr{L}$ be a context schema lattice that includes the set of context schemas $S_{\mathscr{C}} = \{\mathscr{C}_\phi, \{d_1 : \{a_1\}\}, \{d_2 : \{a_2\}\}, \{d_1 : \{a_1\}, d_2 : \{a_2\}\}\}$. Assuming that we have applied $M_1$ and $M_2$ on all contexts in $S_{\mathscr{C}}$ to construct the two distinct typed schema types $S_{\mathscr{C} M_1}$ and $S_{\mathscr{C} M_2}$. From these we can construct two lattices $\mathscr{L}^{M_1}$ and $\mathscr{L}^{M_2}$, which are different typed versions of the general context schema lattice $\mathscr{L}$.

# 5 Tier 3: Context Instance Representation and Calculus

In all practical applications [11,17] the term "context" has been used as "meta information" annotating "certain scenarios" or "happenings". This is achieved by associating "values" (also called "tags") to "dimensions". In our theory we arrive at such "contexts" as "instances" of context schemas. The rationale is to provide a more abstract foundation from which we can generate several "families" of context instances from each typed schema. The advantages include (1) levels of abstractions to conceptualize and manipulate schemas and instances, (2) provide a strong typing for attributes, and (3) achieve a potentially infinite number of context instances corresponding to each "family of typed contexts". This rigorous and disciplined theory will enable the correct development of context toolkit and promote reuse for ubiquitous computing applications.

## 5.1 Context Instance Representation

A Context Instance (CI) is an instantiated TCS in the sense that the attribute names in a TCS are substituted by values from the associated type domain. Hereafter we refer to context instance as context. To formalize, we start with one $\mathscr{C}^M$ be TCS of the lattice $S(\mathbb{D}, \mathbb{A})^M$, and use the substitution notation $[x/v]$ to mean that $v$ is substituted for $x$. Let $\theta$ be a substitution function that assigns to each typed attribute $a^T$ a value from the domain $V$ of values associated with $T$. By a substitution $\theta : \mathscr{C}^M \rightarrow I_1(\mathscr{C}^M)$, we get an instance $I_\theta(\mathscr{C}^M)$ for the typed context schema $\mathscr{C}^M$, where $DIM(I_\theta(\mathscr{C}^M)) = DIM(\mathscr{C}^M), \forall \ < d : A_d^T \ni \in \mathscr{C}^M, \exists \ < d : val^V \ni \in I_\theta(\mathscr{C}^M), val^V = \{[a_i\theta/v_i] \mid v_i \in V\}$. That is, from each node (schema) in $\mathscr{L}(\mathbb{D}, \mathbb{A})$ we can generate a context instance for a fixed substitution. Because an attribute can be substituted by any value from its associated type domain, for each type assignment to an attribute we get a family of contexts generated from one node in $\mathscr{L}(\mathbb{D}, \mathbb{A})$. Therefore, in addition to schema operations we can introduce the operations of the associated type to contexts within a family.

*Example 6.* Let $\theta_1 = \{a_1/1, a2/b, a3/[1-3]\}$. By applying $\theta_1$ on $\mathscr{C}_1^{M_1}$ in Example 5 we get one context $I_1(\mathscr{C}_1^{M_1}) = \{d_1 : [1, \text{``}b\text{''}], d_2 : [\text{``}b\text{''}, [1-3]]\}$. By applying the substitution $\theta_2 = \{a_1/100, a2/e, a3/[2-4]\}$ to $\mathscr{C}_1^{M_1}$, another instance is derived $I_2(\mathscr{C}_1^{M_1}) = \{d_1 : [100, \text{``}e\text{''}], d_2 : [\text{``}e\text{''}, [2-4]]\}$. When $\theta_3 = \{a_1/10, a_2/20, a_3/c\}$ is applied to $\mathscr{C}_1^{M_2}$ we get the new instance $I_3(\mathscr{C}_1^{M_2}) = \{d_1 : [10, 20], d_2 : [20, \text{``}c\text{''}]\}$ of type $M_2$. A noteworthy remark is that operational consistency exists only for contexts within each family.

# 6   Modeling Example

Many different adhoc notations for modeling contexts can be found in [18]. From among them we have chosen "paper submission context" that has been modeled graphically using contextual graphs [13]. This example has been also used in [12]. The actors in "paper submission" process are "publisher, editor, author, and reviewer". They share some activities like "canceling, submitting, checking". However, each actor is independent with respect to many other activities. For instance, editor can edit a paper, but cannot reject a paper, only a reviewer can. We show in the following steps how this context example can be formally represented using our 3-tier context representation. Through this case study the flexibility and generality provided in our model are highlighted (Fig. 1).

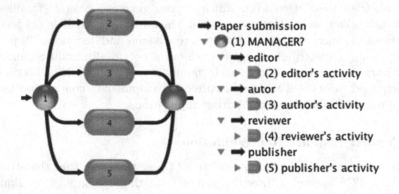

**Fig. 1.** Snapshot of the paper submission example in [13]

**Step 1.** We develop the context schema after identifying a set of dimensions, a set of attributes set, and a set of types from the graphical model. Each actor has information such as "name", "date-of-last-login", thus we find "Info" dimension is necessary. An actor also has "unique activities" and "common activities" shared among all types of actors. Therefore, the two dimensions "Unique", and "Common" should be included in our model. Therefore, the set of dimensions for our model is $\mathbb{D} = \{Info, Unique, Common\}$. The attributes of each dimension can be identified by the information that a dimension holds. "Info" dimension for instance, holds the "name", "lastlogindate" attributes. These attributes can simply be named anything, but meaningful names are used to make attributes readable and comprehensible. Based on example, each author has a list of unique activities, and a list of common activities. Therefore, both dimensions "Unique" and "Common" may have one or more attribute. For the sake of simplicity let us assume they have single attributes $act\_common$, and $act\_unique$. Thus, the set of attributes for our model is $\mathbb{A} = \{name, lastlogindate, act\_common, act\_unique\}$. The types can be customized/user defined, or can be basic types like integer and string. The information in our attributes are either string, integer, or list of a generic type. Therefore, we define the set of types $\mathbb{T} = \{string,$ $date, common, editor, reviewer, publisher, author\}$. The domain of values and operations for each type can be defined: (1) *string*: operations:$\{concat,$ $intersect\}$, domain: set of alphanumeric values; (2) *integer*: operations: $\{+, -\}$, domain: $(date)$; (3) *common* : operations: $\{before, after, add, remove\}$, domain: list of common activities; (4) *editor* : operations: $\{before, after, add, remove\}$, domain: list of unique activities for editor; (5) *reviewer* : operations: $\{before, after, add, remove\}$, domain: list of unique activities for reviewer; (6) *publisher* : operations: $\{before, after, add, remove\}$, domain: list of unique activities for publisher; (7) *author* : operations: $\{before, after, add, remove\}$, domain: list of unique activities for author. Based on the above choice the "Paper Submission Context Schema" is defined as

$$\mathscr{C}_{PS} = \{Info : \{name, lastlogindate\}, Unique : \{activities\}, Common :$$
$$\{activities\}\}.$$

**Step 2.** We assign types to attributes and generate typed schemas. The above schema is general to all types of actors. The types are assigned as below:

$$\mathscr{C}_{PS}^{edi} = \{Info : \{name^{string}, lastlogindate^{date}\}, Unique : \{activities^{editor}\},$$
$$Common : \{activities^{common}\}\}$$

$$\mathscr{C}_{PS}^{rev} = \{Info : \{name^{string}, lastlogindate^{date}\}, Unique : \{activities^{reviewer}\},$$
$$Common : \{activities^{common}\}\}$$

$$\mathscr{C}_{PS}^{pub} = \{Info : \{name^{string}, lastlogindate^{date}\}, Unique : \{activities^{publisher}\},$$
$$Common : \{activities^{common}\}\}$$

$$\mathscr{C}_{PS}^{aut} = \{Info : \{name^{string}, lastlogindate^{date}\}, Unique : \{activities^{author}\},$$
$$Common : \{activities^{common}\}\}$$

**Step 3.** We generate context instances from the typed schema. In this level values are "substituted" to attributes. For instance, an editor instance can be $\mathscr{C}_{PS}^{edi} = \{Info : \{$"Jhon Dazer", "$2017 - 05 - 04$"$\}, Common : \{[submit,$ $cancel, delete]\}, Unique : \{[edit, submit\_notes, contact\_publisher]\}$. We can generate a family of instances for each type assignment.

# 7 Conclusion

The three tier approach introduced in this paper generalizes previous attempts for dimension-based context representation [3, 25, 26], and enriches context calculus. Our approach is general, expressive, and flexible. Whereas the three tiers provide generality through abstraction levels, within tiers 2 and 3 we achieve regularity and extensionality. For certain types, such as "categorical types", categories can be incrementally defined in order to suit the needs of specific application in tier 3. We achieve generating a large number of specialized contexts and can keep track of them using the family structure. Consequently, context calculus remain formal and correct with respect to operations associated with types. It promotes a disciplined approach to generating contexts that are correct with respect to domain semantics, because the choice of dimensions, attributes, and their types are essentially guided by domain semantics. As illustrated in Sect. 6 our formal approach can generate all meaningful contexts, whereas in informal approaches, such as graphical notation, it is possible to identify contexts that are not meaningful. Consequently context calculus implementation based on our formalism will be type-correct, leading to dependable toolkit that can be reused. We are currently working to explore of the algebraic structure of context families, as well as integrating contexts with Datalog programs for contextual reasoning. We are currently working on a reasoning system that will serve to infer new facts from a knowledge-base systems, as well as prove formally whether or not certain critical behavior is satisfied by context-awareness in pervasive computing applications.

# References

1. Akman, V., Surav, M.: The use of situation theory in context modeling. Comput. Intell. Int. J. **13**(3), 427–438 (1997)
2. Alaga, V., Wan, K.: Context based enforcement of authorization for privacy and security in identity management. In: de Leeuw, E., Fischer-Hübner, S., Tseng, J., Borking, J. (eds.) Policies and Research in Identity Management. The International Federation for Information Processing, vol. 261, pp. 25–37. Springer, Boston (2008). https://doi.org/10.1007/978-0-387-77996-6_3
3. Alagar, V., Mohammad, M., Wan, K., Hnaide, S.A.: A framework for developing context-aware systems. EAI Endorsed Trans. Context-Aware Syst. Appl. **14**(1) (2014). https://doi.org/10.4108/casa.1.1.e2
4. Brèzillon, P., Gonzalez, A.I.: Context in Computing: A Cross-Disciplinary Approach to Modeling Real World. Springer, Berlin (2014)
5. Brézillon, P.: Context in human-machine problem solving: a survey. LIP **6**(1996), 029 (1996)
6. Carnap, R.: Meaning and Necessity. Chicago University Press, Chicago (1947). Enlarged Edition 1956
7. Clark, H.H., Carlson, T.B.: Context for comprehension. In: Attention and Performance, pp. 313–330. Lawrence Erlbaum Associates, Hillside (1981)
8. Dey, A.K., Abowd, G.D., Salber, D.: A conceptual framework and a toolkit for supporting the rapid prototyping of context-aware applications. Hum.-Comput. Interact. **16**, 97–161 (2001)
9. Dey, A.K.: Understanding and using context. Pers. Ubiquit. Comput. **5**(1), 4–7 (2001)
10. Dowley, D., Wall, R., Peters, S.: Introduction to Montague Semantics. Reidel Publishing Company, Amsterdam (1981)
11. Bettini, C., et al.: A survey of context modelling and reasoning techniques. Pervasive Mob. Comput. **6**, 161–180 (2009)
12. García, K., Brézillon, P.: A contextual model of turns for group work. In: Christiansen, H., Stojanovic, I., Papadopoulos, G.A. (eds.) CONTEXT 2015. LNCS (LNAI), vol. 9405, pp. 243–256. Springer, Cham (2015). https://doi.org/10.1007/978-3-319-25591-0_18

13. García, K., Brézillon, P.: Contextual graphs for modeling group interaction. In: Brézillon, P., Turner, R., Penco, C. (eds.) CONTEXT 2017. LNCS (LNAI), vol. 10257, pp. 151–164. Springer, Cham (2017). https://doi.org/10.1007/978-3-319-57837-8_12
14. Giunchiglia, F.: Contextual reasoning. Epistemologia, special issue on I Linguaggi e le Macchine 16, 345–364 (1993)
15. Grätzer, S.: Lattice Theory: First Concepts and Distributive Lattices. W. H. Freeman, San Francisco (1971)
16. Guha, R.V.: Contexts: A Formalization and Some Applications, vol. 101. Stanford University Stanford (1991)
17. Held, A., Buchholz, S., Schill, A.: Modeling of context information for pervasive computing applications. In: Proceedings of SCI, pp. 167–180 (2002)
18. Interdisciplinary and Internal Conference Series. Modeling and using context (1997)
19. McCarthy, J.: Notes on formalizing context (1993)
20. McCarthy, J., Buvac, S.: Formalizing context (expanded notes) (1997)
21. Sato, M., Sakurai, T., Kameyama, Y.: A simply typed context calculus with first-class environments. In: Proceedings of FLOPs 2001: the 5th International Symposium on Functional and Logic Programming, pp. 359–374 (2001)
22. Schilit, B., Adams, N., Want, R.: Context-aware computing applications. In: 1994 First Workshop on Mobile Computing Systems and Applications, WMCSA 1994, pp. 85–90. IEEE (1994)
23. Shoham, Y.: Varieties of context. In: Artificial Intelligence and Mathematical Theory of Computation: Papers in Honor of John McCarthy, pp. 393–408 (1991)
24. Wan, K., Alagar, V., Paquet, J.: An architecture for developing context-aware systems. In: Roth-Berghofer, T.R., Schulz, S., Leake, D.B. (eds.) MRC 2005. LNCS (LNAI), vol. 3946, pp. 48–61. Springer, Heidelberg (2006). https://doi.org/10.1007/11740674_4
25. Wan, K.: Lucx: lucid enriched with context. Ph.D. thesis, Concordia University (2006)
26. Wan, K., Alagar, V., Paquet, J.: A context theory for intensional programming. In: Workshop on Context Representation and Reasoning (CRR05). Citeseer, Paris, July 2005
27. Weyhrauch, R.: Prolegomena to a theory of mechanized formal reasoning. Artif. Intell. 13, 133–170 (1980)
28. Winograd, T.: Architecture for context. Hum.-Comput. Inter. 16, 401–419 (2001)

# Transmission Reordering in Self-organizing Network Coordination Framework

Kohji Tomita[✉][iD] and Akiya Kamimura[iD]

National Institute of Advanced Industrial Science and Technology (AIST),
Tsukuba, Ibaraki 305-8568, Japan
{k.tomita,kamimura.a}@aist.go.jp

**Abstract.** By virtue of the rapid progress of IoT technology, communication devices are increasing drastically. Along with the increase, collision of transmission often happens, resulting in restricted throughput. This restriction is mainly caused by a hidden node problem. To resolve that difficulty, a promising methodology is Time Division Multiple Access (TDMA) based on a Pulse Coupled Oscillator (PCO) model. Among them, Self-organizing Network Coordination Framework (SoNCF) presents various benefits. However, in some network topologies, the performance of SoNCF is degraded because the order of random initial phases of nodes is unchanged. As described in this paper, we analyze the effect of transmission ordering on SoNCF using graph theory concepts. We also consider its extension to resolve it through reordering. Its effectiveness was confirmed through simulation.

**Keywords:** Wireless network · Pulse coupled oscillator
Synchronization · Self-organization

## 1 Introduction

Internet of things (IoT) devices including sensor nodes are increasing drastically. This trend is expected to continue because of the rapid progress of IoT technology [4]. The current major protocol for wireless communication uses Carrier-Sense Multiple Access with Collision Avoidance (CSMA/CA). Using CSMA/CA method, declining throughput caused by collision of transmission is a salient issue when many nodes mutually communicate. This degraded performance is mainly attributable to a phenomenon known as a hidden node problem: a node cannot detect two-hop neighbor's transmission and simultaneous transmission results in collision of packets. The Request To Send/Clear To Send (RTS/CTS) mechanism was proposed to mitigate this difficulty, but its effectiveness has remained limited [5].

Unlike these, a promising methodology to resolve the problem is Time Division Multiple Access (TDMA) based on a Pulse Coupled Oscillator (PCO) model. Along this line, much study has been conducted [1–3,6,7].

© ICST Institute for Computer Sciences, Social Informatics and Telecommunications Engineering 2019
Published by Springer Nature Switzerland AG 2019. All Rights Reserved
P. Cong Vinh and V. Alagar (Eds.): ICCASA 2018/ICTCC 2018, LNICST 266, pp. 14–24, 2019.
https://doi.org/10.1007/978-3-030-06152-4_2

Among them, Self-organizing Network Coordination Framework (SoNCF) has various benefits as described below [6].

- In a stable state after convergence, no collision occurs if the connection network topology is unchanged.
- When the topology of connection network changes dynamically, communication timing is adaptively organized in a distributed manner.
- A sub-optimal division number is computed explicitly and shared among nodes.
- When nodes are sending data repeatedly, congestion can be relaxed by using additional slots.

In spite of the benefits described above, in some network topologies, the SoNCF performance is degraded. In SoNCF, each node transmits its data in its own slot one by one. This ordering relation is characterized by a pushing relation among them in the phase domain. The relative order of transmission is decided by the initial randomness of phase assignment to the nodes. The order is not problematic in many cases, but when many long cycles exist in the connection network, the order can take effect.

As described in this paper, we analyze the effect of ordering using concepts in graph theory, and consider its extension to resolve such difficulties. We extend the framework so that the order of transmission can be organized to prevent undesirable pushing of nodes in the phase domain.

## 2  SoNCF

This section presents a review of the framework of SoNCF from [6]. This framework of network coordination where nodes of a wireless network can transmit data without collision is based on TDMA using PCO.

Each node adjusts its transmission timing in consideration of the timing of neighbor nodes. Only nodes within two hops are considered for network coordination. The transmission timing of two-hop neighbors is conveyed via one-hop neighbors.

We can illustrate the concepts in SoNCF through the use of an example. Let us consider a graph in Fig. 1(a) composed of eight nodes. Each circle represents a communication node with its ID number. Each edge represents direct communication possibility. In SoNCF, we separate the transmission timing of each node so that no collision occurs and each node transmits one by one in a local perspective. Figure 1(b) presents an initial random arrangement of phases observed from the global perspective. Each node changes its phase counterclockwise in this figure. We assume that each node transmits at the top position denoted by the dotted line, where node 3 is located. The phase difference between nodes is insufficient. Efficient communication is not possible in this state. The nodes calculate the sub-optimal division number as five, where the optimal division number is four. Based on the value, the nodes mutually interact in a pulse coupled manner and adjust their transmission timing adaptively. Finally, their phase is separated into five groups as in Fig. 1(c). Nodes 1 and 5, for instance, transmit simultaneously but do not cause collision because the nodes are sufficiently separated.

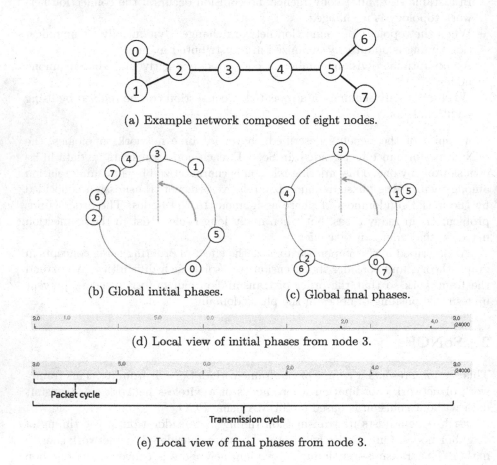

(a) Example network composed of eight nodes.

(b) Global initial phases.          (c) Global final phases.

(d) Local view of initial phases from node 3.

(e) Local view of final phases from node 3.

Fig. 1. SoNCF.

We can also observe how the situation is observed from a node. Each node obtains timing information of one-hop neighbors (called real nodes) directly by receiving communication, and of two-hop neighbors (called virtual nodes) through communication via a real node. Figure 1(d) and 1(e), respectively represent arrangements of neighbors' phases from a local perspective of node 3 in the initial and converged states. In Fig. 1(d), the lower blue node IDs (i.e., nodes 2 and 4) and upper red node IDs (i.e., nodes 0, 1, and 5) respectively represent real and virtual nodes seen from node 3. These linear representations correspond to circular representations in Fig. 1(b) and (c). Phases of nodes 6 and 7 are not known to node 3.

In SoNCF, the duration for a node to send a packet is fixed and called a packet cycle. One cycle of transmission by all the nodes, called a transmission cycle, is calculated by multiplying the packet cycle and the division number as presented in Fig. 1(e). In this paper, the packet cycle and transmission cycle are designated respectively as the packet period and transmission period to avoid confusion with cycles of graphs.

For more details related to SoNCF, one can refer to an earlier report [6].

## 3    Extension by Reordering

### 3.1    Ordering Problem

When nodes are interacting in the framework of SoNCF, the relative phase order of each node is decided by initial random phase assignment. Then, in the original framework, the relative order of transmission among nodes within two-hops does not change.

If the connection topology is tree-like i.e., if the overall system does not include long cycles, then an undesirable pushing situation in the phase domain disappears by itself. However, if the overall system includes many long cycles, then a cycle of pushing nodes could be generated at the time of execution.

The length of a pushing cycle is at least equal to the division number. Each node can use its packet period if they are equal. However, if a pushing cycle is longer than the division number, then an undesirable situation occurs. Such a pushing state reduces the effective length of transmission slot and prevents enjoyment of the full length of transmission. It also increases the danger of collision.

This can be stated more clearly as follows. The nodes involved in the cycle transmit their packets in turn in one transmission period. This transmission means that, for a cycle with length $n$ such that $n > N$, where $N$ is the division number, the overall transmission period is divided into $n$ rather than $N$, giving a shorter duration of sending than the packet period. We designate such cycles as *long pushing cycles*. Moreover, nodes not included in the cycle might be pushed indirectly by nodes in the long pushing cycles. This situation continues. We designate the nodes pushed indirectly by a long pushing cycle as *accompanying nodes*. Actually, cycles in the squared connection graph are a concern.

We distinguish graphs of two kinds and cycles on them.

1. For a *connection graph* $G$ where edges are undirected and where they represent direct communication possibility for the current arrangement of nodes, we consider the *squared connection graph* $G^2$ where edges are between one-hop or two-hop neighbors in the connection graph. Cycles in squared connection graphs are potential pushing cycles at the time of execution. Squared connection graphs and cycles on them do not change unless the network topology is changed.

2. We consider a graph called a *pushing diagram*, where edges are directed and represent the pushing relation in the phase domain between nodes within two-hop neighbors in the connection graph at some moment of execution. Cycles represent the current phase pushing state among nodes, and are a subgraph of the corresponding squared connection graph with a direction in edges. Pushing diagrams are time-dependent.

**Example.** We visualize the situation using the SoNCF simulator [6]. Figure 2(a) presents an example of a connection graph; Fig. 2(b) presents additional information of the pushing relation by blue arrows. The arrows are between one-hop or two-hop neighbors because, in SoNCF, direct interaction of pushing occurs only neighbors within two hops. In this figure, the width of an arrow represents the strength of pushing. This figure depicts a situation in which many pushing relations exist.

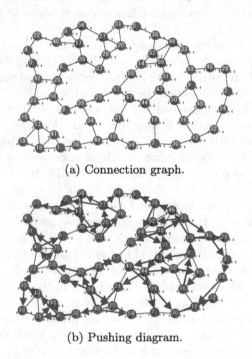

(a) Connection graph.

(b) Pushing diagram.

**Fig. 2.** Connection graph (a) and pushing diagram (b).

Let us consider connected components of the pushing diagram. In the case of a pushing diagram corresponding to Fig. 2(b), where edges are shown by blue arrows, we have two components as in Fig. 3. They are shown based only on a connective relation and are shown irrespective of the location in Fig. 2. Figure 3(a) shows a long pushing cycle as

$$3 \to 40 \to 17 \to 37 \to 20 \to 56 \to 35 \to 26 \to 27 \to 3$$

with length 9. Therefore, the transmission period is divided by 9. Nodes 21 and 52 are accompanying nodes, continuously pushed by the nodes in the cycle. Figure 3(b) includes a long pushing cycle of length 10, with 39 accompanying nodes.

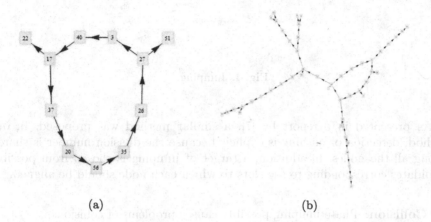

(a)                                                    (b)

**Fig. 3.** Connected components of a pushing diagram.

## 3.2   Phase Jump

Once such state with a long pushing cycle is generated, the original framework maintains the transmission ordering. This state continues unless the network structure changes. We consider resolving such pushing states.

It would be a solution that nodes in the pushing cycle change their relative transmission order appropriately. However, the nodes do not have information of global pushing relation. Accompanying nodes are outside of the cycle but pushed as well from the nodes in the cycle indirectly. Each node cannot decide whether it is in the long pushing cycle or not. The only available information related to pushing is that it is pushed continuously from a neighbor.

**Randomization.** The cause by which a long pushing cycle is generated is that a node is in an inappropriate relative phase position of transmission. If several nodes in the cycle change their order to appropriate positions, then the cycle does not exist any more.

In general, there is an appropriate order of transmission that does not cause a long pushing cycle. In other words, the division number is chosen to satisfy this condition.

Some nodes can detect a cycle because nodes in a long pushing cycle (or accompanying nodes) are pushed continuously by a neighbor node if there is such a long pushing cycle in the network. However, it is difficult to generate an appropriate order directly from a purely local perspective. Therefore, we use a stochastic method. A node that might be in the cycle changes its relative order by jumping to a different position. Figure 4 presents that obtained in the case in which there are eight slots and where a node jumps to an empty slot, which is located three slots ahead.

**Fig. 4.** Jumping.

As presented in a report by [7], a similar method was proposed. In our method, detection of pushing is explicit because the division number is shared among all the nodes. In addition, a target of jumping is chosen from possible candidates corresponding to the slots to which each node should be aligned.

**On Collision.** Phase jumping possibly causes problems of collisions.

In an earlier report of the literature [6], a method of using empty slots without collision was proposed. In that method, a node is guaranteed to perform extra utilization exclusively among its neighbor nodes. The method is based on assigning privilege to a node by exchanging the amount of remaining data to be sent. Then, an empty slot is searched to be used. The emptiness criterion is that the slot is not used by one-hop or two-hop neighbors.

By introducing additional data sent in the packet, reordering while avoiding collision would be possible. In the case treated in this paper, however, to avoid complication, using such additional information is not preferred. Instead, each node jumps at a low probability to reduce collisions.

**Summary.** To summarize the contents above, we use the following method for reordering:

1. Set a minimum threshold of pushing value $th$ to consider and a value $d$ of accumulated pushing value to jump.
2. Calculate the sum of the pushing value in consecutive steps pushed at a strength greater than threshold $th$.
3. The node changes its. transmission timing to an empty slot randomly if the sum exceeds $d$.

The pushing value is calculated as the overlapping rate of its own slot of packet period and its preceding node's slot. Its range is $[0, 1)$. As described herein, we use the following parameter values: $th = 0.05$ and $d = 2.5$.

We implemented this method in the simulator and conducted simulation experiments.

# 4    Simulation and Results

## 4.1    Mesh Network

We first consider a connection network composed of 60 nodes as shown in Fig. 2. We start in a mode without reordering and at the midst of time reordering starts. Figure 5 is a resulting graph showing the change of average pushing values, i.e., the average of the pushing values for all nodes.

Before the reordering starts, the average pushing value is stable at about 0.28 after initial perturbation until time 50. Reordering starts at time 191; phase jumping happens 75 times between time 192 and 205. The average pushing value drops and then remains stable at nearly zero. The occasional positive value after convergence is caused by natural fluctuation because of the phase interaction and is sufficiently small.

The three graphs portrayed in the figure respectively illustrate the pushing state before, during, and after reordering. As the right graph shows, pushing arrows remain, but they are sparse. In appropriate phase ordering, the pushing arrows are weak and disappear soon after appearance, whereas arrows in long pushing cycles are strong, stable, and persistent with nearly constant strength.

This result demonstrates the method's effectiveness.

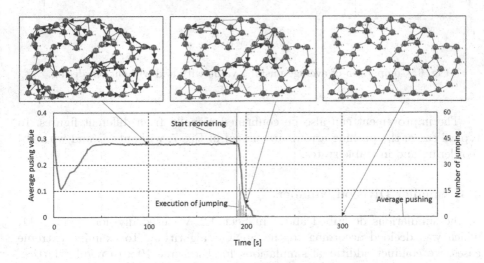

**Fig. 5.** Change of the average pushing value.

## 4.2    Regular Network

Next, let us consider connection networks with $n^2$ nodes arranged in the 2D regular lattice $n \times n$, where $n > 1$. Considering it as an undirected graph, if $n$ is even, there is a Hamiltonian cycle, i.e., a cycle that visits each vertex exactly once. Therefore, one pushing cycle can include all the nodes. It is possible, in principle, that the available transmission period is divided by the number of all nodes $n^2$ in the worst case.

Hereinafter, we consider the case with $n = 10$ and examine the effect of reordering by comparing cases with and without reordering. Figure 6 presents changes of the average pushing values in all nodes for both cases. This is the average of ten runs of simulation each. As the graph shows, the value without reordering is nearly stable at about 0.16 after convergence. However, the value with reordering converges nearly to zero, demonstrating that the pushing state is resolved.

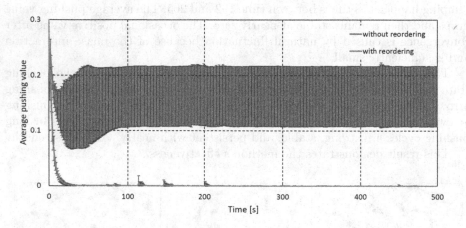

**Fig. 6.** Comparison of average pushing value with and without reordering.

The improvement can also be confirmed visually from different figures. In typical cases, the pushing arrows are shown in Fig. 7, without (a) and with (b) reordering and in stable states.

## 4.3  Smaller Division Number

In the simulations described above in Sect. 4.2, we used division number 11, which was decided according to the SoNCF algorithm. To examine extreme cases, we conduct additional simulations for the same $10 \times 10$ regular lattice. We fix the division number manually and note the convergence of phases. The optimal division number for this graph is 5.

From the conducted simulation, we confirmed that the phase converged to a stable state for division numbers until 7, started from 11. It was difficult to converge for the number 6, a nearly optimal division number, in the current setting of simulation.

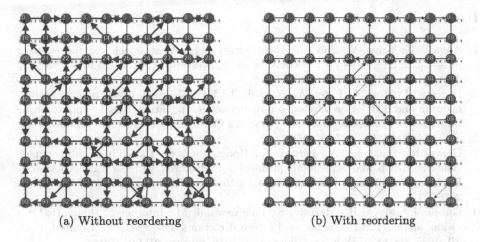

(a) Without reordering                    (b) With reordering

**Fig. 7.** Typical stable states with and without reordering.

## 5    Discussion and Conclusion

We have presented an extension of SoNCF so that the order of transmission is organized in a decentralized manner to an appropriate one. The effectiveness of reordering was confirmed through simulations conducted in mesh and regular lattice networks under various conditions.

The parameter values were chosen empirically. Experimentation showed that these values affect the convergence time but that they have little effect on the convergence. To reduce collision, the stochastic value is useful for $d$. An optimal setting will depend on the calculated division number and the network structure. Further consideration will be necessary.

As stated in the previous section, when the division number is nearly optimal, it is difficult to converge to a stable state. It is difficult to realize in a local manner without using global information.

To use this framework in real applications, further study is required. We assumed for the simulation that the communication condition is sufficiently good and therefore employed a simple model of interference. Actual applications have errors or asymmetry in communication. In addition, energy consumption is expected to be difficult. We have already conducted preliminary experiments using developed communication modules. By coping with the problems described above, we are planning to improve the modules and conduct hardware experiments in future studies.

# References

1. Anglea, T., Wang, Y.: Phase desynchronization: a new approach and theory using pulse-based interaction. IEEE Trans. Signal Process. **65**, 1160–1171 (2017). https://doi.org/10.1109/TSP.2016.2633246
2. Degesys, J., Rose, I., Patel, A., Nagpal, R.: DESYNC: self-organizing desynchronization and TDMA on wireless sensor networks. In: International Symposium on Information Processing in Sensor Networks (PSN), pp. 11–20 (2007). https://doi.org/10.1109/IPSN.2007.4379660
3. Gentz, R., Scaglione, A., Ferrari, L., Hong, Y.-W.P.: PulseSS: a pulse-coupled synchronization and scheduling protocol for clustered wireless sensor networks. IEEE Internet Things J. **3**, 1222–1234 (2016). https://doi.org/10.1109/JIOT.2016.2576923
4. Gubbi, J., Buyya, R., Marusic, S., Palaniswami, M.: Internet of things (IoT): a vision, architectural elements, and future directions. Future Gener. Comput. Syst. **29**, 1645–1660 (2013). https://doi.org/10.1016/j.future.2013.01.010
5. Jayasuriya, A., Perreau, S., Dadej, A., Gordon, S.: Hidden vs. exposed terminal problem in ad hoc networks. In: Proceedings Australian Telecommunication Network and Applications Conference, pp. 52–59 (2004)
6. Kamimura, A., Tomita, K.: Self-organizing network coordination framework enabling collision-free and congestionless wireless sensor networks. J. Network Comput. Appl. **93**, 228–244 (2017). https://doi.org/10.1016/j.jnca.2017.06.002
7. Kubo, Y., Sekiyama, K.: Communication timing control with interference detection for wirelesssensor networks. EURASIP J. Wireless Commun. Networking, Article ID: 54968 (2007). https://doi.org/10.1155/2007/54968

# Context-Aware Parking Systems in Urban Areas: A Survey and Early Experiments

Hafiz Mahfooz Ul Haque[1]([⊠]), Haidar Zulfiqar[2], Sajid Ullah Khan[2], and Muneeb Ul Haque[3]

[1] Department of Software Engineering, The University of Lahore, Lahore, Pakistan
mahfoozul.haque@se.uol.edu.pk
[2] Department of Computer Science, The University of Lahore, Lahore, Pakistan
haidarmalik@live.com, sajid.ullah@cs.uol.edu.pk
[3] SBE, University of Management and Technology, Lahore, Pakistan
hhmuneeb@gmail.com

**Abstract.** Parking spaces have been considered as vital resources in urban areas. Finding parking spaces in jam-packed areas are often challenging, stressful and uncertain for the drivers that cause traffic congestion with a consequent of wastage of time, fuel and increase of pollution. These problems can be addressed using smart parking systems if drivers reserve parking slots in advance. With the proliferation of smart devices in a pervasive computing environment, real-time monitoring of the traffic situation and parking areas is often trivial using context-awareness. Context-awareness has the capability to occupy parking slots dynamically at any time and in any place. However, it is often challenging in busy parking areas because vehicles occupy and leave parking slots very frequently. This paper presents a brief survey on context-aware smart parking systems theoretically as well as practically. We propose a context-aware parking application to assist drivers in finding parking slots dynamically while moving and/or arriving at the destination.

**Keywords:** Context-aware · Smart parking · Distributed reasoning
Sensor · Embedded system

## 1 Introduction

In recent years, transportation has become one of the most essential parts of people's daily lives across the globe. In urban areas, people often prefer to travel using their personal vehicles. These vehicles provide ease, comfort to humans with stress-free driving, discourage public transport services and reduce the risks of getting late. Due to heavy work pressure and anxiety, people usually rush in driving and finding parking slots. Although, it is a fact that traffic is increasing day by day, however, the number of accidents is also increasing accordingly. Accidents are always unplanned events that occur unexpectedly at any time and in any place. In recent years, accidents ratio has been terribly increasing day

© ICST Institute for Computer Sciences, Social Informatics and Telecommunications Engineering 2019
Published by Springer Nature Switzerland AG 2019. All Rights Reserved
P. Cong Vinh and V. Alagar (Eds.): ICCASA 2018/ICTCC 2018, LNICST 266, pp. 25–35, 2019.
https://doi.org/10.1007/978-3-030-06152-4_3

by day. According to the World Health Organization (WHO), it is estimated that around 1.7 million people die in the road accidents every year and around five hundred million people get serious and/or mild injuries [1]. More than 80% of victims can be saved if they are treated within a limited span of time. The core intention is to save the lives of victims and make traffic flow faster and smoother. With the advent of smart technologies and pervasiveness, smart parking, road safety, and route planning and management have been rapidly evolving since the last decade. Thanks to the context-aware vehicular frameworks and applications, that provides a wide range of services to vehicle drivers such as traffic management, smart parking, route planning, collision avoidance controls, suitable assistance, etc. In context-aware computing, smart devices are equipped with various embedded/un-embedded sensors. These devices have the capability to sense and detect, interpret and respond according to the environmental situation. A prime example of this type of application is SFPark [23]. Srikanth et al. proposed a framework that uses sensors embedded in the streets of the city of San Francisco, which shows vacant parking slots. When a user intends to find a parking slot in some area of the city, the application shows a map with marked locations of the vacant parking slots in the designated area. However, the user has to explicitly choose the vacant marked parking slot. To the best of our knowledge, no systematic theoretical frameworks, as well as applications, have been developed yet that assign and maintain the parking slots dynamically at run-time. In this paper, a prototypal context-aware parking application is being developed to assist drivers in finding parking slots dynamically. In particular, when a user registers himself/herself with the application and enters the destination, the system starts acquiring user contextual information (location) while the user is traveling and reserve parking slot automatically on the estimated time of arrival. On arrival at the parking area, the system directs the driver to the reserved parking slots using a guided map. The system calculates the parking duration, and the fee is automatically deducted as the user leaves the parking space.

The rest of the paper is organized as follows. In Sect. 2, we briefly introduce the core notion of context-awareness. In Sect. 3, context-aware vehicular systems have been described. In Sect. 4, we briefly survey smart paring systems with the incorporation of context-awareness. In Sect. 5, we present our proposed context-aware parking application framework and conclude in Sect. 6.

## 2   Context and Context-Awareness

A context is any information that describes the state of an entity like a person, place or object. Context can be a location, weight, people around, time, user activity, social interactions, and these factors may have also other attributes like the weight of an object according to location. The context-awareness relies on context and provides the relevant information or services according to that context [9]. Context-aware applications usually sense the contextual information from the physical environment or grab a particular situation, respond intelligently in such environment and have the ability to build the understanding of the current execution and provide services accordingly [13].

The Context-aware systems are those systems that gather the context of a particular environment or situation and deliver it to the interested entities connected with ubiquitous computing. Context-aware systems provide different devices integrated with multiple sensors that are used to monitor physical environment and individuals to measure their current situations without human involvement and respond accordingly [5,25]. These systems assist the users at any time, anywhere by taking intelligent decisions without human intervention.

## 3   Context-Aware Vehicular System

In recent years, intelligent transportation systems have significantly influenced by context-aware systems. Intelligent transportation systems are incorporating a variety of context-awareness features to facilitate drivers in personalized services ubiquitously such as road safety, the comfort of drivers, analyze traffic condition and suggest appropriate actions accordingly [2,4,10,16–18,24]. Context-aware vehicular applications acquire contextual information related to drivers, vehicle's current state (personalized information such as speed, acceleration, etc), traffic regulations and take appropriate action according to the current situation. Due to rapid technological advancements in the intelligent transportation system, vehicle manufacturers are providing latest features like camera, cruise control, sensors, airbags, GPS, etc. in their vehicles to provide secure, comfortable and hassle-free journey.

Context-aware applications of the transportation system use the driving context information such as information related to the driver, the vehicle state, traffic regulations, available parking lots in different areas etc. and provide assisted support according to the current situation. Context-aware vehicular systems allow the vehicles to communicate with other vehicles and road infrastructure by measuring speed and distance. These systems detect hazardous situation and take decisions intelligently. Majority of these applications are based on a Vehicular Ad-hoc Network (VANET) that collects context data of driving by using the different sensors, cameras and provides inter-vehicular communication capabilities. VANET is a wireless technology for ITS (Intelligent Transportation system) that provides DSRC (Dedicated Short Range Communication) to inter-vehicular communication (vehicle to vehicle) and roadside static infrastructure (vehicle to infrastructure) [12]. VANET has two types of nodes, vehicles OBUs (On-board Units) and RSUs (Road Side Units). The vehicular OBU is used to communicate with other vehicles and RSU. The RSU has multiple network interfaces to connect with other RSUs, vehicles and ISPs (Internet Service Providers). RSU allows OBU to connect using the internet. In VANET, nodes communicate through single-hop and each node can be treated as a router to enable multi-hop communication between the other nodes. VANET uses IEEE 802.11p and IEEE 1609 standards/topology for inter-vehicular communication [20]. In literature, a significant amount of work has been done on Context-aware vehicular systems including Accident detection system [17], smart parking [7,18,26], driver assistance [6], driver behaviour [4], route planning and optimization [24], traffic congestion estimation [16], etc.

# 4   Context-Aware Smart Parking Systems

Since the last decade, traffic congestion is becoming one of the major issues in urban cities. Finding a parking place in urban areas is one of the most challenging and stressful task for the drivers. Drivers often spend their time, suffer stress and waste fuel to find a parking place and thus the waste production of tons of carbon dioxide which is dangerous for human life. There are many smart parking methods that have been proposed by different researchers. In [8], Biondi et al. proposed a smart parking android application that uses GPS to locate the nearest parking areas and BLE (Blue tooth low energy advertising) to provide the contextual information about the adjacent passenger in the vehicle. In this framework, users have to register in the smart parking system and when a user starts driving to the designated place, the application sends GPS position to the remote server after certain intervals until it reaches to the destination and store paths by joining all GPS points. The server stores the maps of designated areas in the database and the paths are compared through an algorithm to estimate the available parking slots. The system architecture consists of smartphones that contain GPS and BLE to gather the contextual information like adjacent users, position, path, and activities of the users. This application presents the result originated by the engine and sends contextual and location information to the engine and provides the nearest parking area. Although the use of Bluetooth technology is a well-suited approach to interconnect devices, however, it may trigger another issue related to heterogeneity, data security, and battery life, which may cause unreliability issue. Adhatarao et al. [3] proposed a smart parking method that sense the vehicle at the entry node and generates parking ID to broadcast over the network. When the vehicle reaches the parking lot, the parking lot sensor detects the presence of a vehicle and the system assigns the ID generated at the entry node to the vehicle parking ID. While leaving the parking lot, the sensor detects free space and the system makes the calculation for easy payment. Though all the smart parking systems are proposed to easily discover and maintain the parking slots in the parking areas. However, users have to do manual requests for discovering and reserving the parking lots every time, even in the same parking area and the slots are not assigned systematically to the users. This may cause inefficiency and inefficacy of the system in maintaining quick response time, light and temperature sensitivity due to high voltage requirements.

In [7], a context-aware on-street parking system was developed by De Montfort University. This project was specifically designed to facilitate the drivers to park their vehicles by automatically locating the freely available and reserved parking places. This context-aware Information system was developed with the incorporation of Vehicular Ad-hoc Networks with the intention of providing more convenient and efficient parking spaces to save fuels and time of the people.

In this system, the parking zones and streets are given the specific identity. So whenever a vehicle sends a request to park the car based on their preferences, the information system automatically locates the desired parking space and reserve the parking space based on the user's preference. In [18], an effort has been made to facilitate the drivers by providing available/reserved parking spaces using contextual knowledge generated. The system has four different parking states including freely available parking spaces to be used by the drivers, reserved parking spaces for pre-booking of parking places, occupied parking spaces and load/unload parking spaces for the quick delivery of goods. These parking states are utilized according to the user's preferences and privileges. To suitably utilize the parking space, the system has two main interfaces; one for the driver and other for the traffic monitoring authorities. In this paper, authors took the advantage of cloud-computing to suitably implement the complex functionalities using smart server. Context-awareness services have been incorporated in the smart server to make its adaptive behavior. Another approach proposed in [26], which describes a PhonePark application to detect the availability of on-street parking places. The architecture is composed of smartphone sensors like GPS, Bluetooth and accelerometer sensors along with the algorithms that can automatically detect the real-time parking/deparking conditions. A parking status detector runs on the smartphone and when it detects the parking/unparking activity of a specific area, it sends the status of parking to the parking availability estimator that is known as the aggregates of parking status detectors (PSD's) notifications. To overcome the false detection of parking places historical availability profile(HAP) construction algorithm is proposed along with the PSD and parking availability estimator(PAE). In [19], Rinne et al. investigates a mobile crowdsourcing approach that describes how smartphone sensors are capable of obtaining contextual information of available parking places without using external infrastructure and discussed the pros and cons of the investigated approach. To detect the available and occupied status of parking places, Google API's activity recognition (in the vehicle, on foot) and Geofencing is used to detect the exit and entrance in the parking area. An Android application has developed to acquire the run-time data from the GPS and API's and automatically send to the server. The server shows real time parking status to the requested drivers according to their preferences and this can be updated either automatically or manually using smartphones.

Kamble et al. [11] presents a prototype of Android centered smart parking application that assists the users in reserving or pre-booking the parking space. In the presented architecture, the user can view and select the parking lot for booking by specifying the parking duration through the application. The system will mark the parking space and provide One Time Password (OTP) to the user to make sure that the specific parking lot is not available for others. The user has to enter the OTP through the keypad in order to open the gate while going in or out from the parking area. In [22] Satre et al. presents an RFID tag based digital parking system. The system architecture consists of GPS, RFID kit, Android and desktop applications, and database. The user can search for the parking lot near to his current location through an Android app. When the user selects the parking lot from the available lots, the app directs the user to the parking lot. The RFID tags contain the user's information and used to allocate and deallocate the parking lots through RFID readers installed at the parking gate. The desktop application assists the administration to keep track of available and unavailable parking lots.

## 5    Proposed Context-Aware Parking Application Framework

Recent years have witnessed the parking problem is one of the crucial issues, more specifically in urban areas that cause road accidents, traffic congestion, time and fuel wastage, environment pollution and driver's stress. Drivers are often unaware of the parking status to their destinations. Literature has revealed a significant amount of work on the smart parking system considering VANET [7,15], cloud computing [14], IoT [21], etc. However, there is a number of quite few frameworks available for context-aware smart parking systems, and these works have not been implemented yet with the intelligent reasoning formalisms to provide fully automated parking support. In addition, to the best of our knowledge, the existing context-aware approaches do not assign parking slots to users dynamically. Users have to explicitly search the parking slots in the specific parking area even if there are many vacant parking places available. Our approach is novel in a sense that we propose a framework that will provide the parking services on the basis of user's preferences automatically. We intend to provide a cost effective context-aware smart parking system for personal vehicles using the smartphone application. The proposed context-aware parking application is being developed to assist drivers in finding a parking slot on real-time, reaching the destination and also allows user to inquire the available parking slots while the user is at home, in office or on the way to the specific parking area.

The application is twofold: one for the user end (client) and other for the service providers (i.e., Parking Bays). Initially, a user has to register through the parking application once using a smartphone only. However, the service provider end needs to fulfill the context-aware smart parking system requirements such as parking area, an entrance sensor, a database system, vehicle presence detection sensor in the designated parking slots and an exit sensor. The proposed application will help three types of users: Registered User with Planned Destination ($RUPD$), Registered User with Unplanned Destination ($RUUD$), and Unregistered User ($UU$). $RUPD$ users need to enter destination prior starting their journey in order to avail parking with fully automated support, $RUUD$ users do not require the destination, however, they can avail parking with semi-automated support, and unregistered users can avail parking with limited automated support. Whenever a registered user with planned destination arrives at the destination, the system assigns a pre-booked parking slot (which is allocated on the estimated time of arrival) to the driver with a directed map to the assigned parking slot through a unique auto-generated One Time

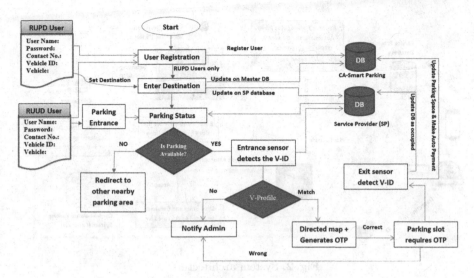

**Fig. 1.** Context-aware parking system activity diagram

Password (OTP). When the vehicle occupies the assigned parking slot, the system requires the OTP through vehicle presence detection sensor from the user and the user will automatically receive SMS about parking slot including slot's occupancy starting time. As the vehicle leaves the reserved parking slot, the system automatically calculates the parking duration and parking fee will be deducted from the user account through the automatic payment method. Whenever *RUUD* user arrives at the destination, the system automatically allocates parking slot to the driver with a map directed to the assigned parking slot that will save the user's time. Note that the registered vehicle numbers are matched with the database in the system at the entrance gate to make the process faster and secure. In case if an unregistered user is willing to park in a smart parking area, then the system automatically captures the car number using the entrance sensor and allocates parking slot at run-time. Un-registered users are provided parking cards at the entrance gate, and these users pay parking fee on exit gate using Auto Paying Machine. If there is no free parking space, then the user will be redirected to the nearby parking areas from the destination. The system activity diagram is shown in Fig. 1 whereas the system architecture can be seen in Fig. 2.

## 5.1 Framework Development Mechanism

To suitably implement the proposed framework, we choose Xcode IDE to develop the smart parking application using Swift 4 programming language. As the system is two-fold in nature, so both kinds of systems (service-provider-end and client-end) are developed using iOS version 11. The application is being connected to the firebase database which usually operates on smartphones. The system consists of a master database (i.e., Context-aware Smart Parking database)

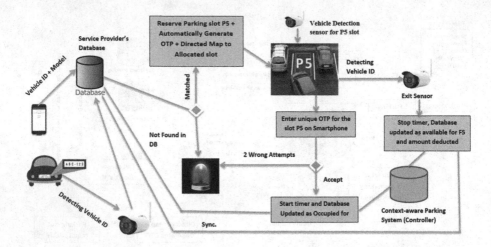

**Fig. 2.** System architecture

and service provider's database. These databases provide different levels of privileges and access grants. The master database keeps records of drivers, vehicles and parking bays along with vacant slots information, whereas service provider's database contains records of its parking slots as well as client's information. The application uses Google maps for route planning, optimization, time and distance calculation. Both firebase and Google maps are third party libraries that have been integrated into the iOS using Pods. As the system is heterogeneous in nature, so users from different localities can register to the application. Whenever a user intends to find the parking slot at the specific parking area, the system lets the user to interconnect to corresponding service provider's database. To suitably implement the complexity and decisiveness of context-aware parking system, we use rule-based reasoning in order to make efficient and correct flow of the system. As the system runs on smartphones, the service-providers-end's smart devices acquire low-level contextual information from surrounding environment regarding parking allocation and client's information and then infers high-level contextual information in order to fulfill the complete parking process. The system consists of hardware components including a server computer, sensors at the entrance and exit of the parking area to detect the number plate of the vehicle through image processing. The vehicle presence detector notifies the system about the presence and absence of the vehicle in the parking slot. Each slot has its own sensor to timely update the system about the status of the parking slot. The server controls all the sensors, database and payment method.

## 5.2   Proposed Application User Interface

The proposed application user interfaces show the design of the user application and processes through which user can request for a parking slot while reaching on the parking area and inquire about the available parking slot in advance.

| (a) Registration Info. | (b) User's Profile | (c) Users &Parking Status | (d) Route to Destination |

**Fig. 3.** Proposed context-aware application user interfaces

The Fig. 3 depicts four different screens. Figure 3(a) is a service provider's home screen where a user can register or login to the application. The purpose of this login screen is to book a parking slot. Figure 3(b) shows the user's profile. In Fig. 3(c), the service provider can see the available, requested and occupied parking slots. Figure 3(d) shows the screen of the RUPD user who is about to arrive at the parking area. Due to space constraint, we illustrate few screenshots of the application only and omit further technicalities.

## 6   Conclusion

In this paper, we first briefly surveyed context-aware smart parking systems and then proposed a prototype of context-aware parking application that assists drivers in finding a parking slot on real-time dynamically while the user intends to arrive at the destination. This system allows registered users to reserve parking slots at the estimated time of arrival in the specified location while the user is at home, in the office or on the way to the destination. In the future work, we will implement the system in a real-time environment. In addition, we upgrade this application for Android devices.

## References

1. Pedestrians and cyclists dying more in road accidents. http://southasia.oneworld.net/archive/globalheadlines/pedestrians-and-cyclists-dying-more-in-road-accidents#.W4mpPM4zapo. Accessed 20 Aug 2018
2. Ngai, E.W.T., Leung, T.K.P., Wong, Y.H., Lee, M.C.M., Chai, P.Y.F., Choi, Y.S.: Design and development of a context-aware decision support system for real-time accident handling in logistics. Decis. Support Syst. **52**(4), 816–827 (2012)

3. Adhatarao, S.S., Alfandi, O., Bochem, A., Hogrefe, D.: Smart parking system for vehicles. In: Vehicular Networking Conference (VNC), 2014 IEEE, pp. 189–190. IEEE (2014)
4. Al-Sultan, S., Al-Bayatti, A.H., Zedan, H.: Context-aware driver behavior detection system in intelligent transportation systems. IEEE Trans. Veh. Technol. 62(9), 4264–4275 (2013)
5. Alemdar, H., Ersoy, C.: Wireless sensor networks for healthcare: a survey. Comput. Networks 54(15), 2688–2710 (2010)
6. Alghamdi, W., Shakshuki, E., Sheltami, T.R.: Context-aware driver assistance system. Procedia Comput. Sci. 10, 785–794 (2012)
7. Alhammad, A., Siewe, F., Al-Bayatti, A.H.: An infostation-based context-aware on-street parking system. In: 2012 International Conference on Computer Systems and Industrial Informatics, pp. 1–6, December 2012
8. Biondi, S., Monteleone, S., La Torre, G., Catania, V.: A context-aware smart parking system. In: 2016 12th International Conference on Signal-Image Technology & Internet-Based Systems (SITIS), pp. 450–454. IEEE (2016)
9. Dey, A.K.: Understanding and using context. Pers. Ubiquit. Comput. 5(1), 4–7 (2001)
10. Hoogendoorn, R.G., Breukink, H.J., van Arem, B.: A context aware intelligent speed adaptation system: a field operational test. In: 2012 15th International IEEE Conference on Intelligent Transportation Systems, pp. 1091–1096 (2012)
11. Kamble, P., Chandgude, S., Deshpande, K., Kumari, C., Gaikwad, K.: Smart parking system (2018)
12. Kenney, J.B.: Dedicated Short-range Communications (dsrc) standards in the United States. Proc. IEEE 99(7), 1162–1182 (2011)
13. Li, X., Eckert, M., Martinez, J.F., Rubio, G.: Context aware middleware architectures: survey and challenges. Sensors 15(8), 20570–20607 (2015)
14. Pham, T.N., Tsai, M., Nguyen, D.B., Dow, C., Deng, D.: A cloud-based smart-parking system based on internet-of-things technologies. IEEE Access 3, 1581–1591 (2015)
15. Rad, F., Pazhokhzadeh, H., Parvin, H.: A smart hybrid system for parking space reservation in VANET. J. Adv. Comput. Eng. Technol. 3(1), 11–18 (2017)
16. Ramazani, A., Vahdat-Nejad, H.: A new context-aware approach to traffic congestion estimation. In: 2014 4th International Conference on Computer and Knowledge Engineering (ICCKE), pp. 504–508 (2014)
17. Ramesh, M.V., Vidya, P.T., Pradeep, P.: Context aware wireless sensor system integrated with participatory sensing for real time road accident detection. In: 2013 Tenth International Conference on Wireless and Optical Communications Networks (WOCN), pp. 1–5 (2013)
18. Rico, J., Sancho, J., Cendon, B., Camus, M.: Parking easier by using context information of a smart city: enabling fast search and management of parking resources. In: 2013 27th International Conference on Advanced Information Networking and Applications Workshops (WAINA), pp. 1380–1385. IEEE (2013)
19. Rinne, M., Törmä, S., Kratinov, D.: Mobile crowdsensing of parking space using geofencing and activity recognition. In: 10th ITS European Congress, Helsinki, Finland, pp. 16–19 (2014)
20. Saini, M., Alelaiwi, A., Saddik, A.E.: How close are we to realizing a pragmatic vanet solution? A meta-survey. ACM Comput. Surv. (CSUR) 48(2), 29 (2015)
21. Saswadkar, A., Kulkarni, C., Ghige, S., Farande, S., Salunke, S.: Mobile application for IoT based smart parking system. Int. J. Eng. Sci. 8, 17337 (2018)

22. Satre, S.M., More, P., Shaikh, S., Mhatre, O., Student, B.: Smart parking system based on dynamic resource sharing. Int. J. Eng. Sci. **8**, 16236 (2018)
23. Srikanth, S., Pramod, P., Dileep, K., Tapas, S., Patil, M.U., et al.: Design and implementation of a prototype smart parking (spark) system using wireless sensor networks. In: International Conference on Advanced Information Networking and Applications Workshops, WAINA 2009, pp. 401–406. IEEE (2009)
24. Wang, Y., Jiang, J., Mu, T.: Context-aware and energy-driven route optimization for fully electric vehicles via crowdsourcing. IEEE Trans. Intell. Transp. Syst. **14**(3), 1331–1345 (2013)
25. Wilson, J., Patwari, N.: See-through walls: motion tracking using variance-based radio tomography networks. IEEE Trans. Mob. Comput. **10**(5), 612–621 (2011)
26. Xu, B., Wolfson, O., Yang, J., Stenneth, L., Philip, S.Y., Nelson, P.C.: Real-time street parking availability estimation. In: 2013 IEEE 14th International Conference on Mobile Data Management (MDM), vol. 1, pp. 16–25. IEEE (2013)

# Stream Pseudo-probabilistic Ciphers

Nikolay Andreevich Moldovyan[1], Dmitriy Nikolaevich Moldovyan[1],
Quang Minh Le[2], Long Giang Nguyen[3], Sy Tan Ho[4],
and Hieu Minh Nguyen[4(✉)]

[1] St. Petersburg Institute for Informatics and Automation
of Russian Academy of Sciences, St. Petersburg 199178, Russia
[2] The Information Technology Institute (ITI),
Vietnam National University, Hanoi, Vietnam
[3] Institute of Information Technology, Vietnam Academy of Science
and Technology, Hanoi, Vietnam
[4] Academy of Cryptography Techniques, Hanoi, Vietnam
hieuminhmta@gmail.com

**Abstract.** The paper considers methods and algorithms for stream pseudo-probabilistic encryption and introduces a novel design of such ciphers. In the known algorithms of such type two independent messages (fake and secret ones) are encrypted simultaneously (with using two different keys, fake and secret) and the produced ciphertext is computationally indistinguishable from the ciphertext produced by process of the probabilistic encryption of the fake message using the fake key. However in the known stream pseudo-probabilistic encryption schemes the algorithms for decrypting the fake and secret messages do not coincide completely. Therefore a potential attacker can use the last fact to distinguish the pseudo-probabilistic encryption from the probabilistic one. To provide resistance to such potential attacks in the paper there are proposed stream pseudo-probabilistic ciphers satisfying criterion of the sameness of the algorithms for decrypting the fake and secret messages. The introduced ciphers are sufficiently fast and represent interest for practical application to provide confidentiality of the communication protocols performed using public channels. The randomized pseudo-probabilistic stream ciphers have been also designed.

**Keywords:** Stream cipher · Pseudo-probabilistic encryption
Probabilistic cipher · Fake message · Secret message

## 1 Introduction

The notion of pseudo-probabilistic (PP) encryption was introduced in [1] as a particular implementation of the shared-key deniable encryption (DE) [2]. The notion of the DE is a special cryptographic primitive suitable for providing resistance to so called coercive attacks [2], i.e., attacks from the part of some potential coercive adversary has power to force a party of the communication session or

© ICST Institute for Computer Sciences, Social Informatics and Telecommunications Engineering 2019
Published by Springer Nature Switzerland AG 2019. All Rights Reserved
P. Cong Vinh and V. Alagar (Eds.): ICCASA 2018/ICTCC 2018, LNICST 266, pp. 36–47, 2019.
https://doi.org/10.1007/978-3-030-06152-4_4

the both parties simultaneously to open the encryption key and the ciphertext after the last has been sent. The paper [2] initiated a lot of investigations devoted to developing secure and efficient protocols for public-key DE [3,4] which have practical interest as a method for preventing vote buying in the internet-voting systems [3] and to provide secure multiparty computations [5].

The shared-key DS algorithms have practical significance as individual method for providing the information protection against unauthorized access in computer and communication systems in the case of coercive attacks. Such application of the shared-key DE algorithms are considered in detail in paper [1] where it had been also shown that for such application it is reasonable to implement the DE algorithms in the form of some PP cipher that generates the ciphertext indistinguishable from the ciphertext generated by some probabilistic encryption procedure applied to transform some fake message with some fake key. Actually the ciphertext contains two messages, the fake and the secret ones that have been encrypted simultaneously, however it is computationally infeasible to distinguish PP encryption process from the probabilistic one while performing cryptanalysis of the ciphertext. The paper [6] describes the block PP encryption algorithms possessing sufficiently high performance and representing practical interest. The papers [1,7] considers the stream DE ciphers, however the ciphers from [1] have sufficiently low performance and the cipher from [7] uses different algorithms for disclosing the fake and the secret message. Any differences between algorithms implementing decryption process while disclosing fake and secret messages can be potentially used by the coercive attacker to distinguish the ciphertext produced as the result of the PP encryption from the ciphertext produced as the result of the probabilistic encryption. Therefore, the criterion of the coincidence of the decryption algorithms for opening the fake and secret messages has practical significance.

Present paper introduces fast stream PP ciphers with the single decryption algorithm for disclosing the fake and secret messages. The paper is organized as follows. Section 2 describes the model of the coercive attack and the design criteria. Section 3 discusses the stream PP cipher proposed in [1]. Section 4 introduces a new stream PP cipher. In Sect. 5 there is considered randomized stream PP cipher. Section 6 concludes the paper.

## 2  Model of the Coercive Attack and Design Criteria

It is assumed that some potential adversary attacks the sender of the encrypted message or/and the receiver after the ciphertext has been sent via a public communication channel. Besides. the adversary has possibility to intercept the ciphertext and the both parties of the communication session to open the following:

- the source text corresponding to the ciphertext;
- encryption and decryption algorithms;
- the source software code used for performing decryption (not encryption) of the ciphertext;
- the encryption key.

Accordingly to [1,6] the resistance to the described potential attack can be provided using the stream PP cipher applied to performing simultaneous encryption of the fake and secret message which produces the ciphertext exactly the same as the ciphertext produced by some stream probabilistic cipher applied to encrypt the fake message (criterion of the computational indistinguishability from probabilistic encryption [1]). Like in the PP ciphers introduced in [1,7] the simultaneous stream encryption of the fake and secret messages is to be performed using two different keys, the fake and secret ones correspondingly. At time of the coercive attack the sender and the receiver of the ciphertext will open the fake message and the fake key. Besides, they will open the stream probabilistic encryption algorithm (called associated probabilistic encryption algorithm [1]) and related stream decryption algorithm. The last two algorithms are attributed to some stream probabilistic cipher called associated probabilistic cipher. The parties of the secure communication session will lie plausible they used the associated stream probabilistic cipher. While using the opened fake key, the decryption procedure of the last cipher will transform the ciphertext into the fake message. Therefore the coercer will have no arguments to expose their lie, until he shows possibility of the alternative decryption of the ciphertext.

Thus, we propose the following design criteria for creating the stream PP ciphers:

- the stream encryption should be performed as simultaneous transformation of two messages, secret one and fake one, using secret and fake keys shared by sender and receiver;
- a stream probabilistic cipher should be associated with the constructed stream PP cipher;
- the associated stream probabilistic cipher should potentially transform the fake message with the fake key into the same ciphertext that is produced by the stream PP cipher;
- disclosing the secret message, while performing cryptanalysis on the base of the known fake massage and the known fake key, should be computationally infeasible;
- the cipher should include encryption and decryption algorithms possessing sufficiently high performance;
- the decryption algorithm should provided independent recovering of the secret and fake messages;
- the algorithms for recovering the fake and secret messages should completely coincide;
- using the fixed-size shared keys should provide performing secure PP encryption of messages having arbitrary length.

# 3   Pseudo-probabilistic of Two Different Messages with the Single Decryption Algorithm for Independent Disclosing Each of the Messages

In the paper [1] the introduced notion of pseudo-probabilistic encryption was illustrated by the proposed stream encryption algorithm based on using some one-way transformation function, for example on the base of some secure hash-function $F_H$. Using the hash-function as the base primitive of the encryption procedure is as follows. Suppose $T$ is a secret message represented as sequence of $u$-bit symbols $t_i$: $T = \{t_1, t_2, \ldots, t_i, \ldots, t_z\}$, for example $u = 4$ to 16.

The following algorithm proposed in [1] performs probabilistic encryption of the message $T$ with using the hash-function $F_H$ and the key $Q$.

## Algorithm for Probabilistic Encryption

1. Set counter $i = 1$ and random 128-bit initialization vector $V$. (The value $V$ is not secret and is to be sent by sender to receiver of the secret message $T$.)
2. Set counter $j = 0$.
3. If $j < 2^{k+1}$, then generate a random $k$-bit ($k > u$) value $r$. Otherwise output the message "The $i$th data block is not encrypted", increment the counter $i = i + 1$ and go to step 2.
4. Compute the value $t = F_H(Q||V||i||r) \bmod 2^u$, where $||$ is the concatenation operation. If $t \neq t_i$, then increment $j = j + 1$ and go to step 3.
5. Set $r_i = r$. If $i \neq z$, then increment $i = i + 1$ and go to step 2. Otherwise STOP.

The described algorithm is a probabilistic procedure. Indeed, it uses random selection of the current ciphertext symbol $r_i$ (see step 3). The size of the output ciphertext $R = \{r_1, r_2, \ldots, r_i, \ldots, r_z\}$ is larger than the size of the source message $T$, since the size of symbols of the input text is larger than the size of the symbols of the output ciphertext ($k > u$). As it was shown in [1] mechanism of random selection some part of the has-function argument, until the hash value takes on the required value of the symbol of the source message, can be put into the base of procedure of simultaneous encryption of two different input message, fake and secret, using two different keys, fake and secret respectively. In this case the generated ciphertext contains both messages and each of the lasts can be decrypted simultaneously with the same decryption algorithm, i. e., the procedure for decrypting the fake message coincide exactly with the procedure for decrypting the secret message. Thus, the encryption procedure of two messages produces the ciphertext that potentially could be produced by process of encrypting only one fake message with using the fake key. Therefore, the distinguishing the ciphertext produced by the process of simultaneous encryption of the fake and secret messages from the ciphertext produced by the process of probabilistic encryption of the fake message will require disclosing the secret message. The process of simultaneous encryption of two messages, called pseudo-probabilistic encryption, is described as follows.

Suppose the sequence $M = \{m_1, m_2, \ldots, m_i, \ldots, m_z\}$, where symbols $m_i$ have size $u$ bits, represents the fake message and $K$ is the fake key. The next algorithm proposed in [1] encrypts the secret $T$ and fake message $M$ with using the secret $Q$ and fake $K$ keys.

## Algorithms for Simultaneous Encryption of Two Messages

1. Set counter $i = 1$ and random 128-bit initialization vector $V$.
2. Set counter $j = 0$.
3. If $j < 2^{k+1}$, then generate a random $k$-bit $(k > 2u)$ value $r$. Otherwise output the message "The $i$th data block is not encrypted", then increment $i = i + 1$ and go to step 2.
4. Compute the values $t = F_H(Q||V||i||r) \bmod 2^u$ and $m = F_H(K||V||i||r) \bmod 2^u$.
5. If $t \neq t_i$ or $m \neq m_i$, then increment $j = j + 1$ and go to step 3.
6. Set $r_i = r$. If $i \neq z$, then increment $i = i + 1$ and go to step 2. Otherwise STOP.

The decryption algorithm corresponding to the both described encryption algorithm is as follows:

## Decryption Procedure

1. Set counter $i = 1$, decryption key $X (X \leftarrow Q$ or $X \leftarrow K)$ and random 128-bit initialization vector $V$.
2. Compute the value $w_i = F_H(X||V||i||r_i) \bmod 2^u$.
3. If $i \neq z$, then increment $i = i + 1$ and go to step 2. Otherwise STOP.

The decryption algorithm outputs the sequence of u-bit data blocks $w_i$: $W = \{w_1, w_2, \ldots, w_i, \ldots, w_z\}$. The correctness of the decryption procedure is evident and $W = M$, if $X = K$, or $W = T$, if $X = Q$. A major drawback of the two encryption algorithms discussed above is applying the mechanism of the exhaustive search for finding the value of each symbol of the ciphertext. On the average, there are required about $2^u$ and $2^{2u}$ trials for selecting appropriate random value $r$ at step 3 of the first and second algorithm respectively. Because of this drawback, their productivity is very low. In order to increase the speed of encryption, the next section proposes an encryption method that is free from using the mentioned mechanism of the exhaustive search.

# 4   Implementation Using Block Encryption Function

## 4.1   General Method for Stream Pseudo-probabilistic Encryption

Suppose that the fake message $M = (m_1, m_2, \ldots, m_i, \ldots, m_z)$ and the secret message $T = (t_1, t_2, \ldots, t_i, \ldots, t_z)$ are represented if the form of the sequences of u-bit symbols $m_i$ and $t_i (i = 1, 2, \ldots, z)$ correspondingly and some secure block encryption function $E_S$ is used to generate the following three key streams $\Gamma$,

$\Gamma'$, and $\Gamma''$ depending on the values of the used block-encryption key $S = K$, $S = Q$, and $S = U$ correspondingly:

$$\Gamma = \{\alpha_1, \alpha_2, \ldots, \alpha_i, \ldots, \alpha_z\},$$
$$\Gamma' = \{\beta_1, \beta_2, \ldots, \beta_i, \ldots, \beta_z\}, \quad \text{and}$$
$$\Gamma'' = \{(\lambda_1, \mu_1), (\lambda_2, \mu_2), \ldots, (\lambda_i, \mu_i), \ldots, (\lambda_z, \mu_z)\},$$

where elements $\alpha_i$, $\beta_i$, $\lambda_i$, and $\mu_i$ represent the $u$-bit symbols. The key stream $\Gamma''$ is generated so that the bit strings $1||\lambda_i$ and $1||\mu_i$, where the sign "$||$" denotes the concatenation operation, represent two mutually irreducible polynomials. The fake key represents the pair $(K, U)$ and the secret key represents the pair $(Q, U)$, where the random subkeys $K$ and $Q$ are generated so that they have different oddness.

Transformation of the pair of the symbols $t_i$ and $m_i$. is performed simultaneously as solving the following system of two linear congruencies:

$$\begin{cases} c_i \equiv m_i \oplus \alpha_i \bmod \eta_i \\ c_i \equiv t_i \oplus \beta_i \bmod \psi_i \end{cases} \tag{1}$$

where $c_i$ is the $i$th symbol of the output ciphertext; $\oplus$ is the bit wise modulo 2 addition operation; $(\eta_i; \psi_i) = (1||\lambda_i; 1||\mu_i)$, if $K$ is odd, and $(\eta_i; \psi_i) = (1||\mu_i; 1||\lambda_i)$, if $K$ is even.

Elements of the key sequences $\Gamma$, $\Gamma'$, and $\Gamma''$ depend on the subkeys $K$, $Q$, and $U$ correspondingly, on sequential number of the message symbol $i$, and on the initialization vector $V$ that is not secret and can be sent by the sender to the receiver via an insecure channel. While using random initialization vector $V$ different pairs of input messages will be encrypted with different triples of the key sequences $\Gamma$, $\Gamma'$, and $\Gamma''$.

Decryption of the $i$th symbol of the fake and secret message is performed as generating the respective elements of the key sequences and using the following two formulas:

$$m_i = c_i \oplus \alpha_i \bmod \eta_i \quad \text{and} \quad t_i = c_i \oplus \beta_i \bmod \psi_i$$

## 4.2    Algorithms for Generating the Key Sequences

Suppose $E_S$ be a secure block encryption function with 128-bit input (for example, AES). The following algorithm performs generation of the elements $\alpha_i$ of the key sequence $\Gamma$ depending on the value $S = K$.

**Algorithm 1.**

1. Set the 64-bit counter $i = 1$ and the value of the random 64-bit initialization vector $V$. (The value $V$ is not secret and is to be sent by sender to receiver of the secret message T).
2. Compute the value $\alpha_i = E_S(V||i) \bmod 2^u$.
3. If $i < z$, then increment the value $i$: $i \leftarrow i + 1$ and go to step 2. Otherwise STOP.

The next algorithm performs generation of the elements $\beta_i$ of the key sequence $\Gamma'$ depending on the value $S = Q$.

**Algorithm 2.**

1. Set the 64-bit counter $i = 1$ and the value of the random 64-bit initialization vector $V$.
2. Compute the value $\beta_i = E_S(V||i) \bmod 2^u$.
3. If $i < z$, then increment the value $i$: $i \leftarrow i + 1$ and go to step 2. Otherwise STOP.

The next algorithm performs generation of the pair of key elements $(\lambda_i, \mu_i)$ of the key sequence $\Gamma''$ depending on the value $S = U$. Note that in frame of the Algorithms 1 and 2 there is executed the same sequence of operations. They differ only by the value of the key used to compute the output value of the block encryption function $E_S(V||i)$.

**Algorithm 3.**

1. Set the 64-bit counter $i = 1$ and the value of the random 64-bit initialization vector $V$.
2. Compute the $2u$-bit value $(\mu_i||\lambda_i) = E_S(V||i) \bmod 2^{2u}$.
3. Compute the greatest common divisor ($gcd$) of the binary polynomials $1||\mu_i$ and $1||\lambda_i$.
4. If $gcd(1||\mu_i; 1||\lambda_i) \neq 1$, then, considering the bit string $\lambda_i$ as binary number, modify the value $\lambda_i$ as follows: $\lambda_i \leftarrow \lambda_i + 1 \bmod 2^u$, where $\leftarrow$ denotes the assignment operation, and go to step 3.
5. If $i < z$, then increment the value $i$: $i \leftarrow i + 1$ and go to step 2. Otherwise STOP.

### 4.3    Algorithm for Stream Pseudo-probabilistic Encryption

The stream pseudo-probabilistic encryption of two input messages $M$ and $T$ is performed as consecutive transformation of the pairs of the symbols $m_i$ and $t_i$ (for $i = 1, 2, \ldots, z$) into the $2u$-bit symbols $c_i$ of the output ciphertext. The pair $(m_i, t_i)$ is transformed as follows:

**Pseudo-probabilistic Encryption Algorithm**
    **Input:** the values $K$, $Q$, $U$, $i$, $t_i$, and $m_i$.

1. Using Algorithm 1 generate the key element $\alpha_i$.
2. Using Algorithm 2 generate the key element $\beta_i$
3. Using Algorithm 3 generate the pair of key elements $(\lambda_i, \mu_i)$.
4. If the value $K$ is even (and the value $Q$ is odd), then define the values $\eta_i = 1||\mu_i$ and $\psi_i = 1||\lambda_i$ and go to step 6.
5. Define the values $\eta_i = 1||\lambda_i$ and $\psi_i = 1||\mu_i$.
6. Compute the $2u$-bit symbol $ci$ of the output ciphertext, using the following formula that describes solution of the system of congruencies (1):

$$c_i = \left[(m_i \oplus \alpha_i)\psi_i(\psi_i^{-1} \bmod \eta_i) \oplus (t_i \oplus \beta_i)\eta_i(\eta_i^{-1} \bmod \psi_i)\right] \bmod \eta_i\psi_i. \quad (2)$$

**Output:** the $i$th ciphertext symbol $c_i$.

Disclosing each of two source message from the ciphertext $C = (c_1, c_2, \dots, c_i, \dots, c_z)$ is performed independently as consecutive transformation of the ciphertext symbols $c_i (i = 1, 2, \dots, z)$ using the following decryption algorithm.

## Common Decryption Algorithm

**Input:** the value $i$, the ciphertext symbol $ci$, the initialization vector $V$, and the decryption key $(W, U)$, where $W = K$ for disclosing the fake message or $W = Q$ for disclosing the secret message $T$.

1. Compute the $u$-bit value $\gamma_i = E_W(V||i) \bmod 2^u$.
2. Compute the $2u$-bit value $(\mu_i||\lambda_i) = E_U(V||i) \bmod 2^{2u}$.
3. Compute the greatest common divisor ($gcd$) of the binary polynomials $1||\mu_i$ and $1||\lambda_i$.
4. If $gcd(1||\mu_i; 1||\lambda_i) \neq 1$, then, considering the bit string $\lambda_i$ as binary number, modify the value $i$ as follows: $\lambda_i \leftarrow \lambda_i + 1 \bmod 2^u$, where denotes the assigning operation, and go to step 3.
5. If $i < z$, then increment the value $i$: $i \leftarrow i + 1$ and go to step 2.
6. If the value $W$ is even, then assign $\sigma \leftarrow 1||\mu_i$ and go to step 8. Otherwise go to step 7.
7. If the value $W$ is odd, then assign $\sigma \leftarrow 1||\lambda_i$.
8. Compute the $i$th symbol $\tau_i$ of the source message: $\tau_i \equiv c_i \oplus \gamma_i \bmod \sigma$.

Execution of the last algorithm for $i = 1, 2, \dots, z$ provides disclosing the fake message $M$, if the fake key $(W, U) = (K, U)$ is used, or disclosing the secret message $T$, if the secret key $(W, U) = (Q, U)$ is used.

The ciphertext produced by the pseudo-probabilistic encryption algorithm potentially can be produced by the following probabilistic encryption algorithm applied to encryption of the fake message with the fake key:

## Associated Probabilistic Encryption Algorithm

**Input:** the values $K$, $U$, $i$, and $m_i$.

1. Using Algorithm 1 generate the key element $\alpha_i$.
2. Using Algorithm 3 generate the pair of key elements $(\lambda_i, \mu_i)$.
3. If the value $K$ is even, then define the values $\eta_i = 1||\mu_i$ and $\psi_i = 1||\lambda_i$ and go to step 5. Otherwise go to step 4.
4. If the value K is odd, then define the value $\eta_i = 1||\lambda_i$ and $\psi_i = 1||\mu_i$.
5. Generate random $u$-bit value $\rho$.
6. Compute the $2u$-bit symbol $c_i$ of the output ciphertext as solution of the following system of congruencies:

$$\begin{cases} c_i \equiv m_i \oplus \alpha_i \bmod \eta_i \\ c_i \equiv \rho \bmod \psi_i \end{cases} \quad (3)$$

**Output:** the $i$th ciphertext symbol $c_i$.

System (3) has solution, since $gcd(\eta_i, \psi_i) = 1$ (see step 4 of Algorithm 3). The solution is described as follows:

$$c_i = \left[(m_i \oplus \alpha_i)\psi_i(\psi_i^{-1} \bmod \eta_i) \oplus \rho\eta_i(\eta_i^{-1} \bmod \psi_i)\right] \bmod \eta_i\psi_i. \qquad (4)$$

The decryption procedure corresponding to the associated probabilistic encryption algorithm is precisely described by the Common decryption algorithm. This fact demonstrates that ciphertext generated by the pseudo-probabilistic encryption algorithm applied to encrypt simultaneously the fake $M$ and secret $T$ messages can be potentially generated by the associated probabilistic-encryption algorithm applied to encrypt the fake $M$ message.

It is easy to see that the initially proposed design criteria are satisfied by the constructed stream pseudo-probabilistic cipher, including the criterion of the computationally indistinguishability from probabilistic encryption. Since the ciphertext contains two different messages, it is potentially possible to show that the ciphertext had not been generated by probabilistic encryption algorithm, however this would require to compute the secret message in the case when the subkey $Q$ is unknown.

Suppose the coercive attacker gets the fake key $(K, U)$. Then he has possibility to compute the sequence of $u$-bit symbols $c_i' = c_i \bmod \psi_i = t_i \oplus \beta_i$. The sequence $C_t = (c_1', c_2', \ldots, c_i', \ldots, c_z')$ represents the intermediate ciphertext obtained as result of encryption the secret message $M$ with using the key stream $\Gamma'$. The last is generated using secure block encryption function $E$ (for example, AES), therefore the generated key stream $\Gamma'$ and the sequence of the ciphertext symbols is computationally indistinguishable from uniform random sequence and computing the message $T$ from $C_t$ is computationally infeasible.

## 5  Randomized Stream Pseudo-probabilistic Cipher

To provide a higher resistance of the stream PP encryption to the coercive attacks at which the attacker has possibility to block the communication channel and to cause repeated encryption of the same source messages in [8] it has been proposed to imbed randomization into the block PP ciphers. Let us consider construction of the randomized stream PP cipher as imbedding randomization mechanism in the PP cipher described in the previous section. The idea of the proposed randomization consists in using two random bit strings, $u$-bit string $\pi$ and $(u+1)$-bit string $R$, at step of computing the ciphertext symbol $c_i$. The last is performed as process of finding solution of the system of the following three congruencies:

$$\begin{cases} c_i \equiv m_i \oplus \alpha_i \bmod \eta_i \\ c_i \equiv t_i \oplus \beta_i \bmod \psi_i \\ c_i \equiv \pi \bmod R \end{cases} \qquad (5)$$

where $R$ is random binary polynomial of the degree $u$ such that the following conditions hold: $gcd(\eta_i, R) = 1$ and $gcd(\psi_i, R) = 1$.

The randomized stream PP encryption of two input messages $M$ and $T$ is performed as consecutive randomized transformation of the pairs of the symbols $m_i$ and $t_i$ (for $i = 1, 2, \ldots, z$) into the $3u$-bit symbols $c_i$ of the output ciphertext. The randomized transformation of the pair of symbols $(m_i, t_i)$ is executed as follows:

### Randomized Pseudo-probabilistic Encryption Algorithm
**Input:** the values $K$, $U$, $i$, $t_i$, and $m_i$.

1. Using Algorithm 1 generate the key element $\alpha_i$.
2. Using Algorithm 2 generate the key element $\beta_i$.
3. Using Algorithm 3 generate the pair of key elements $(\lambda_i, \mu_i)$.
4. If the value $K$ is even (and the value $Q$ is odd), then define the values $\eta_i = 1||\mu_i$ and $\psi_i = 1||\lambda_i$ and go to step 8.
5. Define the values $\eta_i = 1||\lambda_i$ and $\psi_i = 1||\mu_i$.
6. Generate uniformly random $u$-bit string $\pi$.
7. Generate random $(u + 1)$-bit string $R$ such that $gcd(\eta_i, R) = 1$ and $gcd(\psi_i, R) = 1$, where $R$ is interpreted as binary polynomial of the degree $u$.
8. Compute the $3u$-bit symbol $c_i$ of the output ciphertext, using the following formula that describes solution of the system of congruencies (5):

$$c_i = [(m_i \oplus \alpha_i)\psi_i R(\psi_i^{-1} R^{-1} \bmod \eta_i) \oplus (t_i \oplus \beta_i)\eta_i R(\eta_i^{-1} R^{-1} \bmod \psi_i)$$
$$\oplus R\eta_i\psi_i(\psi_i^{-1}\eta_i^{-1} \bmod R)] \bmod \eta_i\psi_i R. \tag{6}$$

**Output:** the ith ciphertext symbol $c_i$ having size equal to $3u$ bits.

The probabilistic stream cipher associated with the described randomized stream PP cipher is described as follows:

### Associated Probabilistic Stream Cipher
**Input:** the values $K$, $U$, $i$, and $m_i$.

1. Using Algorithm 1 generate the key element $\alpha_i$.
2. Using Algorithm 3 generate the pair of key elements $(\lambda_i, \mu_i)$.
3. If the value $K$ is even, then define the values $\eta_i = 1||\mu_i$ and $\psi_i = 1||\lambda_i$ and go to step 5.
4. If the value $K$ is odd, then define the values $\eta_i = 1||\lambda_i$ and $i = 1||\mu_i$.
5. Generate uniformly random $2u$-bit string $\pi$.
6. Generate random $(2u + 1)$-bit string $R$ such that $gcd(\eta_i, R) = 1$, where $R$ is interpreted as binary polynomial of the degree $2u$.
7. Compute the $3u$-bit symbol $c_i$ of the output ciphertext as solution of the following system of two congruencies:

$$\begin{cases} c_i \equiv m_i \oplus \alpha_i \bmod \eta_i \\ c_i \equiv \rho \bmod R \end{cases} \tag{7}$$

**Output:** the $i$th ciphertext symbol ci having size equal to $3u$ bits.

The system (7) has solution, since $gcd(\eta_i, R) = 1$ (see step 6 of the algorithm). The solution is described as follows:

$$c_i = [(m_i \oplus \alpha_i)R(R^{-1} \bmod \eta_i) \oplus \rho\eta_i(\eta_i^{-1} \bmod R)] \bmod \eta_i R. \tag{8}$$

# 6   Conclusion

The design of stream PP cipher with the single decryption algorithm for disclosing the fake message and for disclosing the secret message, depending on the used key (fake or secret respectively) has been proposed. The randomized stream PP cipher constructed by means of embedding a randomization mechanism in the first PP cipher has been also proposed. Each of the introduced stream PP ciphers satisfies criterion of computational indistinguishability from probabilistic encryption. The last fact has been confirmed with presenting the associated probabilistic stream cipher that potentially generates the same ciphertext as the corresponding stream PP cipher. The decryption algorithm relating to the probabilistic cipher exactly coincide with the decryption algorithm relating to the corresponding PP cipher.

In the paper it has been considered the case of equal size of the symbols of the fake and secret messages, however the proposed PP encryption algorithms can be easily extended for the case of different size of the symbols $m_i$ and $t_i$. Analogous remark can be attributed to the size of random bit string mixed with the transformed symbols $m_i$ and $t_i$ in the proposed randomized stream PP cipher.

The proposed designs of stream PP ciphers use the block encryption function $E$ for generating the key streams $\Gamma$, $\Gamma'$, and $\Gamma''$, therefore performance of the introduced two PP ciphers depends on the performance of the used function $E$. It is mentioned case of using the block encryption standard AES as function $E$. Since AES is sufficiently fast for hardware and for software implementations the introduced PP-encryption algorithm have performance sufficient for many potential practical implementations. They have significantly higher performance than the stream PP ciphers described in [1].

To increase the performance it is possible to use block encryption functions having comparatively small size of input data block, for example, 32-, 48-, and 64-bit block ciphers. However detailed consideration of such cases represent individual research topic. It is also interesting to use the hash-functions for generating the key streams $\Gamma$, $\Gamma'$, and $\Gamma''$.

**Acknowledgements.** The reported study was funded by Russian Foundation for Basic Research (project #18 − 57 − 54002 − $Viet\_a$) and by Vietnam Academy of Science and Technology (project #$QTRU$01.08/18 − 19).

# References

1. Moldovyan, N.A., Nashwan, A.A.-M., Nguyen, D.T., Nguyen, N.H., Nguyen, H.M.: Deniability of symmetric encryption based on computational indistinguishability from probabilistic ciphering. In: Bhateja, V., Nguyen, B.L., Nguyen, N.G., Satapathy, S.C., Le, D.-N. (eds.) Information Systems Design and Intelligent Applications. AISC, vol. 672, pp. 209–218. Springer, Singapore (2018). https://doi.org/10.1007/978-981-10-7512-4_21

2. Canetti, R., Dwork, C., Naor, M., Ostrovsky, R.: Deniable encryption. In: Kaliski, B.S. (ed.) CRYPTO 1997. LNCS, vol. 1294, pp. 90–104. Springer, Heidelberg (1997). https://doi.org/10.1007/BFb0052229

3. Barakat, M.T.: A new sender-side public-key deniable encryption scheme with fast decryption. KSII Trans. Internet Inf. Syst. **8**(9), 3231–3249 (2014)

4. Dachman-Soled, D.: On minimal assumptions for sender-deniable public key encryption. In: Krawczyk, H. (ed.) PKC 2014. LNCS, vol. 8383, pp. 574–591. Springer, Heidelberg (2014). https://doi.org/10.1007/978-3-642-54631-0_33

5. Ishai, Y., Kushilevitz, E., Ostrovsky, R., Prabhakaran, M., Sahai, A.: Efficient non-interactive secure computation. In: Paterson, K.G. (ed.) EUROCRYPT 2011. LNCS, vol. 6632, pp. 406–425. Springer, Heidelberg (2011). https://doi.org/10.1007/978-3-642-20465-4_23

6. Moldovyan, N.A., Moldovyan, A.A., Tam, N.D., Hai, N.N., Minh, N.H.: Pseudo-probabilistic block ciphers and their randomization. J. Ambient Intell. Hum. Comput. (2018). https://doi.org/10.1007/1265201807916

7. Moldovyan, N.A., Moldovyan, A.A., Moldovyan, D.N., Shcherbacov, V.A.: Stream deniable-encryption algorithms. Comput. Sci. J. Moldova **24**(1), 68–82 (2017)

8. Moldovyan, A.A., Moldovyan, N.A., Berezin, A.N., Shapovalov, P.I.: Randomized pseudo-probabilistic encryption algorithms. In: Proceedings of 2017 20th IEEE International Conference on Soft Computing and Measurements, SCM 2017, pp. 14–17 (2017)

# jFAT: An Automation Framework for Web Application Testing

Hanh Phuc Nguyen[1,2]([✉]), Hong Anh Le[3], and Ninh Thuan Truong[1]

[1] VNU - University of Engineering and Technology,
144 Xuan Thuy, Cau Giay, Ha Noi, Vietnam
thuantn@vnu.edu.vn
[2] VMU - Vietnam Maritime University,
484 Lach Tray, Le Chan, Hai Phong, Vietnam
phucnh@vimaru.edu.vn
[3] Hanoi University of Mining and Geology,
18 Pho Vien, Bac Tu Liem, Hanoi, Vietnam
lehonganh@humg.edu.vn

**Abstract.** Web technologies have developed rapidly because web application is currently leading the trends of software development. A web-based application is a program that is accessed over a network connection, rather than existing within a device's memory, hence detecting its failures is different from other software systems. Many approaches and tools have been proposed for web testing, however, introducing new frameworks is still an emerging topic in this field. This paper proposes an automation framework running in Java platform for web testing, called jFAT, which integrates with Selenium and TestNG. The paper also illustrates the use of framework with the Bank application case study.

**Keywords:** Automation testing · Web applications · POM

## 1 Introduction

Software applications nowadays are built and worked in web environments, they are also called web-based applications. A web-based application is a program that is accessed over a network connection, rather than existing within a devices memory, it often runs inside a web browser. Their advantage is the ability to share functions, data in the system; support multiple environments working. Therefore, providing quality assurance solutions for web-based applications is becoming more and more important.

Software testing is a technique used widely in software quality assurance. It is a process of executing a program or application with the intent of finding the software bugs. It can also be stated as the process of validating and verifying that a software program or application meets technical requirements that guided its design and development.

© ICST Institute for Computer Sciences, Social Informatics and Telecommunications Engineering 2019
Published by Springer Nature Switzerland AG 2019. All Rights Reserved
P. Cong Vinh and V. Alagar (Eds.): ICCASA 2018/ICTCC 2018, LNICST 266, pp. 48–57, 2019.
https://doi.org/10.1007/978-3-030-06152-4_5

In reality, two methods may be applied to test a software application: manual and automation testing. However, manual testing can become boring and hence error-prone. To avoid these disadvantages and to reduce time and money consuming in testing process, one uses automation testing, in other words an automation tool is used to execute a test case suite.

This paper proposes a Java-based automation testing framework of web-based applications, which integrates with Selenium and TestNG providing features to perform test cases automatically. The contribution of the paper includes (1) module-driven approach to web testing; (2) a high performance and secure framework which is able to execute multiple test scripts at a time.

The remainder of the paper is structured as follows. Section 2 provides some backgrounds of web automation testing. Main work of the paper is presented in Sect. 3 which presents the approach and detailed design of the proposed framework. Followed by Sect. 4, a case study of Bank management system is shown for illustration purposes. Section 5 summarizes the work that relates to this paper research topic. Finally, Sect. 6 concludes the paper and gives some future research directions.

## 2 Background

Automation testing is a method of software testing that uses software tools to perform tests and then compares actual test results with expected results. All of this is done automatically with little or no human intervention. Automation testing includes the following main phases:

- Test tool selection: One of the most important steps before starting automation in any organization is test automation tool selection. Test Tool selection is heavily dependent on the technology which the Application Under Test is built on. Our paper brings the benefit to this phase by providing an automated testing tool for web applications.
- Define the scope of automation: The scope of automation is the area of the Application Under Test will be automated. In order to determine the scope, pay attention to matters such as: scenarios which have a large amount of data; common functionalities across applications; the complexity of test cases; etc
- Planning, Design, and Development: In this phase, you build the strategy and plan for automation. Planning includes establishing an approach to the automation testing framework that consists of the hardware, network, models, tools, and analysis methods. You need to perform the following tasks: Automation tools selected; Framework design and its features; In-Scope and Out-of-scope items of automation; Automation testbed preparation; etc.
- Test execution: This phase involves actual execution of automated tests or integration of the automation framework with built systems. Execution can be performed by means of the automation tool directly or by utilizing the Test Management tool which will trigger the automation tool. This phase also involves verifying the reports generated by automated tests, analyzing the failures and logging appropriate failures as defects in defect tracking system.

– Maintenance: This phase is made to ensure that all automated tests are updated regularly to accommodate changes in application under test so that they remain on purpose and give reliable results.

Testing of Web-based applications is difficult due to its nature of execution environment such as heterogeneity, multi-platform support, autonomy, cooperation, and distribution, etc. Many approaches are proposed to test web applications, these approaches concentrated on the following aspects:

– Functionality Testing: This is used to verify if your product is as per the specifications you intended for it as well as the functional requirements you planned for it in your developmental documentation. Functional testing requires that the tester perform a test of all the links in the site, the format used in the site to send and receive the necessary information from the user. There are also database connections, cookies checks and HTML/CSS verification.
– Usability testing: To verify how the application is easy to use with.
– Interface testing: Performed to verify the interface and the data flow from one system to others. There are three areas that need testing - Application, Web and Database Server.
– Database Testing: Database is one crucial component of your web application and it must be tested comprehensively.
– Compatibility testing: Compatibility testing is performed based on the context of the application.
– Performance Testing: This will guarantee your site's ability to handle all loads.
– Security testing: Performed to verify if the application is secured as data theft and unauthorized access are common issues on web environments.

Our approach will work with the functionality aspect and improve the performance of testing process.

## 3   An Automation Framework for Web Application Testing

In this section, we first introduce the architecture of the proposed automation framework. After that, its detailed design is presented. The proposed testing approach, which is modularity-driven and POM (Page Object Model)-based allows us to develop and maintain test cases more easily. It includes the main steps: (1) Generating POM from web applications; (2) Developing test scripts; (3) Executing test scripts; and (4) Logging the test results.

Following the proposed idea, we construct the jFAT automation framework with the main characteristics as follows

– Web elements are defined at once and reused for all test cases.
– Test cases are constructed in correspondence to certain functionalities of web applications.

Figure 1 depicts the architecture of the proposed framework. Pages and objects are automatically generated from web applications using Selenium Page Object Generator. Two core components of the jFAT are constructing test scripts from POM model and executing test cases using TestNG. First, users develop test cases using POM model. The framework creates test scripts that correspond to test cases based on these models. Then, it converts the test plan defined by users to an XML-based file, which is executable by TestNG. The framework runs the test cases on the browsers by using TestNG and Selenium API. The test results are captured and stored in the file.

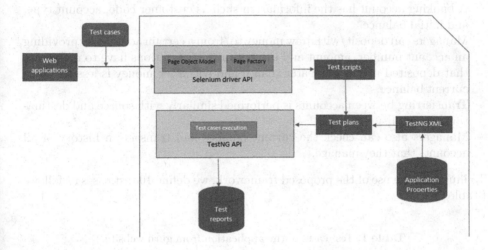

**Fig. 1.** Architecture of jFAT framework

The proposed framework provides security policies to prevent testing scripts from unintentionally accessing resources. The secure model is based on sandbox mechanism deployed in Java platform. Users also can change the security policies by customizing the configuration file, whose format is similar to a policy file of Java.

TestNG and Selenium are integrated into the framework and can be customized by using an XML-based configuration as follows.

```xml
<?xml version="1.0" encoding="UTF-8"?>
<dependency>
    <groupId>org.testng</groupId>
    <artifactId>testng</artifactId>
<version>6.13.1</version>
</dependency>
<dependency>
    <groupId>org.seleniumhq.selenium</groupId>
    <artifactId>selenium-java</artifactId>
    <version>3.8.1</version>
</dependency>
```

# 4    Case Study: Banking Application

In the case study, we take an existing website from Guru99 [1] that simulates banking transactions for managers. The information of customers include full name, birthday, city, email, phone number, and pin code. One customer has several banking accounts. One manager is in charge of many customers and is able to do the following tasks.

- Create, update, delete customers from the banking system.
- Based on the existing information, managers can create accounts for customers. A banking account has the information such as customer code, account type, and initial balance.
- Managers can deposit/withdraw money to/from a certain account by providing an account number, amount and the reasons. Transactions have to make sure that deposited money is greater than 0 and withdrew money is less than the current balance.
- Transferring between accounts is performed similarly with source and destination accounts.
- Managers also can check the current balance and transaction history of all accounts that they manage.

To illustrate the use of the proposed framework, we define 10 test cases as follows (Table 1).

**Table 1.** Test cases of the application from guru website

| No | TC Name | Description |
|----|---------|-------------|
| 1 | TC01 | Create new manager account from guru-bank site |
| 2 | TC02 | Login to guru-bank page |
| 3 | TC03 | Change manager password |
| 4 | TC04 | Create new customer |
| 5 | TC05 | Create new account for customers |
| 6 | TC06 | Change customer account type |
| 7 | TC07 | Deposit to an account |
| 8 | TC08 | Withdraw from an account |
| 9 | TC09 | Transfer between two accounts |
| 10 | TC10 | Delete an account |

Follow the proposed approach, jFAT users need to create classes for pages and objects of home, log in, and register pages. The page classes defined methods which correspond to the functional features of the pages, whilst the object classes defined attributes for web element identifiers.

**Listing 1.** A part of Home page class

```
public void clickFundTransferMenu(){
    waitForElement(hpo.MN_FUND_TRANSFER).click();
}

public void enterAccountID(String payer,String payee){
    waitForElement(hpo.TF_PAYER_ACCOUNT).sendKeys(payer);
    waitForElement(hpo.TF_PAYEE_ACCOUNT).sendKeys(payee);
}

public void enterAmountAndDesc(int amount,String desc){
    waitForElement(hpo.NF_FUND_AMOUNT).sendKeys(String.valueOf(amount));
    waitForElement(hpo.TF_DESCRIPTION).sendKeys(desc);
}
```

**Listing 2.** A part of Home page object class

```
@FindBy(xpath = "//a[contains(text(),'Change Password')]")
public WebElement MN_CHANGE_PASSWORD;

@FindBy(xpath = "//a[contains(text(),'New Customer')]")
public WebElement MN_NEW_CUSTOMER;
```

In order to execute test cases with jFAT, users need to create a test case class whose method shows the steps of a test case. The snippet below show the content of test case TC08.

**Listing 3.** A part of Home page object class

```
 WebDriver driver = drivers.get();
driver.get("http://demo.guru99.com/v4/");
LoginPage loginPage = new LoginPage(driver);
loginPage.enterUserName(un);
loginPage.enterPassword(pw);
HomePage homePage = loginPage.clickSubmit();
homePage.checkManagerID(un);
homePage.clickBalanceEnquiryMenu();
String accid =DataStorage.getData(2).toArray()[0].toString();
homePage.enterAccountID(accid);
homePage.clickSubmitEditForm();
int currentAmount = homePage.saveCurrentAmount();
homePage.clickWithdrawalMenu();
homePage.enterAccountID(accid);
int withdraw = 1200;
homePage.enterAmount(withdraw);
homePage.enterDescription("withdraw");
homePage.clickSubmitEditForm();
homePage.checkRemainingAmount(currentAmount,withdraw);
```

jFAT allows to define a test plan in a text file that indicates which test cases to run and the number of runs. Listing 4 means that the test plan executes *TC01*, *TC02*, *TC03*, *TC09* and *TC02* will be performed twice.

**Listing 4.** A test plan

```
Testsuite|tc01|1
Testsuite|tc02|2
Testsuite|tc03|1
Testsuite|tc09|1
```

In order to run all test cases, the test plan just need to define *Testsuite—All—1*. Figure 2 shows the result of the execution of the test plan 4. It graphically reports that 4 test cases are successful and 01 test case is failed.

**Fig. 2.** Test report of the test plan

# 5    Related Work

Many approaches and tools have been proposed to automation testing. Some of them are applied in industry projects.

Since tests need to be executed repeatedly, such manual tests then have to go through test automation to create scripts or programs out of them. The paper [11] describes a technique to automate test automation. The input to their technique is a sequence of steps written in natural language, and the output is a sequence of procedure calls with accompanying parameters that can drive the application without human intervention.

The paper [6] has proposed to design an automatic software testing framework for web applications based on the Selenium and JMeter. With the use of the software framework, they efficiently improve the extensibility and reusability of automated test. The results of the paper show that the software framework improves software products quality and develop efficiency.

The paper [9] exploits an object-oriented model of a web application as a test model, and proposes a definition of the unit level for testing web application. Based on this model, a method to test the single units of a web application and for the integration testing is proposed. An approach to web application functional testing is provided in the paper.

In recent years, automated web application testing tools have grown to the maturity stage in both quantity and quality. Hower [7] has presented more than 200 both commercial, and free-on-the Web testing tools for Web applications which fall into six categories. The tools are comprised of the last category that is used to assist the functionality testing of Web applications. Therefore, from a general perspective, the tools for Web application functionality testing are classified into three major categories as mentioned here.

Romano et al. [10] developed the tool for the non-functional requirements testing. They were interested in testing the aspects of (i) *Load and performance testing* and (ii) *Navigability testing*. The result of this research may be employed to assess the hosting infrastructure of Web Applications in improving quality, reliability and acceptance of Web applications.

In the line of the web application functional testing, Di Lucca et al. [9] exploited an object-oriented model of a web application as a test model as well as proposed a definition of the unit level for testing web application. A method to test the single units of a web application and for the integration testing is proposed based on this model.

Huang et al. [8] introduced a software tool, named WASATT *(Web Application Scenario Automated Testing Tool)* to support the automated testing for scenario of web-based applications.

The paper [6] has proposed to design an automatic software testing framework for web applications based on the Selenium and JMeter. With the use of the software framework, they efficiently improve the extensibility and re-usability of automated test. The results of the paper show that the software framework improves software products quality and develops efficiency.

Beside approaches presented in the papers, many automation testing tools are also available in market. Test automation tools can be expensive, and are usually employed in combination with manual testing.

Selenium [2] is an open source, popular testing tool that provides playback and recording amenity for regression testing. Recorded script in other languages like Java, Ruby, RSpec, Python, C♯, etc. can be exported using Selenium.

QTP [3] is commonly used for functional and regression testing and accommodates for every major software application and environment. Test creation and maintenance can be simplified by QTP utilising the concept of keyword driven testing. The tester is thus able to build test cases directly from the application. Defects can be fixed faster by comprehensively documenting and replicating defects for developer.

Rational Functional Tester (RFT) [4] is an Object-Oriented automated functional testing tool that is able to deliver automated functional, regression, data-driven testing and GUI testing. It supports a wide variety of protocols and applications like Java, HTML, NET, Windows, SAP, Visual Basic, etc. It is capable of recording and replaying the actions on demand, developers can also be allowed to devise keyword associated script so that it can be re-used.

Silk Test [5] is designed for performing functional and regression testing. Silk test is the primary functional testing product for e-business application. From an object-oriented language perspective, Silk Test uses the concept of an object, classes, and inheritance. Script commands can be converted into GUI commands by Silk Test. Commands can be operated on a remote or host machine on the similar machine. Silk Test can be implemented to recognise the movement of the mouse along with keystrokes. It can be useful for both playback and record method or descriptive programming methods to get the dialogs. All controls and windows of the application under test as objects are identified and all of the attributes and properties of each window are determined by Silk Test.

# 6    Conclusions and Future Work

This paper proposes a module-driven and high performance framework for web testing. The proposed framework, integrated with Selenium and TestNG, allows users to easily develop and perform test plans. The framework also provides a rich and friendly graphical test result reports of all test cases. It has just been done in the initial stage.

In the future, the framework needs to automate some steps to assist users in the development such as automatic extraction of web elements and test script generation. Moreover, we will adopt the data-driven testing approach to separate data and scripts that makes the jFAT more flexible.

**Acknowledgments.** This work has been supported by VNU University of Engineering and Technology under Project QG.16.32.

# References

1. https://www.guru99.com
2. https://www.seleniumhq.org
3. https://www.tutorialspoint.com/qtp/
4. https://www.automation-consultants.com/products/ibm-products/rational-functional-tester/
5. https://www.microfocus.com/products/silk-portfolio/silk-tes

6. Fei, W., Wencai, D.: A test automation framework based on web. In: IEEE/ACIS 11th International Conference on Computer and Information Science, ICIS. IEEE (2012)
7. Hower, R.: Software QA and testing resource center (2006). www.softwareqatest.com
8. Huang, C.-H., Chen, H.Y.: A tool to support automated testing for web application scenario. In: IEEE International Conference on Systems, Man and Cybernetics, SMC 2006, vol. 3, pp. 2179–2184. IEEE (2006)
9. Lucca, G.A.D., Fasolino, A.R., Faralli, F., Carlini, U.D.: Testing web applications. In: International Conference on Software Maintenance, Proceedings, pp. 310–319 (2002)
10. Romano, B.L., et al.: Software testing for web-applications non-functional requirements. In: 2009 Sixth International Conference on Information Technology: New Generations, pp. 1674–1675. IEEE (2009)
11. Suresh, T., Saurabh, S., Nimit, S., Satish, C.: Automating test automation. In 34th International Conference on Software Engineering (ICSE), ICSE, IEEE (2012)

# On the Compliance of Access Control Policies in Web Applications

Thanh-Nhan Luong[1,2]([✉]), Dinh-Hieu Vo[1], Van-Khanh To[1],
and Ninh-Thuan Truong[1]

[1] VNU University of Engineering and Technology,
144 Xuan Thuy, Cau Giay, Hanoi, Vietnam
ltnhan@hpmu.edu.vn, {hieuvd,khanhtv,thuantn}@vnu.edu.vn
[2] Department of Informatics, Hai Phong University of Medicine and Pharmacy,
72A Nguyen Binh Khiem, Ngo Quyen, Hai Phong, Vietnam

**Abstract.** Model-View-Controller (MVC) architecture has commonly used in the implementation of web applications. These systems often incorporate security policies to ensure their reliability. Role-based access control (RBAC) is one of the effective solutions for reducing resources access violations of a system. This paper introduces an approach to check the compliance of a web application under MVC architecture with its RBAC specification. By investigating the system architecture and source code analysis, our approach conducts with extracting a list of resources access permissions, constructing a resources exploitation graph and organizing an access control matrix according to roles of a web application. The approach aims at checking two violation cases of web applications: (i) the presence of unspecified access rules and (ii) the absence of specified access rules. We illustrate the proposed approach by a case study of web based medical records management system.

**Keywords:** Compliance · Access control policy · RBAC
Web applications

## 1 Introduction

Web applications (WAs) which are designed according to Model-View-Controller (MVC) architecture [15] have been using widely in many fields of the social life such as training, e-commerce, healthcare, etc. Besides, these applications are almost executed in the internet environment and their data is transported via difference line types so they include many implicit security risks such as lost data, leak information, refuse users' service requests, or authorize for users incorrectly [10,16]. These problems can cause damage to system resources and users. Therefore, the applications need adequate security policies and mechanisms to ensure the interests of participants.

The confidentiality, integrity, availability, accountability, and non-repudiation are basic security properties of a secure software [12]. However, each type application demands some different properties. In practice, many techniques and

© ICST Institute for Computer Sciences, Social Informatics and Telecommunications Engineering 2019
Published by Springer Nature Switzerland AG 2019. All Rights Reserved
P. Cong Vinh and V. Alagar (Eds.): ICCASA 2018/ICTCC 2018, LNICST 266, pp. 58–69, 2019.
https://doi.org/10.1007/978-3-030-06152-4_6

mechanisms have deployed to guarantee these security properties. Role-based access control (RBAC) [9] is one of the solutions to guard the confidentiality and integrity of software systems. The implementing RBAC within the WAs helps to assign the access rights to users through their roles. This can reduce resources access violations for WAs.

WAs are increasingly complex and programming is prone to errors. In addition, the programmers may not be designers so they may not completely understand about security requirements. Therefore, the application may not be conformed to specified requirements in its model. Furthermore, the cost to repair flaws and overcome the consequence in the maintain stage is much higher than it in the design phase. Checking the compliance of access control policies may detect flaws, reduce costs and increase the reliability of software systems.

Checking the consistency between RBAC policy and its implementation have been explored by some researches [1–3]. However, these studies have not been considered checking of compliance between web applications under MVC architecture and RBAC policies by the static code analysis technique. Our work introduces an approach to deal with this issue. The contribution of this paper includes:

- Firstly, we introduce steps to build the access control matrix according to roles from the source code of WA by the static analysis technique.
- Next, we propose a verification algorithm which can detect two violation cases of WAs: (i) the presence of unspecified access rules and (ii) the absence of specified access rules.
- Lastly, we illustrate proposed approach with a web based medical records management system.

The rest of the paper is organized as follows. Section 2 presents some basic knowledge about RBAC model, MVC architecture. In the next section, we discuss related studies. Section 4 presents a small WA in medical records management system. Our proposed approach is described detail in Sect. 5. We draw some conclusions and future work in the last section.

## 2   Background

The RBAC model and MVC architecture are the background knowledge which is used in our approach. In this section, we briefly describe them.

### 2.1   Role-Based Access Control

The RBAC model [8,9] is depicted in Fig. 1. The *Users, Roles, Permissions, Objects* and *Operations* are five main elements of this model. A user is referred to as the agent that interacts with the system. Users do not perform actions directly but through their roles. The role which is the central component of an RBAC model, represents for a job position in an organization. The *Permissions*

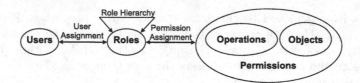

**Fig. 1.** Role-based access control.

includes *Operations* and *Objects*, this means that when users gain a permission, they are allowed to execute an operation on an object.

The principle of least privilege and separation of duty help users in the RBAC model only has sufficiently roles and permissions to carry out their duties. This can prevent attackers from accessing system resources. The *UserAssignment*, *PermissionAssignment* and *RoleHierarchy* are basic relationships of RBAC model. Specifically, a user can be assigned to many roles and a role can have several users. Each role is assigned with some permissions, and defined depending on the regulations of each organization. The inheritances between roles are described in *RoleHierarchy*.

## 2.2   Model-View-Controller Architecture in JavaEE

Model-View-Controller [13,15] is briefly called MVC which has been being a popular software architecture pattern for building web applications with many programming languages like Java, C#, Ruby, PHP, etc. Applications which are designed under MVC architecture aimed at code reuse and parallel development efficiently. Figure 2 depicts the MVC architecture in JavaEE.

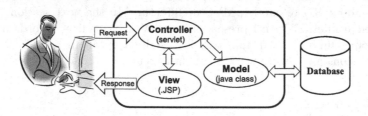

**Fig. 2.** The MVC architecture in JavaEE.

- *Model* is a component of the system that performs requests related to databases from *Controller*. It is the classes *.java* which include methods to connect to databases and interact with data sources.
- *View* includes codes such as *.jsp* to display user's graphical interfaces. It regulates the displayed data formula and communicates with *Controller*. In addition, it also supplies the way to gather data from the input.

– *Controller* creates the synchronization between *Model* and *View* by analyzing the requests. It interacts with *Model* and gets the data to create *View*. In other words, *Controller* is responsible for processing the events that are activated by user's interactions with the application or between processes of the system.

## 3  Related Work

Several papers have previously conducted for verifying web applications' access policies. In this section, we summarize some studies similar to our work.

The research works [1–3] recovered RBAC security model of a dynamic web application for verifying and testing of its security properties. Their approach builds a Prolog-based formal model from UML-based security model of the application. They illustrate proposed approach for analyzing, testing, maintenance, and re-engineering of the web application security. In the testing scenario for unauthorized access, the authors check if a guest user can using the links that an administrator can see. This study is similar to our research about user access, but their problem relates to the testing for unauthorized access. They use both of static and dynamic analysis to recovered SecureUML of WA. However, we only use static analysis on the source code of a WA under MVC architecture.

The paper [11] proposes a tool called SeWAT which is used to model MVC web applications graphically. In addition, the authors implement and validate role-based access control policy with an example of patient management system. The experiments with many realistic applications prove that their technique is useful for checking and deploying access policies of web applications. However, this study did not conduct with source code of WAs.

By using model checking in the design phase, Eun-Hye Choi and Hiroshi Watanabe introduced an approach to verify class specifications of WAs [5]. The authors modeled behavior of WA from its class diagram and method specifications. They proposed two aspects to verify the consistency: (i) between a class specification and a page flow diagram, (ii) between a class specification and a behavior diagram. The approach applied with real specifications of a certain company's developed WA and found several faults of the specifications which had not been detected in actual reviews. Graph-based modeling methods are presented by Di Sciascio *et al.* [6,7] and Castelluccia *et al.* [4]. The authors used model checking techniques to verify the UML design of a WA automatically. They introduced a tool called WAVer [4] which uses Symbolic Model Checking techniques to verify WA designs. The verification is conducted with three main stages: modeling WA in form of Finite State Machine (FSM), formalization of application correctness with CTL formal language, using NuSMV model checker to find a violation of specifications. These studies are only performed in the design phase.

In above presented studies, the works [1–3] analyzed the resources access policy from web application's source code. However, the authors use it for testing. The remained studies have not conducted with source code. In our study, we use static analysis technique to check the conformance of a WA under MVC pattern with its RBAC specification.

# 4    A Case Study

In a medical records management system, the security of patients' information are compulsory task according to regulations in HIPAA (USA's Health Care Insurance Portability and Accountability Act). Medical records must be confidentially kept because they contain private information and they only are used for monitoring and treating diseases or other tasks in regulated law. Medical records have had many risks [14] so protecting them from unauthorized disclosure has been attending.

The process of processing patient records in medical organizations or hospitals is usually attended by receptionist, physician, patient, etc. who have some privileges to do their tasks in the medical records management system. Medical records of patients needs to be secure and it can only read by authorized persons. Table 1 specifies access policy of system.

**Table 1.** RBAC policy to medical record.

| Users | Roles |
|-------|-------|
| Ann | Receptionist |
| Bob | Doctor |
| Tom | Patient |

(a) User-Role assignments.

| Roles | Permissions |
|-------|-------------|
| Receptionist | CreateMedicalRecord |
| Doctor | ReadMedicalRecord UpdateMedicalRecord |
| Patient | ReadMedicalRecord |

(b) Role-Permission assignments

| Permissions | Operation | Object |
|-------------|-----------|--------|
| CreateMedicalRecord | Create | MedicalRecord |
| ReadMedicalRecord | Read | MedicalRecord |
| UpdateMedicalRecord | Update | MedicalRecord |

(c) Permission mapping.

In our case study, the implemented medical records management system is written by J2EE and designed following to the MVC architecture. Medical records are stored in table *MedicalRecord* of the database management system *MySQL*. Figure 3 describes the components *Model, View, Controller*, and roles within our application. Where users must log into the system by their accounts and valid users are assigned some permissions to interact with resources corresponding to their roles in the system. In our example WA, a user assigned role *Doctor* can read, update and delete his/her patients' medical records. Users of role *Patient*, they can only read their medical records. If users are assigned role *Receptionist*, they can create new medical records. Pages *Doctor.jsp, Patient.jsp* and *Receptionist.jsp* help users perform their jobs corresponding to their roles in the organization. We aim at checking the web application's access policy against its specification.

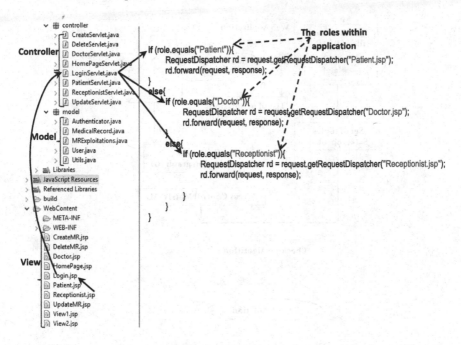

**Fig. 3.** The presence of RBAC and MVC architecture in the medical records management system.

## 5 Our Approach

We use static analysis technique to check the conformance of WAs with specified RBAC policies. Our approach overview is described in Fig. 4. Generally, we use the library $JDT$ in JavaEE to parse each file $*.java$ into an abstract syntax tree (AST). From analyzed ASTs, we extracted the necessary information to serve for each stage of the verification process.

### 5.1 List of Permissions

When users perform their functions within an application, the system has to invokes methods that interact with resources. Firstly, we need to determine the name list of system resources because software application often has may data but some of them are critical resources need to be protected. Next, we specify classes in $Model$ that include resources interaction methods. These methods encompass SQL operations ($Select$, $Insert$, $Delete$, or $Update$) corresponding to action types ($Read$, $Create$, $Delete$, or $Update$) of users. Lastly, we use the static analysis technique to extract these methods into a list of permissions $L = \{\langle mp, ac, rs \rangle\}$. Where, the $mp$ includes class name, return type of method, method name, data type list of parameters; $ac$ is an action type in the action type set $AC$; and $rs$ is an element of the protected resources set $RS$.

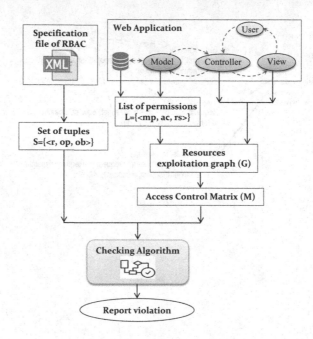

**Fig. 4.** The approach overview.

## 5.2  Resources Exploitation Graph of WA

The component *View* is the set of pages and the *Controller* is used to navigate transitions between pages. We can construct a direct graph which is a resources exploitation graph *G* of the WA. The information of each vertex includes name of each page in the component *View* and list of resources exploitation calls. Our graph is built by following steps:

**Step 1.** Building a diagram of pages according to the following rules:

– Each node of graph is a page in the *View*.
– Edge goes from node A to node B (A ≠ B) iff page A:
    – has a link to page B or
    – is redirected to page B or
    – includes page B.

**Step 2.** By analyzing source code of the component *Controller* and *View* of each page, we can gather all method calls from it and are also presented in the list of permissions *L*. Next we attach them on the information of graph's vertexes. The resources exploitation graph of the example of medical record management system is depicted in Fig. 5.

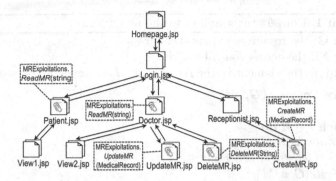

**Fig. 5.** The resources exploitation graph of the medical record management system.

## 5.3 Access Control Matrix

We use a three-dimensional matrix to describe actions on objects of roles within the WAs. It is constructed as follows:

- The first dimension of the matrix is $ROLE$. It contains the set of roles within WA ($R = \{R_1, R_2, .., R_n\}$) that can be taken from analyzing file *.java* of controller that handles login page. Each user logs in to the system through an account ($username, password$). If the login is success then valid users are redirected to the pages corresponding to their roles.
- The second dimension is $ACTION$ which includes all executed atom actions to exploit resources ($AC = \{AC_1, AC_2, .., AC_m\}$).
- The third dimension is $RESOURCES$ which includes list of resources need to be protected ($RS = \{RS_1, RS_2, .., RS_p\}$).

Suppose that, WA includes $n$ roles, $m$ action types, and $p$ resources. The value of an element $M[i][j][k]$ is '*Yes*' if role $R_i$ has permission to perform action $AC_j$ on resources $RS_k$ with $i = 1..n, j = 1..m, k = 1..p$. Users are controlled when they log into system to grant rights according to their roles. By visiting sub-graphs from vertexes corresponding to roles, we can gather all action types which are executed on resources of roles. Algorithm 1 converts the resources exploitation graph to access control matrix and Fig. 6 is the access control matrix of roles in the medical records management system.

## 5.4 Algorithm for Checking Compliance

The inputs of checking algorithm are $S$, $M$, $R$, $AC$, and $RS$, where $M$ is the access control matrix of WA; $S$ is the system resources access policy that is extracted through analyzing *.XML file structure; $R, AC, RS$ are the set of roles, actions, and resources within application respectively. Each tuple $s = \{\langle r, op, ob \rangle\} \in S$ means that role $r$ is allowed to perform operation $op$ on object $ob$ and $S$ is extracted from RBAC policy.

---

**Algorithm 1.** Convert the graph $G$ to the matrix. $M$

---

**Input** : **G**: the resources exploitation graph.
**Output**: **M**: the access control matrix.
**Data** : $r, v$: the element in the set of roles $R$, vertexes $V$, respectively.

**Procedure** Convert(***G, M***)
**begin**
    **foreach** $r \in R$ **do**
        $UnmarkAll(G)$;
        $v \leftarrow GetStartVertex(r)$;
        $Write(G, v, M)$;

**Procedure** Write(***G, v, M***)
**begin**
    **if** $(\neg Mark(v))$ **then**
        **if** $(v.attach \neq \emptyset)$ **then**
            $M \leftarrow Set(v.attach)$;
        $Mark(v) \leftarrow true$;
        $V \leftarrow Adjacent(v)$;
        **if** $(V \neq \emptyset)$ **then**
            **foreach** $v \in V$ **do**
                $Write(G, v, M)$;

---

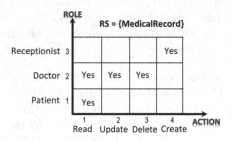

**Fig. 6.** The access control matrix of the medical records management system.

The proposed checking algorithm can detect two violation cases of WAs: the presence of unspecified access rules and the absence of specified access rules. The first case ① shows that there is at least one role executed a permission which is not specified in the access policy of WA. The second case ⑪ shows that specified permissions in the WA's access policy are not implemented inadequately. In two violation cases, the former can lead to leakage resources and it is usually more interested. The later is contradictory with the former but it helps to detect the role's permission shortcoming compared to its specification.

---

**Algorithm 2.** Checking compliance.

**Input**  : **S**: the resources access policy
**M**: the access control matrix of WA
**R, AC, RS**: the set of roles, actions, and resources within application respectively
**Output:** Compliance result
**Data**   : $r, ac, rs$: the element in the set of roles, actions, resources, respectively.

```
Function isConformance(S, M, R, AC, RS)
begin
    foreach rᵢ ∈ R do
        foreach acⱼ ∈ AC do
            foreach rsₖ ∈ RS do
                if M[i][j][k] =' Yes' then
                    m ← {⟨rᵢ, acⱼ, rsₖ⟩};
                    if m ∉ S then
                        | return false; ①
                    else
                        ⌊ S ← S \ {m};

    if (S ≠ ∅) then
        | return false; ⑪
    else
        ⌊ return true;
```

---

# 6   Conclusion and Future Work

Ensuring the security of web systems is a very complex issue. It usually requires the combination of many mechanisms and techniques. Therefore, verification of security policy in web systems is an attractive topic by researchers. In this paper, we have presented an approach to analyze source code of WAs into access control matrix and compare it to their specified policy. The example WA of medical records management system is deployed in the J2EE environment, so the proposed approach use JDT library to analyze source code into AST tree. From those, we extract *Model* into a list of permissions, build resources exploitation graph of WA, and construct access control matrix according to each role within the system. The proposed algorithm can be used to detect two specification violation types: a role executed at least one permission not be presented in access policy; at least one permission specified in access policy not be implemented in the application.

Currently, our case study does not cover all cases of access control policies. In the future, we are planning to investigate the approach with some larger applications in domains such as healthcare system, bank system, etc. In addition, we intend to improve our approach for checking multi-level control and other security properties of WAs. A support tool is developing to check automatically the compliance of access control policy in web applications.

**Acknowledgments.** This work has been supported by VNU University of Engineering and Technology under Project QG.16.32.

# References

1. Alalfi, M.H., Cordy, J.R., Dean, T.R.: A verification framework for access control in dynamic web applications. In: Proceedings of the 2nd Canadian Conference on Computer Science and Software Engineering, pp. 109–113. ACM (2009)
2. Alalfi, M.H., Cordy, J.R., Dean, T.R.: Automated verification of role-based access control security models recovered from dynamic web applications. In: 2012 14th IEEE International Symposium on Web Systems Evolution (WSE), pp. 1–10. IEEE (2012)
3. Alalfi, M.H., Cordy, J.R., Dean, T.R.: Recovering role-based access control security models from dynamic web applications. In: Brambilla, M., Tokuda, T., Tolksdorf, R. (eds.) ICWE 2012. LNCS, vol. 7387, pp. 121–136. Springer, Heidelberg (2012). https://doi.org/10.1007/978-3-642-31753-8_9
4. Castelluccia, D., Mongiello, M., Ruta, M., Totaro, R.: WAVer: a model checking-based tool to verify web application design. Electron. Notes Theor. Comput. Sci. **157**(1), 61–76 (2006)
5. Choi, E.H., Watanabe, H.: Model checking class specifications for web applications. In: 12th Asia-Pacific Software Engineering Conference, APSEC 2005, p. 9. IEEE (2005)
6. Di Sciascio, E., Donini, F.M., Mongiello, M., Piscitelli, G.: AnWeb: a system for automatic support to web application verification. In: Proceedings of the 14th International Conference on Software Engineering and Knowledge Engineering, pp. 609–616. ACM (2002)
7. Di Sciascio, E., Donini, F.M., Mongiello, M., Totaro, R., Castelluccia, D.: Design verification of web applications using symbolic model checking. In: Lowe, D., Gaedke, M. (eds.) ICWE 2005. LNCS, vol. 3579, pp. 69–74. Springer, Heidelberg (2005). https://doi.org/10.1007/11531371_12
8. Ferraiolo, D., Kuhn, D.R., Chandramouli, R.: Role-Based Access Control. Artech House, Norwood (2003)
9. Ferraiolo, D.F., Sandhu, R., Gavrila, S., Kuhn, D.R., Chandramouli, R.: Proposed NIST standard for role-based access control. ACM Trans. Inf. Syst. Secur. (TISSEC) **4**(3), 224–274 (2001)
10. Garg, A., Singh, S.: A review on web application security vulnerabilities. Int. J. Adv. Res. Comput. Sci. Softw. Eng. **3**, 222–226 (2013)
11. Idani, A.: Model driven secure web applications: the SeWAT platform. In: Proceedings of the Fifth European Conference on the Engineering of Computer-Based Systems, p. 3. ACM (2017)
12. Mead, N.R., Allen, J.H., Barnum, S., Ellison, R.J., McGraw, G.: Software Security Engineering: A Guide for Project Managers. Addison-Wesley Professional, Boston (2004)
13. Principe, M., Yoon, D.: A web application using MVC framework. In: Proceedings of the International Conference on e-Learning, e-Business, Enterprise Information Systems, and e-Government (EEE), p. 10 (2015)

14. Rubenstein, S.: Are your medical records at risk? Wall Street J. (2009)
15. Shklar, L., Rosen, R.: Web Application Architecture. Wiley, Hoboken (2009)
16. Touseef, P., Ashraf, M.A., Rafiq, A.: Analysis of risks against web applications in MVC. NFC IEFR J. Eng. Sci. Res. 5 (2017)

# Two-Stage Approach to Classifying Multidimensional Cubes for Visualization of Multivariate Data

Hong Thi Nguyen[1], Thuan My Thi Pham[2], Tuyet Anh Thi Nguyen[3],
Anh Van Thi Tran[4], Phuoc Vinh Tran[6(✉)], and Dang Van Pham[5]

[1] University of Information Technology, Vietnam National University – HCMC,
Ho Chi Minh City, Vietnam
hongnguyen1611@gmail.com
[2] Ho Chi Minh City Open University, Hochiminh City, Vietnam
thuanptm.178i@ou.edu.vn, mythuanpt@gmail.com
[3] Thu Dau Mot University, Binhduong, Vietnam
tuyetnta@tdmu.edu.vn
[4] Ho Chi Minh College of Economics, Hochiminh City, Vietnam
anhttv@kthcm.edu.vn, ttvanh26@gmail.com
[5] Nguyen Tat Thanh University, Hochiminh City, Vietnam
pvdang@ntt.edu.vn
[6] Hochiminh City Open University, Hochiminh City, Vietnam
Phuoc.tvinh@ou.edu.vn, phuoc.gis@gmail.com

**Abstract.** Visualization of multivariate data is a big challenge to problems of visual analytics. A system of data visualization is composed of visual mapping stage and visual display stage. The stage of visual mapping converts data to graph and the stage of visual display shows the graph on screen in accordance with human's retinal perception which is specified by visual features and Gestalt's laws. Based on data characteristics, multidimensional cubes representing multivariate data are classified as non-spatial multidimensional cube for non-spatial data, spatial multidimensional cube for spatio-temporal data, spatio-temporal multidimensional cube for movement data, and 3D-spatio-temporal multidimensional cube for flight data. For a visualization system responding human's retinal perception, multidimensional cubes have to enable analysts to answer elementary questions concerning individual values, variation questions concerning part of data or overall data, and relation questions resulting in the correlation among attributes.

**Keywords:** Visualization · Multidimensional cube · Multivariate data
Visual analytics

## 1 Introduction

Visualization of multivariate data is a big challenge to problems of visual analytics for discovering knowledge from data. The problem to be solved is how to represent multivariate data with only one graph displayed on 2-dimensional screen to enable

© ICST Institute for Computer Sciences, Social Informatics and Telecommunications Engineering 2019
Published by Springer Nature Switzerland AG 2019. All Rights Reserved
P. Cong Vinh and V. Alagar (Eds.): ICCASA 2018/ICTCC 2018, LNICST 266, pp. 70–80, 2019.
https://doi.org/10.1007/978-3-030-06152-4_7

analysts to view the whole. Multidimensional cube representing multivariate data is demanded not only to respond data characteristics but also to satisfy human's retinal perception. Visual representation for analytics enables analyst to answer tasks at different levels. Several types of multidimensional cubes enable to answer not only elementary tasks but also questions concerning the variation of an attribute according to reference variable and/or the correlation among attributes.

A system of data visualization comprises two stages, where the stage of visual mapping converts data to visual graph and the stage of visual display transfers the visual graph to human's eyes. The stage of visual mapping responds the characteristics of data, the stage of visual display satisfies the features of human's retinal perception. Based on the basic Gestalt's principle addressed by Kurt Koffka "The whole is more than the sum of its parts" [1, 2], multidimensional cubes are constituted to represent the whole multivariate data on a graph. This study classifies the cubes as non-spatial multidimensional cube for representing non-spatial data, spatial multidimensional cube for spatio-temporal data, spatio-temporal multidimensional cube for movement data, and 3D- spatio-temporal multidimensional cube for flight data.

The paper is structured as follows. The works in the next item are to consider the characteristics of data and the features of human's retinal perception; in that, data are classified as non-spatial, spatio-temporal, movement, and flight; human's retinal perception is considered according to Gestalt's principles, visual features of graph, and demands of visual analytics. Third item considers knowledge discovery from data as the amplification of data corresponding to the increase of human awareness. Fourth item focuses on the taxonomy of multidimensional cubes for representing various types of data. The final item is conclusion.

## 2 Related Works

### 2.1 Objects

According to the view of geographic information science, everything existing in real world is depicted as field or object. Field is a mapping from a set of spatial positions onto a set of defined values. Each field is represented as a data variable, of which values distribute extensively out non-boundary space. Object refers to an entity occupying a limited spatial area during a time interval and having boundary determined in space. The existence of an object in real world is depicted by its relation with time or/and space [3, 4]. For example, air temperature exists in space as field, vehicle as object.

Technically, values of field are recorded discretely at different locations, data at other positions are inferred from the recorded values. In geographic information systems, Thiesen polygon and Delaunay triangle are utilized to represent attributes as fields. Data depicting object are classified according to the relation of the object with time or/and space as non-spatial data, spatio-temporal data, movement data, flight data. Space-time cube representing the relation between space and time positions of objects by two axes indicating ground positions and other indicating time is utilized to represent spatio-temporal data and movement data [5].

## 2.2   Gestalt's Principle

The Gestalt's principle, proposed by Wertheimer, Koffka, and Kohler, refers to the way human perceives images. Retinal perception enables people to understand the signification of image while looking at it. The basic Gestalt's principle "we see the whole before we see the individual parts that make up that whole" is emphasized by Max Wertheimer [6] and other laws were constituted by several authors [1, 2, 6–8]:

- *Figure/Ground* or *Object/Background*: Human's retinal perception has ability to detect an object from background.
- *Area*: For two overlapping objects, the bigger is perceived as background.
- *Similarity*: Objects which have some similar characteristics are perceived as in a group, where similar characteristics may be shape, color, size, and so on. The similarity can be perceived by human vision or experience. Objects of visual connectedness may be perceived as objects of the same group.
- *Continuation*: Human's retinal perception detects objects arranged on the same line or the same curve as a group. Continual arrangement on a line or curve often is detected easier than other features.
- *Closure*: Human's retinal perception has ability to connect discrete objects, e.g. dashes representing trajectory are cognized as a continual line.
- *Proximity*: Objects close to one another are perceived as in the same group.
- *Synchrony*: Synchrony refers to objects of common state, e.g. turned-on lights are the same group, turned-off lights are the same group.
- *Symmetry*: Human's retinal perception tends to form an imagined point or line as symmetric center of objects
- *Parallelism*: Human's retinal perception cognizes parallel objects as a group, e.g. parallel time axes are considered as one.
- *Common region*: Objects located in the same area determined by boundary are perceived as the same group.
- *Past experience*: Individual or public experiences in the past detect objects of the same group.
- *Focal point:* Focal point is an emphasis point to attract viewers.
- *Law of pregnant:* Human's retinal perception tends to convert ambiguous or complex to simple images.
- *Perspective:* Human's retinal capacity perceives that vertical bar is longer than horizontal bar with respect to two equal bars [2]. Mathematically, human's retinal capacity perceives three dimensions of image shown on 2-dimensional display environment.

## 2.3   Visual Features

Human's retinal perception evaluates the structure of visual graph according to the following features [8–10]:

- *Selection:* Human's retinal perception detects a component of graph or the location of an object on graph.

- *Association:* Human's retinal perception associates the values of a variable or objects of the same characteristic in group.
- *Order:* Human's retinal perception discriminates smaller and larger values of variables, above and below or right and left locations of objects.
- *Quantity:* Human's retinal perception can cognize the ratio of two values which are represented visually.
- *Length:* Length refers to the number of values (elements) of a variable represented on an axis which human can perceive each value.

## 2.4 Visual Analytics

Visual analytics is an approach to analyzing data based on graph representing visually data. For strategy of visual analytics, analysts' available knowledge and experience are utilized to contribute to the process discovering insights of data. Visualization enables people to easily understand data by using their memory and capacity of imagination [11]. Analyst interacts and views graph representing data to find out its insights by answering questions. Accordingly, the findings depend on not only support of technical tools and way interacting on graph, but also analysts' available knowledge and experience with respect to analytical tasks.

Data analysis refers to answer tasks, where each task is composed of two parts, target and constraint. Target is unknown information, goal of analytical task, where goal or target variable may be reference variable or attribute. Constraint is given information, supposition of analytical task, where constraint or supposition variable may be reference variable or attribute [11]. Bertin classified questions as three levels, elementary, intermediate, and overall. Meanwhile, Andrienko classified questions as two levels, elementary and synoptic. At overall or synoptic levels, if the supposition of question is the combination of space and time variables, there are nine levels of supposition [11]. Generally, a combination of $N$ variables results in $3^N$ levels of supposition. Questions constituted from triangle of What, Where, When are elementary questions [12, 13].

In our works, non-elementary questions are divided into variation and relation questions. Variation questions refer to an interval or all values of one attribute to consider the change of the attribute over the interval of the attribute [11, 14]. For questions referring to time, the periodic characteristic of time results in the comparison of values during the same period of year or month. Relation questions refer to several attributes sharing a reference variable to consider whether there is correlation between the attributes, e.g. Rainfall and humidity have high correlation with the number of hand-foot-mouth patients, meanwhile temperature does not correlate nearly with the number of hand-foot-mouth patients [15, 16].

# 3  Two-Stage Approach to Representing Visually Data

## 3.1  The Process Increasing Human Awareness

Knowledge discovery from data is created by the process amplifying data value. From data of vague significance, information is extracted and analyzed to obtain new knowledge, then generalized to become natural or social laws. The amplification of data value corresponds to the increase of human awareness, from unknown to cognition, then understanding, and generalization. In other words, the significance of data is very hard to be cognized when they have not been processed to become information. Knowledge constituted from findings in information can be generalized to become natural of social laws (Fig. 1).

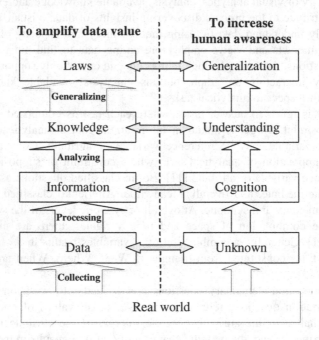

**Fig. 1.** The process amplifying data value corresponding to the process increasing human awareness.

## 3.2  Strategy of Knowledge Discovery from Data

For a strategy of knowledge discovery from data, data are converted to information by model or visualization. In a visual analytics system, human and computer collaborate with one another to utilize human's available knowledge and experience in extracting information and discovering knowledge from data by viewing and thinking. Generally, data analytics system combines model with visualization. Technically, a good system of data analytics enables analysts to switch between model and visualization to obtain more insights as possible (Fig. 2) [17, 18].

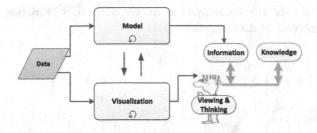

**Fig. 2.** Data analytics system: data are converted to information and knowledge by model approach and/or visualization approach along with the contribution of human.

### 3.3 Two-Stage Approach to Representing Visually Data

A basic system of data visualization is composed of two stages, visual mapping and visual display (Fig. 3). For the stage of visual mapping, data are represented as a graph on coordinates; for the stage of visual display, the graph on coordinates is presented and displayed visually on screen. The visual features of graph are improved at the stage of visual display by integrating retinal variables to increase user's retinal perception [9, 15, 19, 20]. Technically, the two stages closely concern one another, some change in a stage affects another. Mathematically, the stage of visual mapping concerns data more than human's retinal perception, the stage of visual display concerns human's retinal perception more than data.

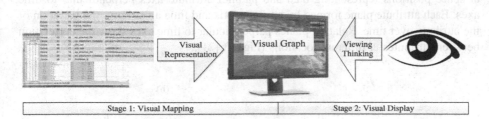

**Fig. 3.** Two-stage approach to representing visually data.

## 4 Taxonomy of Multidimensional Cubes

### 4.1 Non-spatial Multidimensional Cube for Representing Non-spatial Data

Non-spatial multidimensional cube for representing non-spatial data is modified from parallel coordinates, where the common-reference axis is rotated perpendicularly to parallel axes indicating attributes. The variation of attribute is represented on attribute plane formed by the axis of the attribute and the reference axis. Relation plane R may be moved perpendicularly to the reference axis to show the relation between attributes at each reference value or in a reference interval (Fig. 4) [15]. Accordingly, non-spatial multidimensional cube enables analysts to answer elementary, variation, and relation questions in problems of data analytics.

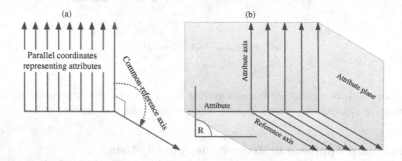

**Fig. 4.** Non-spatial multidimensional cube for representing non-spatial data: (a) The cube is modified from parallel coordinates; (b) Attribute plane for considering the variation of attribute; Relation plane R for considering the correlation between attributes.

## 4.2 Spatial Multidimensional Cube for Representing Spatio-Temporal Data

Spatial multidimensional cube, also called multidimensional map, for representing spatio-temporal data is formed by parallel time axes joining perpendicularly to the map at space positions representing data and parallel attribute axes perpendicular to time axes. Each attribute plane formed by attribute axis and time axis shows the variation of the attribute over time. Relation planes perpendicular to time axes show the correlation between attributes at different locations (Fig. 5) [21].

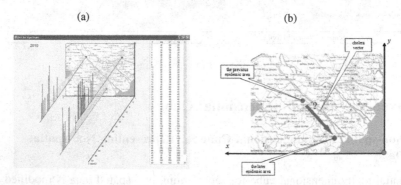

**Fig. 5.** (a) Spatial multidimensional cube representing the data of dengue fever in Angiang, Soctrang, Tiengiang provinces, Vietnam, during 2009-2012; (b) The topology of epidemic intervals in Angiang and Soctrang is asked whether the epidemic propagates from Angiang to Soctrang, cholera germs propagate along the stream of Mekong river (Source [21]).

## 4.3  Spatio-Temporal Multidimensional Cube for Representing Movement Data

Spatio-temporal multidimensional cube is constituted by combining a space-time cube [5] with non-spatial multidimensional cube, where the time axis is shared. A moving object changes locations over time, it takes time to move from a location to another, each time position associates one and only one space position, each space position may associate with one or more time positions. Hence, attributes depending on time may be considered as variables referring to time or space. Spatio-temporal multidimensional cube enables to represent the change of attributes while the location of object does not change (Fig. 6).

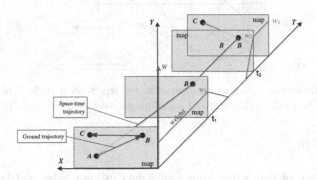

**Fig. 6.** Spatio-temporal multidimensional cube represents movement data of a lorry moving from A to C passing B. The lorry stops at B from $t_1$ to $t_2$ to unload available cargo, its weight decreases from $w_1$ to 0, then load new cargo, its weight increases from 0 to $w_2$.

## 4.4  3D-Spatio-Temporal Multidimensional Cube for Representing Flight Data

3D-Spatio-temporal multidimensional cube for representing flight data combines three cubes, 3D cube, space-time cube, and non-spatial multidimensional cube. In that, 3D cube shares two axes indicating ground positions with space-time cube and space-time cube shares the time axis with non-spatial multidimensional cube. The 3D cube indicates space positions with 2 axes for ground positions and another for elevations; the space-time cube indicates time position; and the non-spatial multidimensional cube indicates attributes referring to time. Each time position on the time axis associates with one and only one space position of flyer on 3D cube; on the contrary, one space position of flyer on 3D cube may associate with one or more time positions on the time axis of space-time cube (Fig. 7) [22, 23].

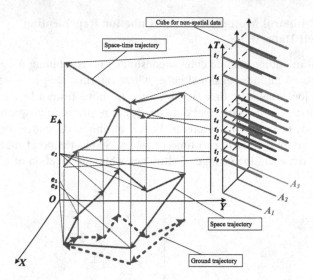

**Fig. 7.** 3D-Spatio-temporal multidimensional cube for representing flight data combines 3D cube with space-time cube and non-spatial multidimensional cube (Source [22]).

## 5   Conclusion

The amplification of data value from vague data to knowledge and laws increases human awareness. In the process of data amplification, approaches of model and visualization are utilized separately or simultaneously to extract information from data. Visualization system represents data as visual graph for human's retinal perception. The system is a two-stage approach to represent visually multivariate data, stage of visual mapping and stage of visual display. The stage of visual mapping is affected by data characteristics. The stage of visual display is affected by human's retinal perception specified by visual features and Gestalt's laws.

Approaching data characteristics, this study classifies multidimensional cubes as non-spatial multidimensional cube for representing non-spatial data, spatial multidimensional cube for spatio-temporal data, spatio-temporal multidimensional cube for movement data, and 3D-spatio-temporal multidimensional cube for flight data. Based on analysts' demands, this study also divides analytical questions into elementary questions referring to individual values of variables, variation questions referring to an interval or overall data of a variable, relation questions referring to data of several variables to study the correlation among attributes at different values of reference.

# References

1. Tuck, M.: Gestalt Principles Applied in Design (2010)
2. Alexandre, D.S., Tavares, J.M.R.S.: Introduction of human perception in visualization. Int. J. Imaging Robot.™ **4**, 60–70 (2010)
3. Yuan, M., Nara, A., Bothwell, J.: Space–time representation and analytics. Ann. GIS **20**, 1–9 (2014)
4. Yuan, M.: Representing complex geographic phenomena in GIS. Cartography Geographic Inf. Sci. **28**, 83–96 (2001)
5. Hagerstrand, T.: What about people in regional science?. In presented at the Ninth European Congress of Regional Science Association (1970)
6. Bradley, S.: Gestalt Principles: How Are Your Designs Perceived? (2010)
7. Graham, L.: Gestalt theory in interactive media design. J. Hum. Soc. Sci. **2**, 1–12 (2008)
8. Few, S.: Data visualization for human perception. In: Soegaard, M., R.F. Dam, Eds., 2nd ed The Encyclopedia of Human-Computer Interaction. Aarhus, Denmark, 2014
9. Bertin, J.: General theory, from semiology of graphics. In: Dodge, M., Kitchin, R., Perkins, C. (eds.) The Map Reader. Theories of Mapping Practice and Cartographic Representation, pp. 8–16. John Wiley & Sons Ltd, London (2011)
10. Green, M.: Toward a Perceptual Science of Multidimensional Data Visualization: Bertin and Beyond. In: ERGO/GERO Human Factors Science, Citeseer (1998)
11. Andrienko, N., Andrienko, G.: Exploratary Analysis of Spatial and Temporal Data - A Systematic Approach. Springer-Verlag, Berlin Heidelberg (2006)
12. Peuquet, D.J.: Representations of Space and Time. Guilford, New York (2002)
13. Peuquet, D.J.: It's about time: a conceptual framework for the representation of temporal dynamics in geographic information systems. Ann. Assoc. Am. Geographers **84**, 441–461 (1994)
14. Aigner, W., Miksch, S., Muller, W., Schumann, H., Tominski, C.: Visualizing time-oriented data—A systematic view. Comput. Graphics **31**, 401–409 (2007)
15. Nguyen, H.T., Tran, A.V.T., Nguyen, T.A.T., Vo, L.T., Tran, P.V.: Multivariate cube integrated retinal variable to visually represent multivariable data. EAI Endorsed Trans. Context-aware Syst. Appl. **4**, 1–8 (2017)
16. Nguyen, H.T., Tran, A.V.T., Nguyen, T.A.T., Vo, L.T., Tran, P.V.: Multivariate cube for representing multivariable data in visual analytics. In: Context-Aware Systems and Applications, Thu Dau Mot, Viet Nam, 2016, pp. 91–100
17. Sacha, D., Stoffel, A., Stoffel, F., Kwon, B.C., Ellis, G., Keim, D.A.: Knowledge generation model for visual analytics. IEEE Trans. Visual Comput. Graphics **20**, 1604–1613 (2014)
18. Keim, D., Andrienko, G., Fekete, J.-D., Görg, C., Kohlhammer, J., Melançon, G.: Visual analytics: definition, process, and challenges. In: Kerren, A., Stasko, John T., Fekete, J.-D., North, C. (eds.) Information Visualization. LNCS, vol. 4950, pp. 154–175. Springer, Heidelberg (2008). https://doi.org/10.1007/978-3-540-70956-5_7
19. Nguyen, H.T., Ngo, D.N.T., Bui, T.T., Huynh, C.N.T., Tran, P.V.: Visualizing Space-Time Map for Bus. In: Cong Vinh, P., Ha Huy Cuong, N., Vassev, E. (eds.) ICCASA/ICTCC - 2017. LNICST, vol. 217, pp. 38–47. Springer, Cham (2018). https://doi.org/10.1007/978-3-319-77818-1_4
20. Bertin, J.: Semiology of graphics: Diagrams, networks, maps. ed: University of Wisconsin (1983)

21. Tran, P.V., Nguyen, H.T., Tran, T.V.: Approaching multi-dimensional cube for visualization-based epidemic warning system - dengue fever. In: presented at the 8th International Conference on Ubiquitous Information Management and Communication, ACM IMCOM 2014, Siem Reap, Cambodia (2014)
22. Hong, N.T., Phuoc, T.V.: Multidimensional cube for representing flight data in visualization-based system for tracking flyer. In: The 5th International Conference on Control, Automation and Information Sciences, Ansan, Korea, 2016, pp. 132–137
23. Tran, P.V., Nguyen, H.T., Tran, T.V., Bui, T.T.: On an Approach to Visualizing Data of Flying Objects. In presented at the IEEE 2014 International Conference on Control, Automation and Information Sciences (ICCAIS 2014), Gwangju, South Korea (2014)

# Proposing Storage Structures and Interpolation Algorithms of 3D Spatial Data

Dang Van Pham[1,2(✉)] and Vinh Cong Phan[1]

[1] Faculty of Information Technology, Nguyen Tat Thanh University,
Hochiminh City, Vietnam
pvdang.tps@gmail.com, {pvdang,pcvinh}@ntt.edu.vn
[2] GUST, Vietnam Academy of Science and Technology, Hanoi, Vietnam

**Abstract.** The rapidly growth urbanization and using high-intensity land in urban areas recently are hot topics interested in researchers of 2-3-4D GIS (2-dimensional, 3-dimensional, and 4-dimensional geographic information system) more and more by the shapes of high-rise buildings (buildings) of diversity and abundance located on limited land funds. This problem is a big challenge for researchers of 2-3-4D GIS, how they can visually represent it into the 2D computer screen. This paper proposes to build space-data storage structures and to develop 3D space data interpolation algorithms (IA and NCA) for visual representation of buildings located on limited land funds in 3D geographical scientific space. This paper also presents experiments by these 3D bodies to represent visualization of buildings. Through these experimental results show able to support the authorities apply for management stages of urban techniques infrastructures in the near future.

**Keywords:** Limited land funds · 2-3-4D GIS · Spatial database · IA and NCA

## 1 Introduction

The increase in population, the demand for education as well as employment, and the policies of receiving immigrants in large cities are always expanding. Therefore, the demand of using high-intensity land [1] requires that we need to develop data structures three-dimensional (3D) space to manage the space object 2-3-4D located on the land fund limited. This management is a major challenge for GIS researchers 2-3-4D, because the shape of the buildings is very rich and diverse in the code samples.

Due to the increasing population and the influx of immigrants into the major cities, leading to more and more land in the urban area, which had limited far more limited. The problem set for the authorities was to develop the planning of buildings, taking the space above the land fund to make up for limited. This is the basis for this paper proposed the structures of spatial data storage and spatial data interpolation algorithms for 3D space.

To build a high-rise building that is the combination of the components as point, line, surface, and blocks. This paper applies the method B-REP (Boundary

© ICST Institute for Computer Sciences, Social Informatics and Telecommunications Engineering 2019
Published by Springer Nature Switzerland AG 2019. All Rights Reserved
P. Cong Vinh and V. Alagar (Eds.): ICCASA 2018/ICTCC 2018, LNICST 266, pp. 81–97, 2019.
https://doi.org/10.1007/978-3-030-06152-4_8

Representations) to represent the object 0-1-2-2.5-3D based on the elements already defined in advance, including: point, line, surface, and blocks. In which, the Line could be the line segment, the arch, the circle; Surface may be flat, the surface polygons created by the circle, cone, the surface of the cylinder; Solid is the expansion of the surfaces to gig the 3D blocks, the blocks can: box, cone, cylinder, the combination of this block or a block of any [2, 3]. Therefore, appropriate B-REP method to gig for the space object has a shape often, artificial, and scalar. B-REP focuses on building objects and relationships between them [4].

The objective of this paper is to propose building the data storage structures and developed the 3D space data interpolation algorithms to visual representation of the high-rise building in 3D geography science space. The construction of the data storage structures in this space in order to minimize the storage of spatial data with the data interpolation algorithms for 3D space, to support to solve some part of land fund management problem limited.

The next section of this paper is organized as follows. Section 2 presents overview of studies, reviews and suggestions. Section 3 performs to develop data storage structures and interpolation algorithms of 3D space data. Section 4 illustrates experiments with the spatial components to build a high-rise building in 3D geography science space. Section 5 presents the results achieved and the development direction in the future. The final section is reference documents.

## 2   The Data Models of 3D and 4D GIS

### 2.1   Overview of the Data Models of 3D and 4D GIS

Over the years, researchers have proposed various models of data space, time, and semantics 3-4D. These models have great contribution in the development history of the 0-1-2-2.5-3-4D GIS. This contribution was evidenced through the GIS model is the author of proposals in the past, as follows.

### 2.1.1   3D Cadastral Model

In 2017, author Yuan Ding and associates [1] proposed the extrusion approach based on non-overlapping footprints (EABNOF) to build the geometry model and topology in the 3D Cadastral Model. EABNOF handles the case of complex 3D blocks. To reach EABNOF, the overlap between the overlapping traces of the input data files will be removed, including the division of the extrusion and processing traces of cadastral objects to fit together. The trace against new cross was born will be extruded to produce the original copies. To build the geometry model and topology for cadastral objects, there are 3 proposed evaluation criteria to identify and remove the excess from the original and then the original version of the composition space the same 3D or the features of the link structure will be incorporated. Special sections of EABNOF approach that groups of authors have applied to 2D data sets. The author team has tested two types of structures on the Pozi verifies EABNOF approach: a complicated building and the furniture. EABNOF based on the traces of the 2D cadastral data sets and especially consistent with areas of the sets of 2D cadastral data to setting 3D cadastral system with lower costs.

### 2.1.2 TUDM Model

TUDM was a model of 4D spatial - temporal data proposed by N.G.T. Anh and coworkers in 2012 [5]. These authors have focused on developing a time dimension to integrate into the known 3D GIS space model. The time dimension in TUDM can be a time or a time period. The birth and extinction time of an object in TUDM can either be in the real world or be recorded in the database. TUDM can represent and store not only the evolutionary history of 0D, 1D, 2D objects but also the life cycle of 3D objects.

### 2.1.3 VRO-DLOD3D Model

The VRO-DLOD3D model was proposed by P.V. Dang and colleagues in 2017 [6]. The author group has researched and developed a visual representation of geographic features (people, buildings and geospatial space) along with relationships (blood relations, social relations, previous conviction relations, previous offence relations and vital relations) in three dimensions at different levels of detail, serving the protection of security and social order and safety in the area. The author group also presents data in forms through a number of typical queries at different levels of detail.

### 2.1.4 UDM Model

UDM (Urban Data Model) was a model of spatial data proposed by Coors in 2003 [7] based on four basic objects POINT, LINE, SURFACE, BODY. UDM uses two elemental objects NODE, FACE. ARC isn't proposed in this model. Each FACE is defined by 3 NODEs, so the model reduces some NODE-ARC, ARC-FACE relationships. Some topology relationships such as NODE are on FACE, NODE in BODY is not described. The obvious advantage of the UDM is the efficient data storage, the object-oriented analysis which is used urban management applications and representation of faces and blocks based on triangulation.

### 2.1.5 CityGML Model

CityGML model by Groger and colleagues proposed in 2007 [8]. The idea behind this model is to build a 3D city model as a model platform and open XML. The main purpose of CityGML is to develop common definitions related to the entities, attributes, and relationships in the model 3D cities to the different applications can share a common data source. CityGML is represented by objects of geometry GML3. This model is based on ISO 19107. Standard CityGML has an attribute not only space but also a semantic attribute. CityGML model supports 5 levels of detail (LOD): LOD0 is the most rugged, mostly 2.5D digital terrain model; LOD1 a block model, the buildings are represented as blocks with flat roofs; in LOD2 more complex buildings can be modeled, complex roof, settings such as stairs and balconies are available; LOD3 allow architectural models, may have detailed the walls, roof, doors gates, etc.; LOD4 completed LOD3 and include internal structure, such as guest rooms, doors, stairs, furniture, etc. It can be shown the same object in different LOD.

Author Kolbe and colleagues in 2009 [9] was used CityGML model and combined building new models for application in a number of German cities. These cities include, buildings, furniture, vegetation, land use, water areas, transportation (streets, rails, etc.) are defined in modules subject matter may be open wide in the future.

### 2.1.6   Improved the CityGML Model

The author group Biljecki and colleagues [10] have improved CityGML model by refining LODs. This improvement increases the level of detail of the detailed CityGML from 5 to 16 the level of detail. This improvement is made using a geometric display. Each level of CityGML is smoothed over 4 times, as illustrated in Fig. 1 (see left and right).

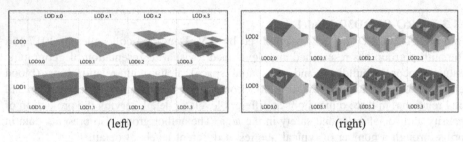

(left)                                              (right)

**Fig. 1.**   Visual illustration of 16 LODs smoother for a residential building [10]

### 2.1.7   ELUDM Model for 2.5D Objects

ELUDM (Enhanced Levels of detail Urban Data Model) was a model proposed by P.V. Dang and coworkers in 2011 [11]. These authors have proposed the addition of LOD (Levels of Detail) and complex links between Surface, Line, Point and LOD to the ELUDM to serve visual representation of 2.5D objects at multiple different levels. User defines the number of levels. The diversity of the visualizing will respond the requirements of different applications. This approach can extend for LOD of objects 3D that not depend on semantic.

### 2.1.8   3D Array Model

Array 3D model was proposed by Rahman in 2005 [2, 3]. Models with simple data structures used to represent most of the 3D object. The 3D elements in the Array have the value 0, 1. In the description that the base value of 0, 1 describes the value that each element in the 3D Array occupied by 3D objects. If a 3D object is being scanned in a 3D array which element of the array is initialized with the initial value 0. After scanning to 3D objects, elements worth 1 present information for 3D objects. If scanning 3D objects with high resolution, the size of the array in each direction will increase as volumetric 3D data should describe also increased and require large storage space.

### 2.1.9  Octree Model

Octree model is an extension of the quadtree into the octal tree. Octree representation is a 3D model based on volume [3, 15]. Octal tree gives us the picture, and this is a method represented by the data structure tree. Generally, an octal tree is defined based on a cube that contains the smallest 3D objects needs performing. Original cube will be divided into 8 cube offspring. An octal tree is based on the decomposition of recursive algorithm follow. Each Node in the tree is or leaf, or 8 seedlings. Each seedling will be checked before being divided into 8 different seedlings.

### 2.1.10  CSG Model

The model CSG was proposed by Rahman in 2008 [2, 3]. CSG performed a 3D object by combining the 3D element has been defined before. The basic 3D blocks such as: cube, cylinder, and sphere. The relationship between the figures includes: transformation and the mathematical treatise storage class. These transformations include translation, rotation, allowed to measure change. The comment class storages include union, intersect and except. CSG is often used in CAD. CSG is very convenient in the calculation of the volume of the object, so the CSG does not conform to the performance for the objects have unusual geometric shapes.

### 2.1.11  Combined Model Between B-REP and CSG

Model B-REP + CSG by Chokri and colleagues were suggested in 2009 [12]. The model is based on the idea of performing 3D objects by combining the two methods of B-REP and CSG. In B-REP models using 4 basic object point, line, surface, and solid. A line is defined by the first and last points 2. A surface is defined from a closed string with or without direction. A surface may be full or empty. Empty_surface to describe the gap. Many surfaces in the same plane make up Composit_surface. A solid is represented by a set of surrounding surfaces. Solid may be full or empty. FULL_-Solid is created by a set of scalar surfaces, so the interior of Solid is not modeled. In CSG element objects include cylinders, spheres, and prisms. A CSG_Composit is the union, intersect, and except of 2 Solids. The inside of Solids is not modeled. The cubes, triangular prisms, polygonal prisms are the derivative objects of the prisms. The advantage of this approach is based on the advantages of the B-REP method, which demonstrates very well the external boundaries that make up the object and the advantage of the CSG approach is the minimization of storage data (Table 1).

**Table 1.** Classification of the models

| Model types | Name of the models |
| --- | --- |
| B-REP (B) | 3D Cadastral Model, TUDM Model, VRO-DLOD3D Model, UDM Model, CityGML Model, Improved the CityGML Model, ELUDM Model |
| VOXEL (V) | 3D Array Model, Octree Model |
| CSG (C) | CSG Model |
| COMBINING B-V-C | B-REP and CSG |

## 2.2   Classification of the Models

The selection 3D data models to represent 3D GIS objects for a specific application will determine the methods of storing, retrieving, managing, treating ways when the show and the obvious required data is also different. A model can combine all areas is not practical. The data models of the authors have proposed a paper analyzes aggregate, and is divided into four main categories as follows:

*Type 1:*   *Representation of 3D objects by B-REP. B-REP method to represent a 3D object-based element has been defined, including: Point, Line, and Surface, Solid. B-REP suitable for representing 3D objects shaped conventional and scalar. B-REP focuses on building objects and the relationships between them [12].*

*Type 2:*   *Representation of 3D objects by voxel elements, such as pixels in 2D GIS. Voxel method represents a 3D object based on ideas split an object into sub-elements, each element is called a voxel child [13]. One element to be considered as a geographical space and is assigned by an integer [14].*

*Type 3:*   *Representation of 3D objects by combining the basic 3D block (CSG) [2].*

*Type 4:*   *Representation of 3D objects by combining three types above*

## 2.3   Proposing Storage Structures and Interpolation Algorithms of 3D Space Data

Through the summarizing and classification models of the authors represent proposed above. We have the following comments below. Through these comments, we propose to build the structures of spatial data storage for the components of a residential building and the interpolation algorithms of 3D space data will be presented in Sect. 3 of this paper.

*Comment 1:*   *The models proposed by authors are most representative of type B-REP.*

*Comment 2:*   *The models proposed by authors are not to mention structure installed in a database management system.*

*Comment 3:*   *The data interpolation algorithms of 3D space has not been mentioned.*

*Comment 4:*   *The combination of the spatial component into a residential building also has not been mentioned.*

# 3   Developing Data Structures and Interpolation Algorithms of 3D Space Data

## 3.1   Developing 3D Space-Data Structures

Spatial data records shapes, sizes, and locations of 3D objects [6]. To manage spatial data is a major challenge for researchers, including insert spatial data, update spatial data, delete spatial data, query spatial data, and query spatial data over time.

However, these are now multiple database management system support the spatial data management, including Oracle database management system, but requires us to use and implement combination the spatial data structure inherent in Oracle to build our own structures effectively.

The EABNOF [1] is a reach extrusion based on non-overlapping traces to build the model geometry and topology in the 3D Cadastral Model. EABNOF handles the case of complex 3D blocks and the overlap between the overlapping traces of the input data will be removed. There are three proposed evaluation criteria to identify and remove the excess from the original and then the original versions of the composition space the same 3D or the features of the link structure will be incorporated. CSG model [2, 3] represents 3D objects by combining 3D elements (cube, cylinder, and sphere) have been defined before. The relationship between the figures includes: transformation (translation, rotation, measure change) and logical operations (union, intersect, and except). B-REP + CSG model [12] represents 3D objects by combining the two methods of B-REP and CSG. B-REP uses four basic objects point, line, surface, and solid to representing 3D objects. The advantage of this approach is based on the advantages of the B-REP method (which demonstrates very well the external boundaries that make up the 2D and 3D object.). Through these three approaches above, we have seen that, the authors have not been mentioned construction of data structures as well as construction of interpolation algorithms of 3D spatial data. These are the premise for this paper proposing development of data structures as well as 3D spatial data interpolation algorithms.

Developing the data structures for the 3D space component and rich diversity of designs is a huge challenge. Within the limits of the paper, we will illustrate the spatial components of a typical building, in order to satisfy the following criteria:

Criterion 1:    *Spatial components can be defined arbitrarily by user.*
Criterion 2:    *Data structures are simple but still are able to govern space components.*
Criterion 3:    *Data structures must conform to spatial data interpolation algorithms.*

In practice, some urban areas are always crowded in all aspects such as housing, people, goods, vehicles, etc. We proposed scenario simulates a number of residential areas, but only set topics centered on residential housing and grab space area on high ground compensate for limited land funds. Figure 2 describes some residential areas today which there are different types of housing and land built on limited funds. The types of buildings have structural diversity, richness of design and challenge us to represent them in 2D computer screen. There are a number of buildings in residential areas are now built based on criteria overhead space taken up for the limited land fund, which see Fig. 2 with Sunny and Bee villa. Bee Villa is built by combining the basic components, including prismatic stand, prismatic triangle, prism quadrilateral, rectangular, square, lines, and points (see Figs. 3 and 4). Figure 5 performs a combination of basic components to form a residential building, these components including object types need management space.

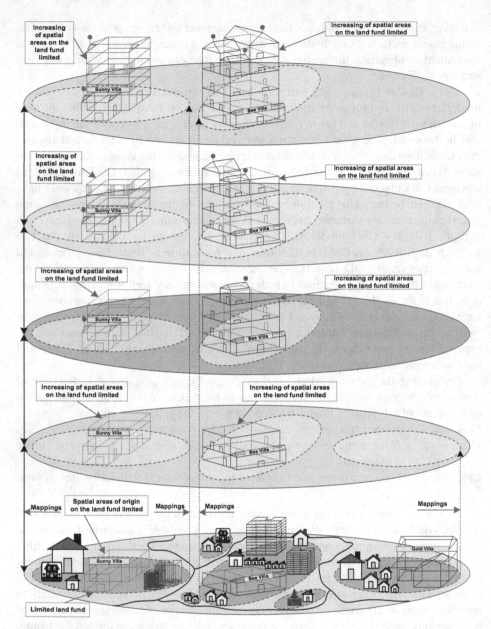

**Fig. 2.** Illustration of some residential area with residential buildings built on high space taken up for the limited land funds

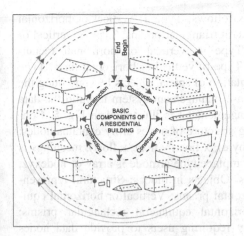

**Fig. 3.** The process of combining the basic components of a residential building on the limited funds

**Fig. 4.** Making combinations of basic components to become a residential building

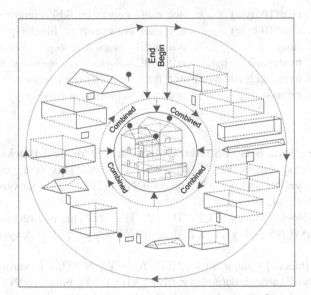

**Fig. 5.** Processing of the basic components of a residential building on limited funds

We categorized the space objects are as follows: Type 1: vertical or horizontal prisms; Type 2: vertical or horizontal equilateral triangular prisms; Type 3: vertical or horizontal equilateral rectangular prisms; Type 4: vertical or horizontal rectangles; Type 5: vertical or horizontal squares; Type 6: vertical or horizontal lines; Type 7: Points. Therefore, we propose the representation of spatial objects by combining the data structures available in the Oracle database management system to build the data structures for the object types need to management takes illustrated in Fig. 5. Construction general structure, including creating structure of nodes array contains nodes: create type nodexyz as object (idn char (10 byte), x float, y float, z float), meanings is object support to single data types; create or replace type arrnode is array of nodexyz, meanings creating 2D object contains nodes. Objects in blocks: Structural representation of the object space is vertical or horizontal prisms; Vertical or horizontal equilateral rectangular prisms; Vertical or horizontal equilateral rectangular prisms; Vertical or horizontal pentagonal prisms by requiring users to provide data nodes bottom, height h, and the type of the object space.

### 3.1.1 Creating Spatial Data Structure of Blocks Form

Table [blocks] (

| | | |
|---|---|---|
| Idvl | char(10 byte) | not null  constraint fkbl references villa(Idvl), |
| Idb | char(10 byte) | not null constraint pk_blocks primary key, |
| Height | float | not null, *--Height is attribute height indentify of object* |
| Typeshape | nvarchar2(50 byte) | not null, *--Vertical:VY or Horizontal: HX or HZ* |
| Description | nvarchar2(100 byte) | not null, *--Describling object of solid form* |
| Arraynode | arrnode | not null *--Arraynode is 2D array* |

);

### 3.1.2 Creating Data Sets of Spatial Objects into Structural Blocks

Insert into [blocks] values('VL1', 'B1', 15, 'VY', N 'This is a vertical prism.', arraynode(nodexyz('N1', x1, y1, z1), nodexyz('N2', x2, y2, z2), nodexyz('N3', x3, y3, z3), nodexyz('N4', x4, y4, z4)));

Insert into [blocks] values('VL1', 'B2', 7, 'HX', N 'This is a rectangular prism.', araynode(nodexyz('N5', x1, y1, z1), nodexyz('N6', x2, y2, z2), nodexyz('N7', x3, y3, z3)));

Insert into [blocks] values('VL1', 'B3', 6, 'VY', N 'This is vertical equilateral rectangular prisms.', arraynode(nodexyz('N8', x1, y1, z1), nodexyz('N9', x2, y2, z2), nodexyz('N10', x3, y3, z3), nodexyz('N11', x4, y4, z4)));

Insert into [blocks] values('VL1', 'B4', 7, 'HX', N 'This is a horizontal rectangular prisms.', arraynode(nodexyz('N12', x1, y1, z1), nodexyz('N13', x2, y2, z2), nodexyz('N14', x3, y3, z3), nodexyz('N15', x4, y4, z4), nodexyz('N16', x5, y5, z5)));

### 3.1.3    Creating Spatial Database Structure of Flatbed Form

Table [flats] (

| | | |
|---|---|---|
| Idvl | char(10 byte) | not null  constraint fk references villa(idvl), |
| Idf | char(10 byte) | not null  constraint pkflats  primary key, |
| Typeshape | nvarchar2(50 byte) | null, --T:Triangle,R:Rectangle,S:Square, Surface |
| Description | nvarchar2(100 byte) | not null, --Describling object of flats form |
| Arraynode | arrnode | not null --Arraynode contains nodes |

);

### 3.1.4    Creating Data Sets of Spatial Objects into Structural Flats

Insert into [flats] values('VL1', 'F1, 'R', N 'This is rectangle.', arraynode (nodexyz ('N17', x1, y1, z1), nodexyz('N18', x2, y2, z2), nodexyz('N19', x3, y3, z3), nodexyz ('N20', x4, y4, z4)));

Insert into [flats] values('VL1', 'F2, 'S', N 'This is square.', arraynode (nodexyz ('N21', x1, y1, z1), nodexyz('N22', x2, y2, z2), nodexyz('N23', x3, y3, z3), nodexyz ('N24', x4, y4, z4)));

Insert into [flats] values('VL1', 'F3, 'L', N 'This is string line.', arraynode (nodexyz('N25', x1, y1, z1), nodexyz('N26', x2, y2, z2)));

Insert into [flats] values('VL1', 'F4', 'P', arraynode(nodexyz('N27', x1, y1, z1)), null, N 'This is point.');

## 3.2    Developing 3D Spatial Data Interpolation Algorithms

Spatial data describes the shapes, sizes, and locations of spatial objects [6]. To represent objects in 3D, we have to provide them with positions in nodes in 3D, and then take into account their shape and size. This paper applies the B-REP [12] approach to represent 3D objects by boundaries. We propose to develop two algorithms: Algorithm 1 is capable of interpolating 3D data and is named Interpolation Algorithm (IA); Algorithm 2 is capable of connecting nodes to form Lines, which represent 3D space objects and is named Nodes Concatenation Algorithm (NCA). We see in Fig. 6 an illustration of the composition of a residential building on a limited ground, and in this context the role of the IA algorithm must be able to interpolation of 3D spatial data and the role of the NCA algorithm must be able to connect the Nodes together to form Lines, to visualize 3D objects. From Fig. 6, we detail the processing of IA and NCA algorithms for visual representation of vertical prisms and horizontal triangular prisms, as follows, we use two IA and NCA algorithms to represent the vertical prism (see Fig. 7), next, we use two IA and NCA algorithms to represent the horizontal triangular prism (see Fig. 8). Two ways of representation above (see Figs. 7 and 8) will illustrate by two IA and NCA algorithms the following:

- **IA (Interpolation Algorithm)**

**Input** : $Type_1$ is pa method, including: $A_2D_1Nodes$ contains 3D spatial datasets originally; H is height; Shape is picture type, nNodes of $A_2DNodes$, flags, $C_2$, $C_3$; $Type_2$ is public variables: $A_2D_2Nodes$, $A_2D_3Nodes$, $C_1=0$, flag=true

**Output:** $A_2D_1Nodes$ contains datasets of 3D space interpolated.

```
01: IA(ref A₂D₁Nodes, h, shape, nNodes, flags)
02:    A₂D₃Nodes = new string[A₂D₁Nodes.Len]; //A₂D₃Nodes contains Nodes
03:    C₂ = 1;
04:    C₃ = 0;
05:    if(flags ==true)
06:       if(flag==true)    //Test first picture
07:          A₂D₃Nodes =A₂D₂Nodes = A₂D₁Nodes;
08:          C₁ = C₃ = nNodes;
09:          flag=flase;
10:       else if (flag==false)    //Test the next picture
11:          for(i=0;i<=A₂D₁Nodes.Upper(0)&&A₂D₁Nodes[i,0]!=null;i++,C₁++,C₃++)
12:             for(j=0; i<= A₂D₁Nodes.Upper(1); j++)
13:                switch(j)
14:                   case 0: //--IDN
15:                      A₂D₂Nodes[C₁, j] = "N"+ riseIndexNodes;
16:                      A₂D₃Nodes[C₃, j] = A₂D₂Nodes[C₁, j]; break;
17:                   case 1: //--x
18:                      A₂D₂Nodes[C₁, j] = A₂D₁Nodes[i, j];
19:                      A₂D₃Nodes[C₃, j] = A₂D₂Nodes[C₁, j]; break;
20:                   case 2: //--y
21:                      A₂D₂Nodes[C₁, j] = A₂D₁Nodes[i, j];
22:                      A₂D₃Nodes[C₃, j] = A₂D₂Nodes[C₁, j]; break;
23:                   case 3: //--z
24:                      A₂D₂Nodes[C₁, j] = A₂D₁Nodes[i, j];
25:                      A₂D₃Nodes[C₃, j] = A₂D₂Nodes[C₁, j]; break;
26:                end switch
27:             end for j
28:          end for i
29:       end if
30:    end if
31.    if(shape == "VY" || shape == "HX" || shape == "HZ") //3D spatial data interpolation
32:       for(i=0; i<=A₂D₂Nodes.Upper(0) && C₂++<=nNodes; i++, C₁++, C₃++)
33:          for(j=0; j<=A₂D₂Nodes.Upper(1); j++)
34:             switch(j)
35:                case 0: //--IDN
36:                   A₂D₂Nodes[C₁, j] = "N" + riseIndexNodes;
37:                   A₂D₃Nodes[C₃, j] = A₂D₂Nodes[C₁, j];   break;
38:                case 1: //--x
39:                   A₂D₂Nodes[C₁, j] = A₂D₁Nodes[i, j] + (shape=="HX"?h:0);
40:                   A₂D₃Nodes[C₃, j] = A₂D₂Nodes[C₁, j];   break;
```

```
41:          case 2: //--y
42:              A₂D₂Nodes[C₁, j] = A₂D₁Nodes[i, j] + (shape=="VY"?h:0);
43:              A₂D₃Nodes[C₃, j] = A₂D₂Nodes[C₁, j];   break;
44:          case 3: //--z
45:              A₂D₂Nodes[C₁, j] = A₂D₁Nodes[i, j] + (shape=="HZ"?h:0);
46:              A₂D₃Nodes[C₃, j] = A₂D₂Nodes[C₁, j];   break;
47:        end switch
48:      end for j
49:    end for i
50:  end if
51:  A₂D₁Nodes=A₂D₃Nodes; //Assign data after 3D spatial data interpolation
52:  End IA;
```

- **NCA (Nodes Concatenation Algorithm)**

**Input** : $A_2DNodes$ contains datasets of 3D spatial data; Shape is picture type.
**Output**: $A_2DLines$ contains datasets of Lines connected by Nodes

```
01: NCA(A₂DNodes, out A₂DLines, Shape)
02:  CNodes = 0;                                    //Summarizing of nodes current
03:  A₁DNodes = new string[A₂DNodes.Len]; //A₁DNodes contains all Nodes of A₂DNodes
04:  A₂DLines  = new string[A₂DNodes.Len]; //Containing datasets of lines connect by Nodes
05:  for(i = 0; i<= A₂DNodes.Upper (0); i++)   //A₂DNodes copy IDN each Node
06:    if(A₂DNodes[i, 0] == null) then break;  //Exit for when meets IDN = null
07:    A₁DNodes[i] = A₂DNodes[i, 0];            //Copy IDN from A₂DNodes into A₁DNodes
08:    CNodes++;                                      //Count Nodes
09:  end for
10:  col = midI = rowI = 0;
11:  for(i=0; i<CNodes; i++)                    //Plan 1: concatenation bottom prism
12:    midI = i;
13:    A₂DLines[i, col++] = "L" + riseIndexLines; //Create Index for Line
14:    A₂DLines[i, col++] = A₁DNodes[midI];     //Copy IDN of A₁DNodes in each row i
15:    if(midI==CNodes)  //Rear array append with array middle element
16:        A₂DLines[i, col++] = (Shape is true)?A₁DNodes[0]:A₁DNodes[midI/2];
17:        col =0;
18:        rowI = i;               //Save row order to i of A₂Dlines, to update next for row i
19:        break;                  //Exit for
20:    end if
21:    if (Shape is true)     //Comment: T:Triangle, R:Rectangle, S:Square, S:Surface, L:Line
22:        A₂DLines[i, col++] = A₁DNodes[midI];
23:    else                        //Comment: Blocks
24:        A₂DLines[i, col++]=(midI==(CNodes/2))?A₁DNodes[0]:A₁DNodes[midI];
25:    end if
26:    col=0;                      //Reset for col of rowI
27:  end for
28:  for(i=0; i< CNodes/2 && Shape not true; i++) //Plan 2: concatenation_height of prism
29:    A₂DLines[rowI + i + 1, col++]="L" + riseIndexLines; //Create Index for Line
30:    A₂DLines[rowI + i + 1, col++]=A₁DNodes[i];  //Copy IDN first A₁DNodes in A₂DLines
31:    A₂DLines[rowI + i + 1, col++]=A₁DNodes[(CNodes/2)+i]; //Copy IDN
32:    col=0; //Reset for col of rowI
33:  end for
34: End NCA;
```

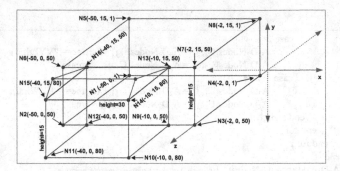

**Fig. 6.** A combination of a residential building or villa on a narrow ground

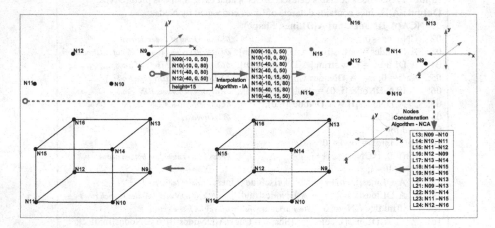

**Fig. 7.** Representation of vertical prisms by IA and NCA algorithms

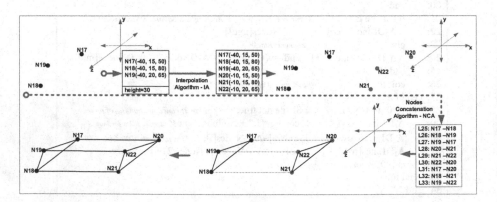

**Fig. 8.** Representation of horizontal triangular prisms by IA and NCA algorithms

## 4   Experiments

In this section, we have detailed the data storage structures and interpolation algorithms of 3D spatial data, and have seen the challenges and difficulties of 3D spatial data processing. To illustrate the results of this study in Sect. 3, we perform an empirical installation on Oracle database administration and C# programming language [16–18]: two IA and NCA algorithms; Data structures include: structure representing spatial objects that are prismatic or vertical; The triangular prism is either vertical or horizontal, by the users providing the bottom data, height h, and type of shape of the object. Experimental results are visual representations of spatial components of a residential building located on a narrow ground (see Figs. 9 and 10).

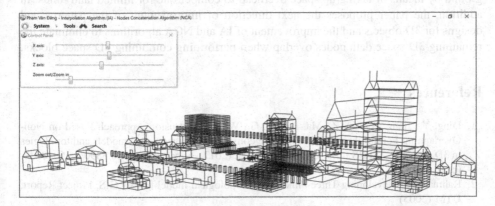

**Fig. 9.** A representation of urban areas including residential buildings and villas

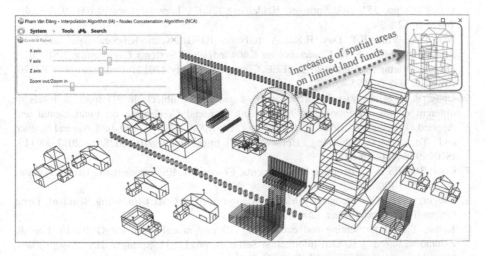

**Fig. 10.** The form illustrating space components is grouped into a residential building

## 5   Conclusion

This paper analyzes and synthesizes 3-4D space, time, and semantic data models proposed by authors in the past. These models have contributed greatly to the long history of the development of GIS. The paper classifies models into four main categories, namely, type 1 represents 3D objects by boundaries (B-REP); Type 2 represents 3D objects by voxel elements; Type 3 represents 3D objects by combining basic 3D blocks (CSG); Type 4 represents 3D objects by combining these three types. By classifying and making these observations, we propose the construction of data structures and interpolation algorithms of 3D spatial data, which the authors did not mention are detailed in the paper. Subsequently, the paper has been experimentally set up by combining spatial components to build residential buildings located on narrow ground by means of taking up space overhead to compensate for limited land funds. In addition, the paper proposes the next direction of improvement of the patterns and designs for 3D objects and the improvement of IA and NCA algorithms to eliminate the remaining 3D space data nodes overlap when performing combining 3D space blocks.

## References

1. Ding, Y., Jiang, N., Yu, Z., Ma, B., Shi, G., Wu, C.: Extrusion Approach Based on Non-Overlapping Footprints (EABNOF) for the construction of geometric models and topologies in 3D cadasters. ISPRS Int. J. Geo-Inf. 6(8), 232 (2017). https://doi.org/10.3390/ijgi6080232. (cc by 4.0)
2. Rahman, A.: Developing Three-dimensional topological model for 3D GIS. Project Report, UTM (2005)
3. Rahman, A.: Spatial data modeling for 3D GIS. Springer, Heidelberg (2008). https://doi.org/10.1007/978-3-540-74167-1
4. Tet-Khuan, C., Abdul-Rahman, A., Zlatanova, S.: 3D spatial operations in geo DBMS environment for 3D GIS. In: Gervasi, O., Gavrilova, Marina L. (eds.) ICCSA 2007. LNCS, vol. 4705, pp. 151–163. Springer, Heidelberg (2007). https://doi.org/10.1007/978-3-540-74472-6_12
5. NG, T.A., Vinh, P.T, Duy, H.K..: A study on 4D GIS spatio-temporal data model. In: Proceedings of IEEE 4th Conference on Knowledge and Systems Engineering, KSE 2012, Danang, Vietnam, August 2012. IEEE Computer Society (2012). Order Number P4670. ISBN-13: 978-0-7695-4760-2
6. Dang, P.V., et al.: Visual representation of geographic objects in 3D space at levels of different details. In: Proceeding of the 10th National Conference on Fundamental and Applied IT Research – FAIR 2010, Da Nang, 17–18/08/2017, pp. 979–988. Natural Science and Technology Publishing House (2017). https://doi.org/10.15625/vap.2017.000115. ISBN: 978-604-913-614-6
7. Coor: 3D-GIS In: Networking Environments, Computers, Environment and Urban Systems, pp 345–357 (2003)
8. Groger, et al.: City Geography Markup Language (CityGML) Encoding Standard. Open Geospatial Consortium Inc. (2007)
9. Kolbe, T.H.: Representing and exchanging 3D city models with CityGML. In: Lee, J., Zlatanova, S. (eds.) 3D Geo-Information Sciences, pp. 15–31. Springer, Heidelberg (2009). https://doi.org/10.1007/978-3-540-87395-2_2

10. Biljecki, F., Ledoux, H., Stoter, J.: An improved LOD specification for 3D building models. Comput. Environ. Urban Syst. **59**, 25–37 (2016)
11. Dang, P.V., et al.: Levels of Detail for Surface in Urban Data Model, International Conference on Future Information Technology, vol. 13, pp. 460–464. ICFIT, Singapore (2011). ISBN 978-981-08-9916-5
12. Chokri, K., Mathieu, K.: A simplified geometric and topological modeling of 3D building enriched by semantic data: combination of surface-based and solid-based representations. In: ASPRS 2009 Annual Conference Baltimore, Maryland (2009)
13. The Three Dimensional Visualization & Analysis of Geographic Data, by: James Swanson Maps.unomaha.edu/Peterson/gis/Final_Projects/1996/Swanson/GIS_Paper.html.    Accessed Apr 2017
14. Lieberwirth, U.: 3D GIS voxel-based model building in archaeology. Archaeopress, Oxford (2008)
15. Gröger, G., et al.: Representation of a 3D city model in spatial object-relational databases. In: XXth ISPRS Congress, Geo-Imagery Bridge- ing Continents, Commission 4, ISPRS (2004)
16. A Tool for visualizing 3D Geometry Models. http://www.codeproject.com/Articles-/42992/ A-Tool-for-Visualizing-D-Geometry-Models-Part. Accessed Nov 2017
17. Oracle Spatial User's Guide and Reference, Release 9.0.1, Part Number A88805-01, June 2001. Accessed Nov 2017
18. Elem_Info_Arraying: An alternative to SDO_UTI-L.GetNumRings and querying SDO_E-LEM_INFO_it  self.  http://www.spatialdbadvisor.com/oracle_spatial_tips_-tricks/89/sdo_utilget_numrings-an-alternative. Accessed May 2017

# Visually Analyzing Evolution of Geographic Objects at Different Levels of Details Over Time

Dang Van Pham[1,2(✉)] and Phuoc Vinh Tran[3]

[1] Faculty of Information Technology, Nguyen Tat Thanh University,
Hochiminh City, Vietnam
pvdang@ntt.edu.vn, pvdang.tps@gmail.com
[2] GUST, Vietnam Academy of Science and Technology, Hanoi, Vietnam
[3] Hochiminh City Open University, Hochiminh City, Vietnam
phuoc.tvinh@ou.edu.vn

**Abstract.** Evolutionary history of geographic objects (EHGO$_S$) in three-dimensional (3D) space at different levels of details (DLOD$_S$) over time is due to natural law or imposed by humans and always goes on every day. To represent visualization this evolutionary history, this paper proposes visual analysis of EHGO$_S$ at DLOD$_S$ over time, results of visual analysis are a model of representation of visualization of GO$_S$ at DLOD$_S$ over time, this model is called TLOD$_S$. Time is the class that records the time of formation and loss of GO$_S$. Time in this paper is divided into three main categories and integrate into the TLODs model, namely legal time (LT$_S$), event time (ET$_S$), and database time (DT$_S$). When manipulating queries can be either point of time or period of time in three types of time. This paper presents the experimental setup of the TLOD$_S$ model in Oracle 11G and incorporating in C# to represent typical forms. Experimental results show that it can be applied to the management of urban technical infrastructure in practice.

**Keywords:** Geographic objects · DLOD$_S$ · TLOD$_S$ · Visual analysis
Visual representation

## 1 Introduction

Geographic objects (GO$_S$) are objects in 3D space. Afterwards temporal geography is developed, GO$_S$ are objects of space and time [1]. The design of 3-4D GIS data model will directly impact to visual representations of data, storing of data, retrieving of data, and analyzing visualization of data for geographical objects in 3D space. And especially more important when designing a 3-4D GIS data model, this 3-4D GIS data model must be able to answer users' questions raised by various criteria that belong to field of regulation.

Throughout the long history of GIS development, lots of the 3-4D GIS data models were proposed, but most of these models only represent 2.5-3D objects. This paper summarizes the research as follows: Cadastral 3D model was proposed by author Ding and colleagues in 2017 [2]; the TUDM model was proposed by the author team Anh

© ICST Institute for Computer Sciences, Social Informatics and Telecommunications Engineering 2019
Published by Springer Nature Switzerland AG 2019. All Rights Reserved
P. Cong Vinh and V. Alagar (Eds.): ICCASA 2018/ICTCC 2018, LNICST 266, pp. 98–115, 2019.
https://doi.org/10.1007/978-3-030-06152-4_9

and colleagues in 2012 [3]; the VRO-DLOD3D model was proposed by Dang and colleagues in 2017 [1]; the CityGML model was proposed by Groger and colleagues in 2008 [4]; the author team Kolbe and colleagues have expanded the CityGML model in 2009 [5]; the author team Biljecki and colleagues improved the CityGML model by 2016 [6]; the author team Dang P.V. and colleagues proposed the ELUDM model for 2.5D objects in 2011 [7]; the author team Anh and colleagues proposed ELUDM model for 2.5-3D objects in 2011 [8]; the author team Löwner and colleagues proposed a new LoD and multi-representational concept for the CityGML model in 2016 [9]; The CityGML-TRKBIS.BI model was proposed by Aydar and colleagues to respond the need to establish 2-2.5-3D national Turkey by 2016 [10], etc. These researches will be presented in detail in Sect. 2. By summarizing the above-mentioned researches, we have found that no author group refers to the visualization of the evolutionary history of $GO_S$ in 3D space at the $DLOD_S$ over time.

$EHGO_S$ ($GO_S$ include: housing, population, geographical space, furniture, etc.) at the $DLOD_S$ over time is very diversified and complex. Diversity is represented in the design, style, size, and color of the $GO_S$. Complexity is represented in spatial dimension, linkage between geographic objects and time dimension. In particular, the evolutionary history of $GO_S$ in urban technical infrastructures is now of great interest by urban managers, as the management of $GO_S$ which is a residential building in residential areas is a very hot topic today. People must take advantage of the high space to make up for the limited land fund.

The objective of this paper is to visualize the $EHGO_S$ in 3D space at $DLOD_S$ over time. Result in representing $EHGO_S$ is an extremely important stage in the development of urban planning today. Thanks to the management of the evolutionary history of these geographic objects, we can see the development and disappearance process of $GO_S$. At different levels of details at the same time, $GO_S$ will be born and gone, and such management is essential for levels of urban infrastructure in the future. When demonstrating blocks 2-2.5-3-3.75-4D, we are interested in how to display these objects at $DLOD_S$ over time. These details depend on the different needs of the application, location, or different requirements for the same application. In computer graphics $DLOD_S$ are often used a lot. $DLOD_S$ are the hierarchy of resolution when compared to the real world. $DLOD_S$ is a quick representation of a 3D space model, indicates the degree of voltage abstraction for objects. $DLOD_S$ of a low level object are called low resolution levels, otherwise called high resolution. When performing an object into a computer, we need to represent it in such a way that it is in the real world.

The remainder of paper is organized as follows. Section 2 presents overview of GIS data models and comments and suggestions. Section 3 performs a visual analysis of the evolutionary history of $GO_S$ in 3D space at $DLOD_S$ over time and with some illustrations. Section 4 illustrates experiments. Conclusion is in Sect. 5.

## 2  The GIS Data Models

### 2.1  Overview of the GIS Data Models

Throughout the long history of the development of 0-dimensional, one-dimensional, two-dimensional, 2.5-dimensional, three-dimensional, 3.75-dimensional, and four-dimensional geographic information systems (0-1-2-2.5-3-3.75-4D GIS), including the great contributions of researchers on GIS, they have proposed many spatial, temporal, and semantic data models. These models are chosen as the premise for the development of residential GIS management systems over time, management of urban technical infrastructure, mining management, disaster management, land management, or epidemiological management, etc. These models are illustrated detail below.

#### 2.1.1  3D Cadastral Model

In 2017, author Ding and associates [2] proposed the extrusion approach based on non-overlapping footprints (EABNOF) to build the geometry model and topology in the 3D Cadastral Model. EABNOF handles the case of complex 3D blocks. To reach EAB-NOF, the overlap between the overlapping traces of the input data files will be removed, including the division of the extrusion and processing traces of cadastral objects to fit together. The trace against new cross was born will be extruded to produce the original copies. To build the geometry model and topology for cadastral objects, there are 3 proposed evaluation criteria to identify and remove the excess from the original and then the original version of the composition space the same 3D or the features of the link structure will be incorporated. Special sections of EABNOF approach that groups of authors have applied to 2D data sets. The author team has tested two types of structures on the Pozi verifies EABNOF approach: a complicated building and the furniture. EABNOF based on the traces of the 2D cadastral data sets and especially consistent with areas of the sets of 2D cadastral data to setting 3D cadastral system with lower costs.

#### 2.1.2  TUDM Model

TUDM was a model of 4D spatial - temporal data proposed by Anh and coworkers in 2012 [3]. These authors have focused on developing a time dimension to integrate into the known 3D GIS space model. The time dimension in TUDM can be a time or a time period. The birth and extinction time of an object in TUDM can either be in the real world or be recorded in the database. TUDM can represent and store not only the evolutionary history of 0D, 1D, 2D objects but also the life cycle of 3D objects.

#### 2.1.3  VRO-DLOD3D Model

The VRO-DLOD3D model was proposed by Dang and colleagues in 2017 [1]. The author group has researched and developed a visual representation of geographic features (people, buildings and geospatial space) along with relationships (blood relations, social relations, previous conviction relations, previous offence relations and vital relations) in three dimensions at different levels of detail, serving the protection of security and social order and safety in the area. The author group also presents data in forms through a number of typical queries at different levels of detail.

### 2.1.4  CityGML Model

CityGML model by Groger and colleagues proposed in 2008 [4]. The idea behind this model is to build a 3D city model as a model platform and open XML. The main purpose of CityGML is to develop common definitions related to the entities, attributes, and relationships in the model 3D cities to the different applications can share a common data source. CityGML is represented by objects of geometry GML3. This model is based on ISO 19107. Standard CityGML has an attribute not only space but also a semantic attribute. CityGML model supports 5 levels of detail (LOD): LOD0 is the most rugged, mostly 2.5D digital terrain model; LOD1 a block model, the buildings are represented as blocks with flat roofs; in LOD2 more complex buildings can be modeled, complex roof, settings such as stairs and balconies are available; LOD3 allow architectural models, may have detailed the walls, roof, doors gates, etc.; LOD4 completed LOD3 and include internal structure, such as guest rooms, doors, stairs, furniture, etc. It can be shown the same object in different LOD.

### 2.1.5  Improved the CityGML Model (a)

Author Kolbe and colleagues in 2009 [5] was used CityGML model and combined building new models for application in a number of German cities. These cities include, buildings, furniture, vegetation, land use, water areas, transportation (streets, rails, etc.) are defined in modules subject matter may be open wide in the future.

### 2.1.6  Improved the CityGML Model (b)

The author group Biljecki and colleagues [6] have improved CityGML model by refining LOD. This improvement increases the level of detail of the detailed CityGML from 5 to 16 the level of detail. This improvement is made using a geometric display. Each level of CityGML is smoothed over 4 times, as illustrated in Fig. 1 (see left and right).

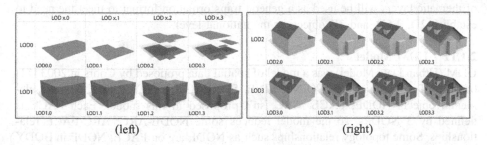

(left)                                                                    (right)

**Fig. 1.**  Visual illustration of 16 LODs smoother for a residential building [6]

### 2.1.7  ELUDM Model for 2.5D Objects

ELUDM (Enhanced Levels of detail Urban Data Model) was a model proposed by Dang P.V. and coworkers in 2011 [7]. These authors have proposed the addition of LOD (Levels of Detail) and complex links between Surface, Line, Point and LOD to the ELUDM to serve visual representation of 2.5D objects at multiple different levels.

User defines the number of levels. The diversity of the visualizing will respond the requirements of different applications. This approach can extend for LOD of objects 3D that not depend on semantic.

### 2.1.8    ELUDM Model for 2.5-3D Objects

The ELUDM model was proposed by the author team Anh and colleagues in 2011 [8]. The author team proposed adding more complex linkages to the existing data model to improve visibility for Surface Objects (2.5D) and Body (3D). The author team also proposed to remove semantic objects to become the purest spatial data model. This new model is capable of rendering 2.5D and 3D objects at detailed levels. Users can define multiple levels of detail.

### 2.1.9    The Multi-representational Concept for CityGML

The author team Löwner and colleagues proposed a new LoD concept and multi-representational concept [9] for the CityGML model that allowed the user to define LoDs arbitrarily. The author team also proposed using the concept of multi-representation as a meta-model to allow users to define more than one LoD concept for the CityGML3.0 model.

### 2.1.10    The CityGML-TRKBIS.BI Model Extending from CityGML Model

The author team Aydar and colleagues proposed the creation of a geographic data model for Turkey 3D [10], which is compatible with OGG International's CityGML code. The author team has also prepared an ADE called CityGML-TRKBIS.BI created by extending the existing specialized modules of the CityGML model according to the needs of the TRKBIS geographic data model. All thematic data sets in the TRKBIS geographic data model were modified to generate large-scale 3D geographic data models for Turkey 3D. The 3D geographic data model developed for the construction of thematic layers will be used as a general transformation format to meet the need to establish 2D, 2.5D, and 3D objects at the national level.

### 2.1.11    UDM Model

UDM (Urban Data Model) was a model of spatial data proposed by Coors in 2003 [11] based on four basic objects POINT, LINE, SURFACE, BODY. UDM uses two elemental objects NODE, FACE. ARC isn't proposed in this model. Each FACE is defined by 3 NODEs, so the model reduces some NODE-ARC, ARC-FACE relationships. Some topology relationships such as NODE are on FACE, NODE in BODY is not described. The obvious advantage of the UDM is the efficient data storage, the object-oriented analysis which is used urban management applications and representation of faces and blocks based on triangulation.

### 2.1.12    3D Array Model

Array 3D model was proposed by Rahman in 2005 [12, 13]. Models with simple data structures used to represent most of the 3D object. The 3D elements in the Array have the value 0, 1. In the description that the base value of 0, 1 describes the value that each element in the 3D Array occupied by 3D objects. If a 3D object is being scanned in a 3D array which element of the array is initialized with the initial value 0. After scanning to 3D objects, elements worth 1 present information for 3D objects. If scanning 3D objects with high resolution, the size of the array in each direction will increase as volumetric 3D data should describe also increased and require large storage space.

### 2.1.13    Octree Model

Octree model is an extension of the quadtree into the octal tree. Octree representation is a 3D model based on volume [13, 14]. Octal tree gives us the picture, this is a method represented by the data structure tree. Generally, an octal tree is defined based on a cube that contains the smallest 3D objects needs performing. Original cube will be divided into 8 cube offspring. An octal tree is based on the decomposition of recursive algorithm follow. Each Node in the tree is or leaf, or 8 seedlings. Each seedling will be checked before being divided into 8 different seedlings.

### 2.1.14    CSG Model

The model CSG was proposed by Rahman in 2008 [12, 13]. CSG performed a 3D object by combining the 3D element has been defined before. The basic 3D blocks such as: cube, cylinder, and sphere. The relationship between the figures includes: transformation and the mathematical treatise storage class. These transformations include translation, rotation, allowed to measure change. The comment class storages include union, intersect and except. CSG is often used in CAD. CSG is very convenient in the calculation of the volume of the object, so the CSG does not conform to the performance for the objects have unusual geometric shapes.

### 2.1.15    The Method Boundary Representations (B-REP)

The method B-REP (Boundary Representations) uses to represent the object 0-1-2-2.5-3D based on the elements already defined in advance, including: point, line, surface, and blocks. In which, the Line could be the line segment, the arch, the circle; Surface may be flat, the surface polygons created by the circle, cone, the surface of the cylinder; Solid is the expansion of the surfaces to gig the 3D blocks, the blocks can: box, cone, cylinder, the combination of this block or a block of any [12, 13]. Therefore, appropriate B-REP method to gig for the space object has a shape often, artificial, and scalar. B-REP focuses on building objects and relationships between them [15].

### 2.1.16    Combined Model Between B-REP and CSG

The B-REP+CSG model by Chokri and colleagues were suggested in 2009 [16]. The model is based on the idea of performing 3D objects by combining the 2 methods of B-REP and CSG. In B-REP models using 4 basic object point, line, surface, and solid. A line is defined by the first and last points 2. A surface is defined from a closed string (Closed-string) with or without direction. A surface may be full or empty. Empty_-surface to describe the gap. Many surfaces in the same plane make up Composit_-surface. A solid is represented by a set of surrounding surfaces. Solid may be full or empty. FULL_Solid is created by a set of scalar surfaces, so the interior of Solid is not modeled. In CSG element objects include cylinders, spheres, and prisms. A CSG_Composit is the union, intersect, except of 2 Solids. The inside of Solids is not modeled. The cubes, triangular prisms, polygonal prisms are the derivative objects of the prisms. The advantage of this approach is based on the advantages of the B-REP method, which demonstrates very well the external boundaries that make up the object and the advantage of the CSG approach is the minimization of storage data.

## 2.2    Classification of the Data Models

Selecting 3D data models to represent 3D GIS objects for a particular application will determine the storage methods, access methods, management methods, and processing methods when display and data bindingness will also be different. A model can combine all fields is not practical. The data models were proposed by the authors will be analyzed and synthesized in this paper. It was divided into four main categories, and had the following categories of data models (see Table 1).

**Table 1.**  Classification of the models

| Model types | Name of the models |
| --- | --- |
| B-REP (B) | 3D Cadastral model, TUDM model, VRO-DLOD3D model, UDM model, CityGML model, Improved the CityGML model (a and b), ELUDM model for 2.5D, ELUDM model for 2.5-3D, Multi-representational concept (MRC) for CityGML model, CityGML-TRKBIS.BI model extending from CityGML model |
| VOXEL (V) | 3D Array Model, Octree Model |
| CSG (C) | CSG Model |
| COMBINING B-V-C | B-REP and CSG |

Type 1:    Representation of 3D objects by B-REP. B-REP method to represent a 3D object-based element has been defined, including: Point, Line, Surface, and Solid. B-REP suitable for representing 3D objects shaped conventional and scalar. B-REP focuses on building objects and the relationships between them [15].

Type 2:    Representation of 3D objects by voxel elements such as pixels in 2D GIS. Voxel method represents a 3D object based on ideas split an object into sub-elements, each element is called a voxel child [17]. One element to be considered as a geographical space and is assigned by an integer [18].

Type 3:    Representation of 3D objects by combining the basic 3D blocks [12, 13].

Type 4:    Representation of 3D objects by combining three types above

## 2.3    Commentation and Suggestion TLODs Data Model

Through the synthesis and classification of data models suggested by the authors in the past, we have the following observations. Through the below comments, we have some suggestions as follows: (1) Combining space components to become residential buildings or villas located on limited land funds, (2) Applying B-REP method for new TLODs model, and (3) Visually analyzing evolution of geographic objects to build TLOD$_S$ data model. The TLOD$_S$ model is capable of answering users' questions about the topic: "Visual representation the evolutionary history of geographic objects at different levels of details in the 3D geographic space over time". Within the scope of this paper, we only analyze, construct and manage geographic objects that are residential buildings or villas. In the next section, we perform a visual analysis of these GOs to integrate these GOs into entities such as LOD$_S$, PRISM$_S$, SURFACE$_S$, LINE$_S$, POINT$_S$, TIME$_S$, MDY$_S$, and TIMETYPE$_S$.

> *Comment 1: Most models use the B-REP method.*
> *Comment 2: The models have not mentioned to represent GO$_S$ at DLOD$_S$ over time.*
> *Comment 3: The combination of space components to become a residential building also has not yet been mentioned.*
> *Comment 4: Most models represent only one-level for the 3D-block except the CityGML, MRC, CityGML-TRKBIS.BI, and ELUDM models which represent 2.5-3D objects at the detail levels, but these models also do not mention the evolutionary history of GO$_S$ at DLOD$_S$ over time. In addition, the CityGML, Improved CityGML, MRC, and CityGML-TRKBIS.BI models are 3D models which have rich semantics. CityGML has four or five detail levels, while MRC and CityGML-TRKBIS.BI have an arbitrary level of details; ELUDM model is a non-semantic model and has an arbitrary level of details.*

# 3    Development of TLODS Model

## 3.1    Visual Analysis the EHGO$_S$ at DLOD$_S$

To construct 3D objects that are residential buildings or villas, this paper integrates spatial components from various PRISM$_S$ (**BP$_S$** and **BC$_S$**), SURFACE$_S$ (**S$_S$**), LINE$_S$ (**L$_S$**), and POINT$_S$ (**P$_S$**) objects to form residential buildings or villas and apply the B-REP method for demonstrating these spatial components. We illustrate some residential areas to visually analyze the evolutionary history of residential buildings or villas at different levels of details over time located on limited land funds. Figure 2 illustrates the results of a visual analysis of the evolution history of the villa named "Bee Villa" at various different levels of details located on a limited land funds. Through the results of visual analysis of Fig. 3, we performed the results of Fig. 3 in database of TLOD$_S$ model (see Table 2) and will be experimentally installed in the next Sect. 4.

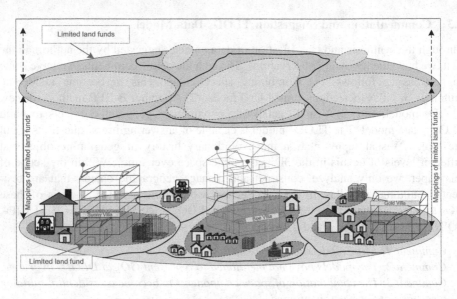

**Fig. 2.** An illustration of residential areas with residential houses or villas located on limited land funds

### 3.2   To Develop TLOD$_S$ Data Model

The time class is used to map during the creation progress of one or more GO$_S$ at DLOD$_S$, such as a villa or residential house. This mapping will keep track of the EHGO$_S$ at DLOD$_S$. There are three types of time to be applied [19] (Fig. 4), which are: (1) Legal time (LT$_S$) is the effective time in the legal document *(with month-day-year-hour:minute:second start and month-day-year-hour:minute:second end on the legal document)*; (2) Event time (ET$_S$) is time of start of formation and end of loss in the real world *(with month-day-year-hour:minute:second start and month-day-year-hour:minute:second end in the real world)*; (3) Database time (DT$_S$) is the start and end time of recording in the database *(with month-day-year-hour:minute:second start and month-day-year-hour:minute:second end in the database)*. Forms of time include: point of time or period of time (Fig. 5), we have:

-   The link between TIME$_S$ and TIMETYPE$_S$ indicates the time format of three types of time (Fig. 4).
-   The link between TIME$_S$ and MDY$_S$ indicates the time format of either instant time or interval time (Fig. 5).

At one level DLOD$_S$ can have multiple PRISM$_S$ A, SURFACE$_S$ A, LINE$_S$ A, and POINT$_S$ A created for a villa or residential building over time. Thus, we created a four-branch connection that indicates a PRISM$_S$ A, SURFACE$_S$ A, LINE$_S$ A, and POINT$_S$ A will either be created or lost and will be visualized at different levels of details, some DLOD$_S$ for a villa or a residential building over time. Corresponding to visual representation data models for villas or residential buildings at a different level of details over time, we have:

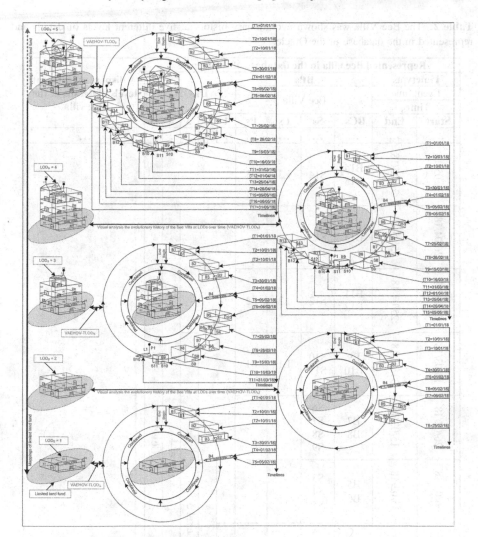

**Fig. 3.** Visual analysis the evolutionary history of Bee Villa (shown in Fig. 2) at DLOD$_S$ over time is located on a limited land funds.

- The four-branched linkage between four DLOD$_S$ objects, PRISM$_S$(Children), PRISMsP (Parent) and TIME$_S$ indicates that a PRISM$_S$ will be generated or lost at a certain interval time *(For example, a PRISM$_S$ A is born from January 1, 2018 to March 30, 2018, and from May 05, 2018 to May 28, 2018 PRISM$_S$ A will be lost.)* and will be visualized at the DLOD$_S$ level and for any villa (see Fig. 6).
- The four-branched linkage between the four DLOD$_S$, SURFACE$_S$, PRISMsP (Parent), and TIME$_S$ indicates that a SURFACE$_S$ will be born or lost at a certain period of time *(For example, a SURFACE$_S$ A is born from January 10, 2018 to*

**Table 2.** The Bee Villa was shown evolutionary history at five different levels of details and represented in the database of the Oracle.

| Represented Bee villa in the database of the Oracle | | | | | | | | | | | A display of different levels of details of the Bee villa |
| Timetypes | | BPs | | | | DLODs | | | | | |
| Event time | | Bee Villa | | | | | | | | | |
| Times | | | | | | | | | | | |
| Start | End | BCs | Ss | Ls | Ps | 1 | 2 | 3 | 4 | 5 | |
| ... | ... | ... | ... | ... | ... | . | . | . | . | . | ... |
| 06/05/18 | 31/05/18 | B14 B15 | S14 | L3 | P3 | | | | | | LODS = 5 |
| 26/04/18 | 05/05/18 | B13 | S13 | | | | | | | | |
| 01/04/18 | 25/04/18 | B11 B12 | S12 | L2 | P2 | | | | | | LODS = 4 |
| 16/03/18 | 31/03/18 | B9 B10 | S10 S11 | L1 | P1 | | | | | | |
| 26/02/18 | 15/03/18 | B7 B8 | S6 S7 S8 S9 | | | | | | | | LODS = 3 |
| 06/02/18 | 25/02/18 | B5 B6 | S3 S4 S5 | | | | | | | | |
| 01/02/18 | 05/02/18 | B4 | | | | | | | | | LODS = 2 |
| 10/01/18 | 30/01/18 | B2 B3 | S2 | | | | | | | | LODS = 1 |
| 01/01/18 | 10/01/18 | B1 | S1 | | | | | | | | Limited land fund |

Level 1   Level 2   Level 3   Level 4   Level 5

Mappings of limited land fund

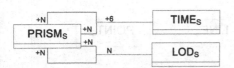

**Fig. 4.** Data model expresses linkage between TIME$_S$ and TIMETYPE$_S$

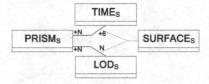

**Fig. 5.** Data model expresses linkage between TIME$_S$ and MDY$_S$

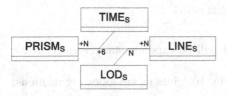

**Fig. 6.** Data model expresses linkage between PRISMsP (Parent), PRISM$_S$ (Children), TIME$_S$, and LOD$_S$.

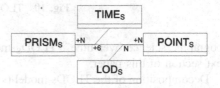

**Fig. 7.** Data model expresses linkage between PRISMsP (Parent), SURFACE$_S$, TIME$_S$, và LOD$_S$.

**Fig. 8.** Data model expresses linkage between PRISMsP (Parent), LINE$_S$, TIME$_S$, và LOD$_S$.

**Fig. 9.** Data model expresses linkage between PRISMsP (Parent), POINT$_S$, TIME$_S$, và LOD$_S$.

*March 15, 2018, and from May 10, 2018 to May 30, 2018 SURFACE$_S$ A will be lost.*) and will be visualized at any DLOD$_S$ level and for which villa (see Fig. 7).

- The four-branched linkage between the four DLOD$_S$, LINE$_S$, PRISMsP (Parent), and TIME$_S$ objects indicates that a LINE$_S$ will be generated or lost at a particular interval time (*For example, a LINE$_S$ A is born from Jan 1, 2018 to March 30, 2018, and from May 05, 2018 to May 25, 2018, LINE$_S$ A takes over.*) and will be visualized at the DLOD$_S$ level of detail and for any villa (see Fig. 8).

- The four-branched linkage between the four DLOD$_S$, POINT$_S$, PRISMsP (Parent), and TIME$_S$ indicates that a POINT$_S$ will be generated or lost at a certain time interval (*For example, a POINT$_S$ A is generated from January 1, 2018 to March 30, 2018, and from May 12, 2018 to May 20, 2018, POINT$_S$ A will be lost.*) and will be visualized at any DLOD$_S$ level and for any villa (see Fig. 9).

Through the visual analysis of the geographic objects and integration of entities PRISM$_S$, SURFACE$_S$, LINE$_S$, POINT$_S$, LOD$_S$, TIME$_S$, MDY$_S$ and TIMETYPE$_S$, we have come up with a new proposal model called TLOD$_S$ (see Fig. 10). TLOD$_S$ model is capable of answering users' questions/queries related to the topic "Visual representation of the evolutionary history of GO$_S$ at different levels of details in space of 3D

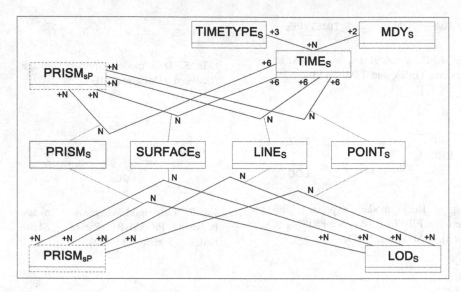

**Fig. 10.**  TLOD$_S$ data model

geographic science over time". TLOD$_S$ model will be experimentally verified in the next section of this paper.

Decomposition of the TLODs model (see Fig. 10) gives us the following relations:

PRISMsP(#IDBP, NAME, DESCS)
PRISMs(#IDB, HEIGHT, TYPESHAPE, DESCRIPTION, ARRAYNODE)
SURFACEs(#IDS, TYPESHAPE, DESCRIPTION, ARRAYNODE)
LINEs(#IDL, TYPESHAPE, DESCRIPTION, ARRAYNODE)
POINTs(#IDP, TYPESHAPE, DESCRIPTION, ARRAYNODE)
LODs(#IDLOD, NAME, DESCS)
PRISMLODs(#IDBP, #IDB, #IDLOD, DESCS)
SURFACELODs(#IDBP, #IDS, #IDLOD, DESCS)
LINELODs(#IDBP, #IDL, #IDLOD, DESCS)
POINTLODs(#IDBP, #IDP, #IDLOD, DESCS)
TIMETYPEs(#IDTT, NAME, DESCS)
MDYs(#IDMDY, MDY, HMS)
TIMEs(#IDT, IDMDY$_{begin(b)}$, IDMDY$_{end(e)}$, IDTT, DESCS)
PRISMTIMEs(#IDBP, #IDBC, IDT$_{bLTs}$, IDT$_{eLTs}$, IDT$_{bETs}$, IDT$_{eETs}$, IDT$_{bDTs}$, IDT$_{eDTs}$)
SURFACETIMEs(#IDBP, #IDS, IDT$_{bLTs}$, IDT$_{eLTs}$, IDT$_{bETs}$, IDT$_{eETs}$, IDT$_{bDTs}$,IDT$_{eDTs}$)
LINETIMEs(#IDBP, #IDL, IDT$_{bLTs}$, IDT$_{eLTs}$, IDT$_{bETs}$, IDT$_{eETs}$, IDT$_{bDTs}$, IDT$_{eDTs}$)
POINTTIMEs(#IDBP, #IDP, IDT$_{bLTs}$, IDT$_{eLTs}$, IDT$_{bETs}$, IDT$_{eETs}$, IDT$_{bDTs}$, IDT$_{eDTs}$)
*Notation: # is primary key.*

# 4   Experiments

In this section, we perform a $TLOD_S$ model implementation in Oracle 11G and associated with the C# programming language to present the form through a number of typical queries [20–22]. We will extract a villa named "Bee Villa" in a residential area (see Fig. 11) to perform a visual demonstration of the villa's evolution at different levels of details. These experimental results demonstrate that the $TLOD_S$ model is capable of answering users' questions on the subject "Visual representation of the evolutionary history of $GO_S$ at different levels of details in the space of three-dimensional geographic science over time". Queries will require users to provide the required input parameters, the obtained results are 3D space objects at different levels of details over time. The following are some typical queries and are accompanied by experimental results.

**Query 1:** Find and display the "Bee Villa" with construction time from [T1 = 01/01/2018, T2 = 31/03/2018], knew T1, T2 as period of time and type of event time ($ET_S$). The information of details of the show include: The villa image and details of each space component of the "Bee Villa" from T1 to T2 (see Fig. 12).
**Input:**      The "Bee Villa" that has time from T1 to T2 is a type of $ET_S$.
**Output:**   The image of the villa and time details of each space component of the "Bee Villa" villa from T1 to T2

**Query 2:** Find and display the "Bee Villa" with construction time from [T1 = 01/01/2018, T2 = 31/05/2018], knew T1, T2 is the time period and is type of $ET_S$ and only display at detail level $LOD_S = 5$. Display information includes: villa image and construction time details of each spatial component of "Bee Villa" at $LOD_S = 5$ and T1 to T2 (Fig. 13).
**Input:**      The "Bee Villa", time from T1 to T2, type of $ET_S$, and at $LOD_S = 5$
**Output:**   The villa image and timing details of each space component of the "Bee Villa" at $LOD_S = 5$ and T1 to T2

**Query 3:** Find and display the "Bee Villa" at detail level $LOD_S = 4$ over type of $ET_S$. The display information includes: The villa is built at $LOD_S = 4$ and enclosed with details of the evolution of spatial components at this level.
**Input:**      The "Bee Villa" and at level $LOD_S = 4$ over type of $ET_S$ (Fig. 14).
**Output:**   The villa image is built at $LOD_S = 4$ detail level and included with details of the evolutionary history of spatial components at this level over type of $ET_S$

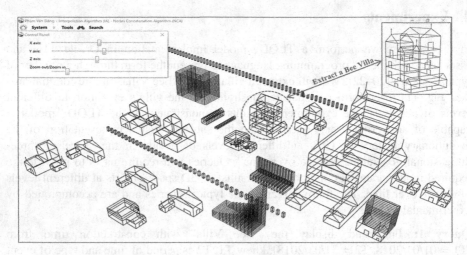

**Fig. 11.** A representation of urban areas including residential buildings and villas

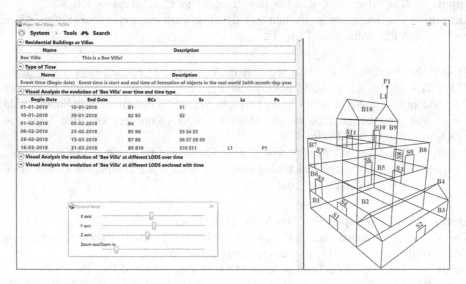

**Fig. 12.** The picture of "Bee Villa" and details of the time of construction of each space component of this villa from T1 to T2

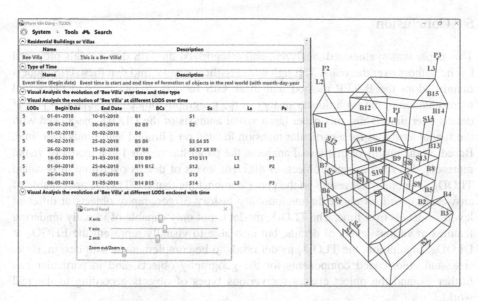

**Fig. 13.** The image of "Bee Villa" and detailed construction time for each spatial component of this villa at LOD$_S$ = 5 from T1 to T2

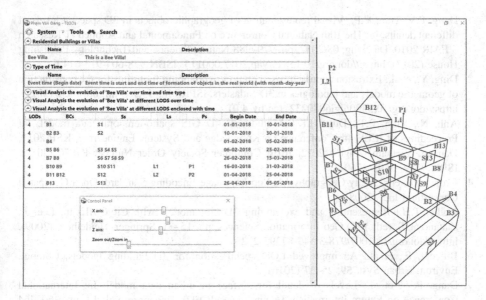

**Fig. 14.** The picture of the "Bee Villa" and enclosed with details of the evolutionary history of the spatial components at this level over type of ET$_S$

# 5 Conclusion

This paper was synthesized, analyzed, and categorized the GIS data models proposed by the authors over the years. Through this classification, we find that these GIS models mainly adopt the B-REP method and these GIS models do not refer to the visual representation of the evolutionary history of the geography objects at different levels of details over time. Thus, this paper has a visual analysis of the $DLOD_S$ associated with the spatial attributes for a particular mansion located on a limited land funds over time. Based on the results of this visual analysis, the paper has resulted in a model of visual representation of geography objects at different levels of details over time, it is called $TLOD_S$. The empirical results in the paper demonstrate that the $TLOD_S$ are capable of answering questions about the evolutionary history of geography objects at different levels of details over time. The $TLOD_S$ model is not only capable of visually rendering features at various levels of details, but also able to visually represent the $EHGO_S$ at $DLOD_S$. In addition, the $TLOD_S$ model needs to be complemented with design, style, size, and color-coded components for the geography objects, and in particular can further expand the object classes for various types of objects according to the real world.

# References

1. Dang, P.V, Tran, V.P.: Visual representation of geographic objects in 3D space at levels of different details. In: The 10th National Conference on Fundamental and Applied IT Research – FAIR 2010, Da Nang, 08/2017, pp. 979–988 Natural Science and Technology Publishing House (2017). https://doi.org/10.15625/vap.2017.000115. ISBN 978-604-913-614-6
2. Ding, Y., et al.: Extrusion approach based on non-overlapping footprints for the construction of geometric models and topologies in 3D cadasters. ISPRS Int. J. Geo-Inf. **6**(8), 232 (2017). https://doi.org/10.3390/ijgi6080232. (cc by 4.0)
3. Anh, N., Vinh, P.T., Duy, H.K.: A study on 4D GIS spatio-temporal data model. In: Proceedings of IEEE 4th Conference on Knowledge and Systems Engineering, KSE 2012, Danang, Vietnam, August 2012. IEEE Computer Society Order Number P4670 (2012). ISBN 978-0-7695-4760-2
4. Groger, G., et al.: City Geography Markup Language Encoding Standard. Open Geospatial Consortium Inc. (2008)
5. Kolbe, T.H.: Representing and exchanging 3D city models with CityGML. In: Lee, J., Zlatanova, S. (eds.) 3D Geo-Information Sciences, pp. 15–31. Springer, Heidelberg (2009). https://doi.org/10.1007/978-3-540-87395-2_2
6. Biljecki, F., et al.: An improved LOD specification for 3D building models. Comput. Environ. Urban Syst. **59**, 25–37 (2016)
7. Dang, P.V., et al.: Levels of detail for surface in urban data model. In: International Conference on Future Information Technology – ICFIT, Singapore, vol. 13, pp. 460–464 (2011). ISBN 978-981-08-9916-5
8. Anh, N.G., Vinh, P.T., Vu, T.P., Van Pham, D., Sy, A.T.: Representing multiple levels for objects in three-dimensional GIS model. In: The 13th International Conference on Information Integration and Web-Based Applications & Service (iiWAS2011), pp. 495–498. ACM Press, Vietnam (2011). ISBN 978-1-4503-0784-0

9. Löwner, M.O., et al.: Proposal for a new LOD and multi-representation concept for CityGML. ISPRS Ann. Photogramm. Remote Sens. Spat. Inf. Sci. **IV**(2/W1), 3–12 (2016)
10. Aydar, S.A., et al.: Establishing a national 3D geo-data model for building data compliant to CityGML: case of Turkey. In: The International Archives of the Photogrammetry, Remote Sensing and Spatial Information Sciences, vol. XLI-B2, 2016 XXIII ISPRS Congress, 12–19 July 2016, Prague, Czech Republic (2016)
11. Coors, V.: 3D-GIS in networking environments. Comput. Environ. Urban Syst. **27**(4), 345–357 (2003)
12. Rahman, A.A.: Developing three-dimensional topological model for 3D GIS. Project Report, UTM (2005)
13. Rahman, A.A.: Spatial Data Modeling for 3D GIS. Springer, Berlin (2008). https://doi.org/10.1007/978-3-540-74167-1
14. Gröger, G., et al.: Representation of a 3D city model in spatial object-relational databases. In: XXth ISPRS Congress, Geo-Imagery Bridging Continents, Commission 4 (2004)
15. Tet-Khuan, C., Abdul-Rahman, A., Zlatanova, S.: 3D spatial operations in geo DBMS environment for 3D GIS. In: Gervasi, O., Gavrilova, M.L. (eds.) ICCSA 2007. LNCS, vol. 4705, pp. 151–163. Springer, Heidelberg (2007). https://doi.org/10.1007/978-3-540-74472-6_12
16. Chokri, K., Koehl, M.: A simplified geometric and topological modeling of 3D building enriched by semantic data: combination of surface-based and solid-based representations. In: ASPRS 2009 Annual Conference Baltimore, Maryland (2009)
17. Swanson, J.: The Three Dimensional Visualization & Analysis of Geographic Data. Maps. unomaha.edu/Peterson/gis/Final_Projects/1996/Swanson/GIS_Paper.html. Accessed Apr 2017
18. Lieberwirth, U.: 3D GIS Voxel-Based Model Building in Archaeology. Archaeopress, Oxford (2008)
19. Dang, P.V., Tran, V.P.: Developing TPS data model in 3D GIS for management the population data. In: The 9th National Conference on Fundamental and Applied IT Research – FAIR'9, Can Tho, 08/2016, pp. 573–582. Natural Science and Technology Publishing House (2016). https://doi.org/10.15625/vap.2016.00071. ISBN 978-604-913-472-2
20. A Tool for Visualizing 3D Geometry Models. http://www.codeproject.com/Articles-/42992/A-Tool-for-Visualizing-D-Geometry-Models-Part. Accessed Nov 2017
21. Oracle Spatial User's Guide and Reference, Release 9, Part Number A88805-01, June 2001. https://docs.oracle.com/cd/A91202_01/901_doc/appdev.901/a88805/title.htm. Accessed Nov 2017
22. Elem_Info_Arraying: An alternative to SDO_UTI-L.GetNumRings and querying SDO_E-LEM_INFO_it self. http://www.spatialdbadvisor.com/oracle_spatial_tips_-tricks/89/sdo_utilget_numrings-an-alternative. Accessed Dec 2017

# A Conceptual Model of Consumers' Purchase Intention on Different Online Shopping Platforms

Attasit Patanasiri[1]([⊠]) [iD] and Donyaprueth Krairit[2]

[1] College of Social Communication Innovation, Srinakharinwirot University,
114 Sukhumvit23, Bangkok 10110, Thailand
attasitp@g.swu.ac.th
[2] NIDA Business School, National Institute of Development Administration,
118, Sereethai Road, Klongchan, Bangkapi, Bangkok 10240, Thailand

**Abstract.** The first objective of this paper is to provide a more comprehensive conceptual model which can be utilized in the examination of the effects of stimuli on online consumers' behavior and their decision making processes when they are contemplating a particular purchasing action or environment on various online shopping platforms. The proposed conceptual model was constructed by exploiting one of the theoretical framework of consumer behavior, the Stimulus-Organism-Response Model (S-O-R Model), as a base model and incorporating various related literature in the context of online shopping platforms into the base model and then develop into a conceptual framework. The second objective is to present the proposed conceptual model which can be utilized to study the differences of online consumers' behaviors on different online shopping platforms. The variables that were incorporated with the S-O-R Model include website interactivity (active control and reciprocal communication), perceived risk, social identity, website involvement (affective involvement and cognitive involvement), flow (perceived enjoyment, concentration, and curiosity), and purchase intention.

**Keywords:** E-commerce · Social-commerce
Stimulus-Organism-Response Model

## 1 Introduction

Currently, with the rapid changes of technologies which leading to several newly emerging technologies, people have been extremely impacted with this phenomenon in various aspects ranging from the way they live their daily lives to the way they organize their businesses. One of the newly emerging technologies that has been impacted people the most in various dimensions is social media including social network services. Besides the impact on people's daily lives, social media has extremely impacted on e-commerce industry. Social media has enormously transformed the environments of the e-commerce industry from product-oriented environment to social-oriented and customer-oriented environments. The newly emerging transformation of e-commerce has been recognized as s-commerce or social-commerce. Furthermore, s-commerce has

© ICST Institute for Computer Sciences, Social Informatics and Telecommunications Engineering 2019
Published by Springer Nature Switzerland AG 2019. All Rights Reserved
P. Cong Vinh and V. Alagar (Eds.): ICCASA 2018/ICTCC 2018, LNICST 266, pp. 116–125, 2019.
https://doi.org/10.1007/978-3-030-06152-4_10

been not only absolutely impacted on the environments of the e-commerce industry but also has been incredibly impacted on online consumers' behavior and their decision making processes.

This paper is aimed to present a comprehensive model that can be utilized to investigate the effects of stimuli on online consumers' purchase intention of different online shopping platforms including the platforms evolved by those newly emerging technologies.

## 2   Literature Review

### 2.1   Stimulus-Organism-Response Model

Stimulus-Organism-Response Model is the theoretical framework created in the area of cognitive approach. Moreover, it is a model among many well-known consumer behavior models. The objective of this model is to study and understand consumer's decision making processes in various level ranging from individual, groups, to organizations. The major objective that many researchers exploit the S-O-R model in the research studies is to evaluate how stimulus affects consumers and their behavior. The model was separated in to three parts including, stimulus, organism, and response. Stimulus part could be environmental or social stimuli. Moreover, the stimulus affects the second part of the model, organism part. Response is the result from the effect of the antecedents to the organism part. Bray [3] discussed in his study that consumers' processing of information is influenced by their past experiences. Furthermore, these experiences influence the consumers on what is the information they will seek and receive as well. The S-O-R Model can be depicted in Fig. 1.

**Fig. 1.** Stimulus-Organism-Response Model

In the context of online platforms, Haung [9], a major researcher who used the S-O-R Model, suggested that the stimulus part of the S-O-R Model could be online stimuli which influence consumers' organic experiences. Furthermore, these online stimuli can subsequently affect the response part of the model as well. Eroglu, Machleit and Davis [7] also suggested that the stimuli are directly related to the application's technological features. Furthermore, they also similarly stated the same suggestion as Huang [9] in that these stimuli also have influences on the organic experiences of consumers. Haung [9] suggested that environmental cues can act as stimuli in the S-O-R Model and both affectively and cognitively affect consumers' reactions. In the context of online shopping, Eroglu et al. [7] suggested that stimuli are directly related to the design features of the platform which are used to interact with the users. For the organism, Eroglu et al. [7] also defined the definition of this part as the cognitive or affective (emotional) systems of consumers. These systems include consumers' feelings, schema, cognitive network, and so forth. Additionally, the response of the consumers in this context can be in various formats ranging from conscious response to unconscious response and nonvisible (internal) response to visible (external) response.

## 2.2    Website Interactivity

In the context of online shopping platforms and social network services, Huang [9] suggested that an online shopping platform and a social network service need the capabilities of web-based communication and interactive technology in order to provide the interactivity to their users (consumers). This cooperative capability is called website interactivity. Jiang, Chan, Tan and Chua [10] suggested that there are two aspects of website interactivity that consumers encounter or engage with while they are making decision on their online purchases, mechanical interactivity and social interactivity. Jiang et al. [10] utilized active control and reciprocal communication as the demonstrations of mechanical interactivity and social interactivity consecutively. Huang [9] stated in his research study that interactivity has significant effects on both website involvement and consumers' flow experience.

Active control is defined as the capability to select information and conduct an interaction [9]. However, many research studies define active control as interactivity that allows consumers to communicate synchronously with the online shopping platforms and other users. Jiang et al. [10] suggested that active control is an essential component that influences users to interact with technologies.

Reciprocal communication is defined as the ability of communication between two or more entities [9, 10]. A user can experience reciprocal communication via communication tools provided by a web site, i.e. email or live chat. The main objective of providing communication tools is to provide the channels to users to involve in connection with online shopping platforms. Some research studies have suggested that reciprocal communication increasing could heighten communication intimacy and could lessen the relationship uncertainty between users and the online shopping platforms.

## 2.3    Social Identity

In the context of social network services, Huang [9] suggested that "social identity occurs when people seek to evaluate in-group similarities and out-group distinctiveness in social comparisons." Therefore, he defined social identity as "a user self-esteem and commitment to groups in a social networking site." Likewise, Cheung and Lee [5] also defined social identity as "the self-awareness of one's membership in a group, as well as the emotional and evaluative significance of this membership."

Cheung and Lee [5] and Huang [9] suggested that social identity composes of three major components, evaluative social identity, cognitive social identity, and affective social identity. Additionally, Cheung and Lee [5] also defined evaluative social identity as "the evaluation of self-worth on the basis of belonging to a particular group," cognitive social identity as "the self-categorization process renders the self stereotypically interchangeable with other group members, and stereotypically distinct from outsiders," and affective social identity as "a sense of emotional involvement with the group, which is characterized by identification with, involvement in, and emotional attachment to the group." While, Huang [9] also defined evaluative social identity as an "indicator of the evaluation of self-worth to an online group," cognitive social identity as "the process of self-categorization into an online group," and affective social identity as "a sense of emotional attachment to the online group." From the research study of Cheung and Lee [5], they suggested that evaluative social identity, cognitive social identity, and affective social identity should be treated as first-order component and social identity should be conceptualized as a second-order latent construct.

In many previous research studies, many researchers discovered significant impacts of social identity in many dimensions. Kwon and Wen [13] suggested that, from the previous research studies, the researchers discovered the significant impact of social identity on attitude. While, Arnett, German and Hunt [2] and Simon [19] suggested in their research studies which can be implied that people with high social identity tend to perceive in-group feeling and tend to prefer a group that can provide positive self-image to them. Moreover, this perceived in-group feeling can positively distinguish these people from out-group feeling as well. Clément, Noels and Doeneault [4] discovered that users with social identity need communication support from the platforms. This can be implied that these users perceive a social network service as a useful tool because it can provide the collaboration capability to them. Song and Kim [20] recommended that social identity is a significant determinant that has an effect on the intention to use a system, a service, or a specific technology.

### 2.4 Perceived Risk

From the classical decision theory, the variation in distribution, possibilities, and subjective values of possible outcomes are the sources of risk. Additionally, the theory of consumer's perceived risk stated that the sources of perceived risk are from the uncertainty and prospectively undesirable outcomes resulting from a purchase. Many research studies stated that the higher the risk the consumer perceive; the lower probability they will purchase the products or services. Nevertheless, consumers can reduce the risk by adopting many risk reduction strategies, i.e. gathering more information before making decision on their purchases.

In the context of online shopping platforms, perceived risk can be classified into nine dimensions including perceived financial risk (economic risk), perceived performance risk, perceived social risk, perceived physical risk, perceived psychological risk, perceived time-loss risk, perceived personal risk, perceived privacy risk, and perceived source risk. However, from these nine dimensions, Lim [14] continued to identify the sources of these risks and then classified them into four sources including technology, vendor, consumer, and product. First, perceived technology risk was defined as "the degree to which individuals believe that if they purchase products or services through the Internet, they will suffer losses caused by the Internet and its related technology" [14]. Secondly, perceived vendor risk was defined as "the degree to which individuals believe that if they purchase products or services through the Internet, they will suffer losses caused by Internet vendors" [14]. Thirdly, perceived consumer risk was defined as "the degree to which individuals believe that if they purchase products or services through the Internet, they will suffer losses caused by social pressure. Social pressure refers to pressure individuals receive from their families, friends, or colleagues" [14]. Finally, perceived product risk was defined as the degree to which individuals believe that if they purchase products or services through the Internet, they will suffer losses caused by products" [14]. However, Lim [14] found that, for online consumers of B2C e-commerce, there are only three sources of risk that have been perceived, perceived technology risk, perceived vendor risk, and perceived product risk. Vijayasarathy and Jones [21] and Lim [14] suggested that perceived risk has a significant effect on consumers' online shopping behaviors in an online shopping situation. As a result, perceived risk is proposed to be the stimuli part of the model.

## 2.5 Website Involvement

In the context of online shopping platforms and social network services, the concept of purchase involvement has been widely exploited in many research studies. From previous research studies, the researchers confirmed the moderating effect of involvement on purchase intention [7, 16, 22]. On the other hand, some research studies have paid more attention on website involvement because the researchers believe that it is a long-term involvement with direct influencing power on shaping consumers' behaviors.

From previous research studies, there are two aspects of website involvement that have been mostly investigated, affective involvement and cognitive involvement [9–11, 23]. Eroglu et al. [7] and Koufaris [12] suggested that affective or emotional involvement and cognitive involvement of consumers can be enhanced through the interactions with websites. Eroglu et al. [7] also suggested that the features of websites, i.e. sound, animation, color, website information, can enhance affective involvement because these features can enhance users' happiness and experiences while they are shopping on those websites. Moreover, website cues, i.e. images, price, and description of a product, sales policies, can enhance cognitive involvement as well. Kim and Lennon [11] demonstrated about cognitive involvement that "the cognitive state concerns issues regarding how online shoppers interpret information provided online and form thoughts and beliefs toward the service/product being provided." They also demonstrated about affective involvement that "users can also be affectively involved with a social networking site through features such as friend messages, photos, music, movies, chat windows, and game activities." Huang [9] stated that the higher involvement consumers have; the higher positive online experiences consumers gain.

In this context, Huang [9] defined involvement as "a consumer's overall subjective feelings of personal relevance." Whereas, Jiang et al. [10] defined involvement as "the perceived relevance of the website based in the inherent needs, values, and interests of the consumer." Additionally, in this context, there is a variation in defining the definitions of affective and cognitive involvement. Jiang et al. [10] defined affective involvement as "affective involvement is associated with "emotional, hedonistic" and is derived from value-expressive or affective motives." They also defined cognitive involvement as "cognitive involvement is associated with rational, thinking, and is induced by utilitarian or cognitive motives." Whereas, Kim and Lennon [11] defined affective involvement as "affective responses reflect emotions and feelings evoked by environmental stimuli" and cognitive involvement as "cognitive responses describe consumers' internal mental processes and states, and involve memory, knowledge structures, imagery, beliefs and thoughts."

## 2.6  Flow

The origin of flow theory is from the psychology, but, it has been exploited to deal with optimal user experiences in various contexts, especially, technology usage [15]. The theory of flow has been exploited to describe a state of people in which "people are so involved in an activity that nothing else seems to matter" [6]. In the state of flow, people lose their self-consciousness and feel that they have the power to control their environment because all of their awareness is totally used in focusing on the activity that they are performing. Flow is recognized as a complex concept that researchers can operationalize it through various dimensions. Nevertheless, there are four dimensions or constructs that many research studies exploited in their works to measure flow including enjoyment, concentration, perceived control, and curiosity.

Recently, most of the researchers in the context of online consumer experiences or online consumer behavior have been initially paid their attentions to study flow [1, 8, 12, 18]. The reason behind this phenomenon is that people can develop positive emotions naturally when they are being in the state of flow because flow is a highly enjoyable and absorbing experience [9]. For online consumers, online environments of the websites can generate flow by involving consumers with those environments. Huang [9] suggested that users who enjoy their existence in virtual platforms are more likely to invest more time and money in purchasing the products available on that platforms. From previous research studies, researchers discovered the positive relations between flow and purchase intention and between flow and return intention in the context of online shopping and website usage [12, 17]. As a result, flow theory is proposed as a part of the organism part of the conceptual model.

## 2.7  Purchase Intention

Huang [9] suggested that purchase intention is one among many forms of consumers' online experiences. Moreover, consumers' responses aroused from purchase intention can be in various forms and reactions ranging from consciously purchase product(s) to unconsciously purchase product(s) [9]. In the research study of Huang [9], he demonstrated that online experience can be classified into two categories, direct product experience and indirect product experience. Direct product experience occurs when a consumer interacts with a product and directly obtain information from this action. Indirect product experience come from consumer's experience about a product and is mediated by an advertising. Furthermore, direct product experience has significant influence on consumer's expectation toward a purchase.

From previous research studies, the results showed that affective involvement, cognitive involvement, and flow significantly affect consumers' purchase intention.

# 3 Proposed Conceptual Model

The conceptual model was constructed based on the S-O-R Model and the combination of literature. The first major objective of the conceptual model is to provide more comprehensive model that can be utilized to study the differences of online consumers' actions on various online shopping platforms. Furthermore, this conceptual model is aimed to be utilized as a metric to capture those differences. The second major objective is to provide a conceptual model which can be exploited to examine the effects of stimuli on online consumers' behavior and their decision making processes. The details of the proposed conceptual model are discussed as follows.

## 3.1 Online Stimuli

According to the S-O-R Model and related literature, there are four variables which can be representatives of the stimuli (S) part of the S-O-R Model and are included in the conceptual model. The descriptions of these variables are as follows.

**Active Control:** The intention of this variable is to capture the degree of controlling capability that the platforms allow users to choose information and guide their interactions with the platforms.

**Reciprocal Communication:** The intention of this variable is to capture the degree of the ability of two-way communication tools that the platforms provided to their users.

**Perceived Risk:** The intention of this variable is to capture the different types of risks that the users perceived while they are contemplating a particular purchasing action.

**Social Identity:** The intention of this variable is to capture the different types and the degree of enhancing capability that the online shopping platforms can motivate their users to participate in the platforms' activities.

## 3.2 Online Experience and Purchase Intention

According to the S-O-R Model and related literature, there are four variables which can be representatives of the organism (O) part of the S-O-R model and are included in the conceptual model. The descriptions of these variables are as follows.

**Affective Involvement:** The intention of this variable is to capture the affective or emotional needs of online consumers.

**Cognitive Involvement:** The intention of this variable is to capture the degree of the online consumers' capabilities in the interpretation of online information that affects their thought about the products.

**Perceived Enjoyment:** The intention of this variable is to capture online consumers' perceived enjoyment arousing while they are contemplating a particular purchasing situation.

**Concentration:** The intention of this variable is to capture online consumers' attention arousing while they are contemplating a particular purchasing situation.

**Curiosity:** The intention of this variable is to capture online consumers' curiosity arousing while they are contemplating a particular purchasing situation.

Finally, the response part (R) of the S-O-R model can be represented by purchase intention and is included in the conceptual model. The intention of this variable is to capture online consumers' willingness to buy product(s) from online shopping platforms. The conceptual model of can be depicted in Fig. 2.

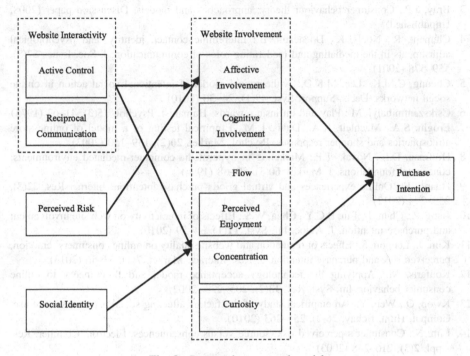

**Fig. 2.** Proposed conceptual model

## 4  Conclusion

The proposed conceptual model is aimed to provide more comprehensive model that can be exploited to study the differences of online consumers' behaviors on several online shopping platforms. Additionally, it can be exploited to examine the effects of stimuli on online consumers' behavior and their decision making processes. However, this proposed conceptual model will be tested in further study.

# References

1. Animesh, A.P., Yang, S.B., Oh, W.: An odyssey into virtual words: exploring the impacts of technological and spatial environments on intention to purchase virtual products. MIS Q. 35(3), 780–810 (2011)
2. Arnett, D.B., German, S.D., Hunt, S.D.: The identity salience model of relationship marketing success: the case of non-profit marketing. J. Market. 67(2), 89–105 (2003)
3. Bray, J.P.: Consumer behaviour theory: approaches and models. Discussion paper (2008, Unpublished)
4. Clément, R., Noels, K., Doeneault, B.: Interethnic contact, identity, and psychological adjustments in the mediating and moderating roles of communication. J. Soc. Issues 57(3), 559–578 (2001)
5. Cheung, C.M.K., Lee, M.K.O.: A theoretical model of intentional social action in online social networks. Decis. Support Syst. 49(1), 24–30 (2010)
6. Csikszentmihalyi, M.: Play and intrinsic rewards. Humanist. Psychol. 15(3), 41–63 (1975)
7. Eroglu, S.A., Machleit, K.A., Davis, L.M.: Empirical testing of a model of online store atmospherics and shopper responses. Psychol. Market. 20(2), 139–150 (2003)
8. Hoffman, D.L., Novak, T.P.: Marketing in hypermedia computer-mediated environments: conceptual foundations. J. Market. 60(3), 50–68 (1996)
9. Huang, E.: Online experiences and virtual goods purchase intention. Internet Res. 22(3), 252–274 (2012)
10. Jiang, Z., Chan, J., Tan, B.C.Y., Chua, W.S.: Effects of interactivity on web site involvement and purchase intention. J. Assoc. Inf. Syst. 11(1), 34–59 (2010)
11. Kim, J., Lennon, S.: Effects of reputation and website quality on online consumers' emotion, perceived risk and purchase intention. J. Res. Interact. Market. 7(1), 33–56 (2013)
12. Koufaris, M.: Applying the technology acceptance model and flow theory to online consumer behavior. Inf. Syst. Res. 13(2), 205–223 (2002)
13. Kwon, O., Wen, Y.: An empirical study of the factors affecting social network service use. Comput. Hum. Behav. 26(2), 254–263 (2010)
14. Lim, N.: Consumer's perceived risk: source versus consequences. Electron. Commer. Res. Appl. 2(3), 216–238 (2003)
15. Lu, Y., Zhou, T., Wang, B.: Exploring Chinese user's acceptance of instant messaging using the theory of planned behavior, the technology acceptance model, and the flow theory. Comput. Hum. Behav. 25(1), 29–39 (2010)
16. Manganari, E.E., Siomkos, G.J., Rigopoulou, I.D., Vrechopoulos, A.P.: Virtual store layout effects on consumer behaviour: applying an environmental psychology approach in the online travel industry. Internet Res. 21(3), 326–346 (2011)
17. Moon, J.W., Kim, Y.G.: Extending the TAM for a world-wide-web context. Inf. Manage. 38(4), 217–230 (2001)
18. Novak, T.P., Hoffman, D.L., Yung, Y.F.: Measuring the customer experience in online environments: a structural modeling approach. Mark. Sci. 19(1), 22–44 (2000)
19. Simon, B.: Identity in Modern Society: A Social Psychological Perspective. Blackwell, Oxford (2004)
20. Song, J., Kim, Y.J.: Social influence process in the acceptance of a virtual community service. Inf. Syst. Front. 8(3), 241–252 (2006)

21. Vijayasarathy, L.R., Jones, J.M.: Intentions to shop using internet catalogues: exploring the effects of product types, shopping orientations, and attitudes towards computers. Electron. Markets 10(1), 29–38 (2000)
22. Wang, K., Wang, E.T.G., Farn, C.K.: Influence of web advertising strategies, consumer goal-directedness, and consumer involvement on web advertising effectiveness. Int. J. Electron. Commer. 13(4), 67–95 (2009)
23. Zaichkowsky, J.L.: Conceptualizing involvement. J. Advertising 15(6), 1–14 (1986)

# MVMO with Opposite Gradient Initialization for Single Objective Problems

Thirachit Saenphon[(⊠)]

Chulalongkorn University, Bangkok, Thailand
thirachits@gmail.com

**Abstract.** The objective of this paper is to describe an opposite gradient initialization concept with mean-variance mapping optimization (OGI-MVMO). OGI-MVMO is an optimization based on the actual manifold of objective function whereas original MVMO based stochastic optimization. Generating the new candidate solution to speed up the solution finding and accuracy of solution are important purposes. The OGI-MVMO algorithm consist of 2 steps: the primary step is generating new solution by OGI and also the second step is mutation between every of selected candidate solution supported the mean and variance of the population. The results showed that OGI-MVMO algorithm has better performance than other algorithm include the original MVMO for 15 real-parameter single objective functions.

**Keywords:** Continuous function
Mean-variance mapping optimization
Opposite gradient initialization search · Optimization

## 1 Introduction

The black-box continuous optimization is solving a global optimization solution without explicit knowledge of the form or structure of the objective function. Mean-variance mapping optimization (MVMO) [4] is a mapping function described by the mean and shape variables which both of them are derived from $n$ the best solutions save in the specific archive. MVMO applied to solve the optimization problem such as wind farm [1], electricity pricing [6]. To generate a new offspring before the mutation, the technique based on MVMO also remain use the randomness without consider the interesting population on the real searching surface of the objective function.

An importance task in evolutionary algorithms is a generating first population with neighboring to an expect best solution. Random initialization is appreciated for generating new candidate solutions and selecting low scoring solutions to maximize or minimize the objective function. The geometric structure of the

© ICST Institute for Computer Sciences, Social Informatics and Telecommunications Engineering 2019
Published by Springer Nature Switzerland AG 2019. All Rights Reserved
P. Cong Vinh and V. Alagar (Eds.): ICCASA 2018/ICTCC 2018, LNICST 266, pp. 126–135, 2019.
https://doi.org/10.1007/978-3-030-06152-4_11

objective function is not relevant as a part of solution to generate a new off-spring and searching process. The use of searching solutions on a manifold of objective function using opposite gradient search was first introduced in [7]. Fast Opposite Gradient Search (FOGS) does not depend on meta-heuristic search as the others' but it searches the manifold to find the locations with zero gradients and minimum values of objective function.

A new combining approach to improve the accuracy of solution with the better initial population for solving the single objective optimization problem was proposed. The research present an opposite gradient to generate some new offspring and searching a better solution from these first population with mean-variance mapping technique. The technique is called the opposite gradient initialization combined with mean-variance mapping optimization (OGI-MVMO). The method focused on how to enhance a step of generating a new offspring and how to search the better solution. This research also applied mapping function for mutation operation on the basic of the mean and variance of the n-best solutions to adjust the better candidate solution in the black-box problem functions which their surface are difficult and alter dependence on the composite function.

This article has the following sections; Sect. 2, Mean-Variance Mapping Optimization, Opposite Gradient Initialization and the combining OGI and MVMO algorithm are described. Experimental result and analysis are given in Sect. 3. Discussion the experimental results are given in Sect. 4. Finally, the conclusion is given in Sect. 5.

## 2    Concept of Proposed Algorithm

Our proposed algorithm consists of two main concepts. The first concept concerns the generating new offspring along the manifold of the objective function. The second concept focuses on search of the best solution using an adaptation of mean-variance mapping optimization. The detail of each concept is in the following sections.

### 2.1    Concept of Opposite Gradient Initialization

For a vector in a $D$-dimensional space of the objective function, OGI tries to generate some new offspring in the locations of the manifold whose the first derivative $(F'(x))$ are approximate zero since these locations must be the best solution. $\nabla F(x)$ is the unique vector field that satisfies $F'(x) \approx \nabla F(x)$ for vector field $x$.

Let $\mathbf{P}^{(\alpha)}$ and $\mathbf{P}^{(\beta)}$ be any two vectors on the manifold of the objective function $F(\mathbf{P}^{(i)})$. The point with zero of the gradient must lay on between $\mathbf{P}^{(\alpha)}$ and $\mathbf{P}^{(\beta)}$ if $\nabla F(\mathbf{P}^{(\alpha)})$ and $\nabla F(\mathbf{P}^{(\beta)})$ are difference sign value. A new vector can be computed from a distance $\delta$. The value of $\delta$ can be computed by the following equation.

$$\delta = \frac{|\nabla F(\mathbf{P}^{(\beta)})|}{|\nabla F(\mathbf{P}^{(\alpha)})| + |\nabla F(\mathbf{P}^{(\beta)})|} \times ||\mathbf{P}^{(\beta)} - \mathbf{P}^{(\alpha)}|| \times w \qquad (1)$$

A constant $w \in R^+$. After computing $\delta$, two new vectors are generated and computed from $\mathbf{P}^{(\alpha)} + \delta$ and $\mathbf{P}^{(\beta)} - \delta$. These two new vectors are the new offspring which used to be the first population for MVMO in the next step. The principal procedure of the proposed algorithm is as follows.

---

**Algorithm 1.** Proposed hybrid opposite gradient initialization with mean-variance mapping algorithm

---

1:  Initialize algorithm parameters and Generation of initial population
2:  **while** Terminating conditions are not satisfied **do**
3:      $NP$ is a size of $Q$
4:      **for** $1 \leq k \leq NP$ **do**
5:          Fitness evaluation $F(\mathbf{P}^{(\alpha)})$.
6:          Fill or Update individual point using two archives.
7:          Classification of good gradient vectors and good fitness values.
8:          Fill the good gradient vectors in the first archive and some vectors with good fitness values in the second.
9:          Using opposite gradient initialization algorithm as described in Algorithm 2 to compute new set of candidate solutions.
10:         Fill or Update individual point using solution archives.
11:         Mutation through mapping of $m$ selected dimensions using local mean and variance.
12:     **end for**
13: **end while**

---

The main procedure begins with an initialization step where the algorithm parameter settings are defined and the first generation of population is generated by OGI within their search boundaries for a set of total number of candidate solutions. It ensures that the generated offspring will always in the search boundaries before fitness evaluation or local search execute. Furthermore, the first generated offspring is relative a local minimum. The heart of the algorithm is contained in the while loop in which for each fitness evaluation of each point, local search, updating the solution archive, fitness and gradient classification of points into selected parents point and offspring generation are performed. The main algorithm is terminated when the termination criterion is satisfied.

According to continually-updated archive in MVMO technique [4], each point has a fixed size compact memory that continuously fill and updated solution archive associated to it, the data stored in the archive are n-best offspring in a descending order of fitness to be knowledge for guiding the search direction. Only a new better solution of each point in the archive can replace later on every fitness evaluation or local search.

In this step of algorithm, the classification of good opposite gradient point and good fitness value for selection to be parents in the opposite gradient algorithm is included. In each generation, two new vectors are generated and lay in between two vectors of opposite gradients in the previous generation. Therefore, the new vectors are computed and lay on the reducing search space. If one of them gives a better cost function, then this new vector along with another vector in the first generation, whose value of cost function is in an acceptable range and its gradient that is opposite to the new vector, is used to generate a new vector in the next generation. Otherwise, any two vectors in the first generation, whose values of cost function are in an acceptable range and their gradients are opposite to each other, are newly selected to generate two new vectors in the second generation.

All $\mathcal{NP}$ vectors are ranked according to their local the best cost function and classified into two groups: Let $\mathcal{G}^+$ be sets of vectors whose gradients of cost function are positive and $\mathcal{G}^-$ be those whose gradients of cost function are negative. All vectors in $\mathcal{G}^+$ and $\mathcal{G}^-$ are already sorted in descending order according to their values of gradient. At the end of algorithm, the locations with zero gradient will be obtained. The detail of this step is given in Algorithm 2.

---

**Algorithm 2.** Opposite Gradient Initialization algorithm for generating new offspring

---

1: Set $count = 1$
2: Separate the vector in archive to $\mathcal{G}^+$ and $\mathcal{G}^-$ groups.
3: **while** $count \leq \mathcal{NP}$ **do**
4:     Let $\mathbf{P}^{(\alpha)}$ be the first vector of $\mathcal{G}^+$ and $\mathbf{P}^{(\beta)}$ be the first vector of $\mathcal{G}^-$.
5:     Compute vector $\mathbf{P}^{(1)}$ from $\mathbf{P}^{(\alpha)}$ and $\mathbf{P}^{(2)}$ from $\mathbf{P}^{(\beta)}$ by using equation (1).
6:     Replace $\mathbf{P}^{(\alpha)}$ with $\mathbf{P}^{(1)}$ in $\mathcal{G}^+$ if $|\nabla F(\mathbf{P}^{(1)})| < |\mathbf{P}^{(\alpha)}|$.
7:     Replace $\mathbf{P}^{(\beta)}$ with $\mathbf{P}^{(2)}$ in $\mathcal{G}^-$ if $|\nabla F(\mathbf{P}^{(2)})| < |\mathbf{P}^{(\beta)}|$.
8:     Set $count = count + 1$.
9: **end while**

---

The new offspring from this step is filled and updated in solution archive, which stores its n-best offspring in descending order of fitness and serve for guiding the search direction. The size of solution archive is not vary along the entire process. After every point evaluate their fitness and local search, each point update its archive takes place only if the new solution is better than those in the archive.

## 2.2    Combined Mean-Variance Mapping Optimization

The objective of adapting Mean-Variance Optimization as a part of our algorithm is to improve the solution searching process so that the possible best solution can be found in fewer generations. The steps of procedure of MVMO for combine with OGI for the continuous problem are described as follows:

## 3    Experimental Simulation and Analysis

The proposed algorithm and the three other algorithms (NBIPOPaCMA [2], PVADE [5], MVMO [4]) were implemented for testing the performance of these

---

**Algorithm 3.** Combine the MVMO with OGI searching process

---

1: Set the parameters including $iter_{max}$, $d_r$, $\triangle d_0$, $f^*_{s\_ini}$, $f^*_{s\_final}$, number of points $(NP)$
2: Get the initial points which in the range [-100,100] from OGI step algorithm 2.
3: Set $k = 1$, $k$ denotes point counters
4: **while** $iter_{max}$ is not reached **do**
5:     Calculate the cost function $f$ for the problem, store $f_{best}$ and $x_{best}$ in archive.
6:     Increase $i = i + 1$
7:     **if** $i < iter_{max}$ **then**
8:         Check the point for the global best, collect a set of individual solutions.
9:         The $i - th$ point is discarded from the optimization process if the $f_i$ is greater than every $f_n$ in archive
10:        **if** the point is deleted **then**
11:            Increase $k = k + 1$ and go to step 5
12:        **else**
13:            Create offspring generation with algorithm 2
14:        **end if**
15:    **else**
16:        Create offspring generation with algorithm 2
17:    **end if**
18:    **if** $k < NP$ **then**
19:        increase $k = k + 1$ and go to step 5
20:    **end if**
21: **end while**

---

algorithms, the experimental results were compared with those of the other three algorithms based on 15 test functions on Real-Parameter Single Objective Optimization [3]. In Liang et al. [3], the complete description of the problem definition functions can be found. The set of test functions is uni-modal function. Search range is $[-100, 100]^D$. The optimization is terminated upon completion of the maximum number of function evaluations. In this section, the description of the parameter set-up (Sect. 3.1), the experimental results (Sect. 3.2) are presented.

## 3.1 Parameter Set-Up

All optimization problems are deciphered by utilizing OGI-MVMO with 150 points. The selected parameters for OGI-MVMO were summarized in Table 1. The first column denotes the names of parameters and the second column shows the value of each parameter.

## 3.2 Experimental Results

This paper present best, worst, median, mean and standard deviation of the error value between the best fitness values. The results are shown in Tables 2 and 3 respectively.

Table 1. Parameter setting of our proposed algorithm.

| Parameters | Values |
|---|---|
| $f^*_{s\_ini}$ | 1 |
| $f^*_{s\_final}$ | 20 |
| $\gamma$ | 15 |
| $d_r$ | 1 |
| $\delta d_0$ | 0.05 |
| $NP$ | 150 |
| Archive size | 5 |
| Maximum number of function evaluations $iter_{max}$ | 100000 |
| Number of experimental runs in each function | 50 |

OGI-MVMO has capability to search the solution with zero error values for all function in all runs for 10D. The better result for each problem is highlighted in boldface. The result of tests show that OGI-MVMO can successfully solve problems without considering the local search strategy. Thus, OGI-MVMO is an appropriate technique to solve continuous problems.

Solving basic multi-modal functions: For 10D case issues, OGI-MVMO has capability to achieve the results with zero error values for all test function problem except F14, F15. However, the accuracy of the results that are obtained also are terribly satisfactory compared to the compared algorithms.

From the previous tables, OGI-MVMO outperformed others on 15 single objective functions while also get the good results as other 3 techniques on 10 function problems. It means using an opposite gradient initialization, rather than using a random start of the population, close to the best answer, and speed up the search. The examples for performance comparison are shown in Fig. 1. The figures have been also plotted average error (compared to the optimal solution) vs. the number of evaluations (for $D = 10$ dimensions) in Fig. 1. Note that the y-axis (average best value for all 50 run times) is logarithmic scale. Experiments have been repeated 50 times to plot the average error values. (a)–(c) F9, F14, and F15 with D = 10.

## 4    Discussion

The present methodology works on 2 significant ideas. The primary concept is to applied the manifold of objective function perform as a component of initializing and generating a candidate solution. The subsequent generation of solution is created based on the gradient of manifold of objective function. The last significant concept is searching the improve solution by collect the solution in an archive for locating the mean and variance to map a brand new probability of the better solution. These 2 ideas perform along well to attain since the geometrical structure of the cost function manifold and can relieve some problem of the important issues.

**Table 2.** Result of the comparison from different algorithms for $F1 - F5$

| Algorithms | Best | Worst | Median | Mean | Std. |
|---|---|---|---|---|---|
| F1 | | | | | |
| NBIPOPaCMA | 0.00E+00 | 0.00E+00 | 0.00E+00 | 0.00E+00 | 0.00E+00 |
| PVADE | 0.00E+00 | 0.00E+00 | 0.00E+00 | 0.00E+00 | 0.00E+00 |
| MVMO | 0.00E+00 | 0.00E+00 | 0.00E+00 | 0.00E+00 | 0.00E+00 |
| OGI-MVMO | 0.00E+00 | 0.00E+00 | 0.00E+00 | 0.00E+00 | 0.00E+00 |
| F2 | | | | | |
| NBIPOPaCMA | 0.00E+00 | 0.00E+00 | 0.00E+00 | 0.00E+00 | 0.00E+00 |
| PVADE | 0.00E+00 | 7.97E+02 | 0.00E+00 | 1.57E+01 | 1.12E+02 |
| MVMO | 0.00E+00 | 0.00E+00 | 0.00E+00 | 0.00E+00 | 0.00E+00 |
| OGI-MVMO | 0.00E+00 | 0.00E+00 | 0.00E+00 | 0.00E+00 | 0.00E+00 |
| F3 | | | | | |
| NBIPOPaCMA | 0.00E+00 | 0.00E+00 | 0.00E+00 | 0.00E+00 | 0.00E+00 |
| PVADE | 0.00E+00 | 5.03E-03 | 0.00E+00 | 9.87E-05 | 7.05E-04 |
| MVMO | 0.00E+00 | 0.00E+00 | 0.00E+00 | 0.00E+00 | 0.00E+00 |
| OGI-MVMO | 0.00E+00 | 0.00E+00 | 0.00E+00 | 0.00E+00 | 0.00E+00 |
| F4 | | | | | |
| NBIPOPaCMA | 0.00E+00 | 0.00E+00 | 0.00E+00 | 0.00E+00 | 0.00E+00 |
| PVADE | 0.00E+00 | 2.25E-01 | 0.00E+00 | 4.41E-03 | 3.15E-02 |
| MVMO | 0.00E+00 | 0.00E+00 | 0.00E+00 | 0.00E+00 | 0.00E+00 |
| OGI-MVMO | 0.00E+00 | 0.00E+00 | 0.00E+00 | 0.00E+00 | 0.00E+00 |
| F5 | | | | | |
| NBIPOPaCMA | 0.00E+00 | 0.00E+00 | 0.00E+00 | 0.00E+00 | 0.00E+00 |
| PVADE | 0.00E+00 | 8.66E-04 | 0.00E+00 | 1.70E-05 | 1.21E-04 |
| MVMO | 0.00E+00 | 0.00E+00 | 0.00E+00 | 0.00E+00 | 0.00E+00 |
| OGI-MVMO | 0.00E+00 | 0.00E+00 | 0.00E+00 | 0.00E+00 | 0.00E+00 |

**Table 3.** Result of the comparison from different algorithms for $F6$–$F15$

| Algorithms | Best | Worst | Median | Mean | Std. |
|---|---|---|---|---|---|
| F6 | | | | | |
| NBIPOPaCMA | 0.00E+00 | 0.00E+00 | 0.00E+00 | 0.00E+00 | 0.00E+00 |
| PVADE | 0.00E+00 | 9.89E+00 | 9.81E+00 | 7.09E+00 | 4.25E+00 |
| MVMO | 0.00E+00 | 0.00E+00 | 0.00E+00 | 0.00E+00 | 0.00E+00 |
| OGI-MVMO | 0.00E+00 | 0.00E+00 | 0.00E+00 | 0.00E+00 | 0.00E+00 |

*(continued)*

**Table 3.** (*continued*)

| Algorithms | Best | Worst | Median | Mean | Std. |
|---|---|---|---|---|---|
| F7 | | | | | |
| NBIPOPaCMA | 0.00E+00 | 1.60E+01 | 3.27E−08 | 0.14E+01 | 0.48E+01 |
| PVADE | 3.13E−05 | 1.08E+01 | 2.64E−03 | 3.22E−01 | 1.53E+00 |
| MVMO | 6.34E−03 | 6.34E−03 | 6.34E−03 | 6.34E−03 | 0.00E+00 |
| OGI−MVMO | 0.00E+00 | 0.00E+00 | 0.00E+00 | 0.00E+00 | 0.00E+00 |
| F8 | | | | | |
| NBIPOPaCMA | 3.63E−08 | 1.70E−08 | 1.03E−08 | 1.03E−08 | 9.48E−09 |
| PVADE | 2.01E+01 | 2.05E+01 | 2.04E+01 | 2.03+01 | 7.12E−02 |
| MVMO | 2.02E+01 | 2.02E+01 | 2.02E+01 | 2.02E+01 | 8.93E−02 |
| OGI−MVMO | **0.00E+00** | 6.21E−08 | 4.34E−08 | 1.54E−07 | 1.0253E−07 |
| F9 | | | | | |
| NBIPOPaCMA | 1.94E−08 | 2.53E+01 | 8.83E−01 | 3.85E+00 | 9.48E−09 |
| PVADE | 8.15E−03 | 3.66E+00 | 1.44E+00 | 1.56E+00 | 9.77E−01 |
| MVMO | 5.20E−01 | 2.43E+00 | 8.50E−01 | 8.32E−01 | 6.81E−01 |
| OGI−MVMO | **0.00E+00** | 9.66E−08 | 4.39E−08 | 7.15E−08 | 4.69E−08 |
| F10 | | | | | |
| NBIPOPaCMA | 1.00E−08 | 6.70E−08 | 2.88E−08 | 3.26E−08 | 1.91E−09 |
| PVADE | 0.00E+00 | 1.77E−01 | 3.94E−02 | 5.05E−02 | 3.82E−02 |
| MVMO | 1.01E−02 | 3.69E−02 | 1.36E−02 | 1.67E−02 | 2.18E−02 |
| OGI−MVMO | **0.00E+00** | 3.94E−08 | 2.98E−08 | 3.04E−08 | 7.88E−09 |
| F11 | | | | | |
| NBIPOPaCMA | 0.00E+00 | 6.70E−08 | 2.88E−08 | 3.26E−08 | 1.91E−09 |
| PVADE | 0.00E+00 | 1.19E+01 | 3.39E+00 | 3.94E+00 | 2.34E+00 |
| MVMO | 0.00E+00 | 5.97E+00 | 0.00E+00 | 2.25E+00 | 1.38E−02 |
| OGI−MVMO | 0.00E+00 | 1.11E−08 | 4.04E−09 | 4.89E−09 | 3.75E−09 |
| F12 | | | | | |
| NBIPOPaCMA | 0.00E+00 | 1.05E+00 | 1.50E−04 | 3.50E−01 | 1.91E−09 |
| PVADE | 9.95E−01 | 1.61E+01 | 4.97E+00 | 5.92E+00 | 3.69E+00 |
| MVMO | 1.98E+00 | 1.57E+01 | 5.97E+00 | 5.95E+00 | 1.38E+00 |
| OGI−MVMO | 0.00E+00 | 3.56E−05 | 4.41E−08 | 4.80E−08 | 7.64E−09 |
| F13 | | | | | |
| NBIPOPaCMA | 0.00E+00 | 5.68E+00 | 2.74E−04 | 7.8E−01 | 1.77E+00 |
| PVADE | 0.00E+00 | 2.13E+01 | 8.07E+00 | 8.63E+00 | 4.79E+00 |
| MVMO | 1.98e+00 | 1.97e+01 | 5.69E+00 | 9.14e+00 | 9.36E+00 |
| OGI−MVMO | 0.00E+00 | 3.82E−05 | 4.76E−02 | 1.09E−05 | 1.37E−05 |

(*continued*)

**Table 3.** (*continued*)

| Algorithms | Best | Worst | Median | Mean | Std. |
|---|---|---|---|---|---|
| F14 | | | | | |
| NBIPOPaCMA | 2.19E+01 | 7.67E+02 | 3.77E+02 | 3.52E+02 | 2.14E+02 |
| PVADE | 4.13E+01 | 5.28E+02 | 1.55E+02 | 1.79E+02 | 1.09E+02 |
| MVMO | 3.41E+00 | 2.18E+01 | 3.72E+00 | 8.05E+00 | 7.68E+00 |
| OGI−MVMO | **2.02E−05** | 2.80E−05 | 2.68E−05 | 2.57E−05 | 4.86E−06 |
| F15 | | | | | |
| NBIPOPaCMA | 6.89E+00 | 2.41E+02 | 1.05E+02 | 1.19E+02 | 9.01E+01 |
| PVADE | 3.74E+02 | 1.13E+03 | 7.96E+02 | 7.85E+02 | 1.72E+02 |
| MVMO | 1.97E+02 | 6.67E+02 | 5.48E+02 | 5.62E+02 | 9.99E+01 |
| OGI−MVMO | **2.69E−05** | 7.31E−02 | 6.85E−02 | 3.23E−02 | 3.44E−02 |

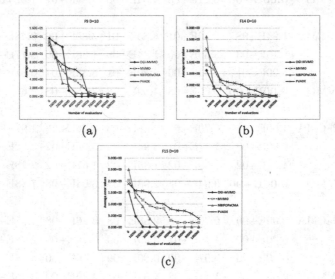

**Fig. 1.** Examples for performance comparison between OGI-MVMO, NBIPOPaCMA, PVADE, MVMO. F9, F14, and F15 are selected because the OGI-MVMO outperforms others.

## 5   Conclusion

This paper proposed an algorithm that combines the concept of opposite gradient initiation and the mean variance mapping optimization(OGI-MVMO) for solving the single continuous objective function problems. The algorithm contributed two important issues. The first issue is the opposite gradient initialization technique on the manifold of objective function. The opposite gradient analyses the manifold and generate a new offspring to the global search. The step of mean-variance mapping optimization is the second issue to utilize the result from opposite gradient initialization implementation to enhance the power of global searching. From the experimental results, the best solution quality and average solution quality of OGI-MVMO algorithm showed that OGI-MVMO is attractive for solving single objective functions.

# References

1. Erlich, I., Shewarega, F., Feltes, C., Koch, F., Fortmann, J.: Determination of dynamic wind farm equivalents using heuristic optimization. In: Proceedings of 2012 IEEE Power and Energy Society General Meeting, San Diego, USA (2012)
2. Loshchilov, I.: CMA-ES with restarts for solving CEC 2013 benchmark problems. In: Proceedings of Proceedings of IEEE Congress on Evolutionary Computation (CEC), Cancun, Mexico, pp. 369–376 (2013)
3. Liang, J., Qu, B.Y., Suganthan, P.N., Hernandez-Diaz, A.G.: Problem definitions and evaluation criteria for the CEC 2013 special session on real-parameter optimization. Technical reportTR2012, Cancun, Mexico (2013)
4. Rueda, J.L., Erlich, I.: Hybrid mean-variance mapping optimization for solving the IEEE-CEC 2013 competition problems. In: Proceedings of IEEE Congress on Evolutionary Computation (CEC), Cancun, Mexico, pp. 1664–1671 (2013)
5. Coelho, L.D., Ayala, H.V.H., Freire, R.Z.: Population's variance-based Adaptive Differential Evolution for real parameter optimization. In: Proceedings of IEEE Congress on Evolutionary Computation (CEC), Cancun, Mexico, pp. 1672–1677 (2013)
6. Holtschneider, T., Erlich, I.: Optimization of electricity pricing considering neural network based model of consumers' demand response. In: Proceedings of 2013 IEEE Symposium Series on Computational Intelligence, Singapore (2013)
7. Saenphon, T., Phimoltares, S., Lursinsap, C.: Combining new Fast Opposite Gradient Search with Ant Colony Optimization for solving travelling salesman problem. Eng. Appl. Artif. Intell. **35**, 324–334 (2014)

# Context Based Algorithm for Social Influence Measurement on Twitter

Alaa Alsaig[(✉)], Ammar Alsaig, Marwah Alsadun, and Soudabeh Barghi

Computer Science and Software Engineering, Concordia University, Montreal, Canada
{al_alsai,a_alsaig,m_alsadu,s_arghi}@encs.concordia.ca

**Abstract.** The social media became one of the most effective method for marketing and for information propagation. Therefore, measuring users influence is important for organizations to know which user to target to successfully spread a piece of information. Twitter is one of the social media tools that is used for information propagation. The current methods for measuring influence of Twitters users, use ranking algorithms that focus on specific criteria such as number of followers or tweets. However, different cases creates different needs in measuring influence. Each need could include different elements with different priority. One of these cases is local businesses which need to propagate information within a specific context such as location. That is, the most influential user for such a business is the one that has the highest number of followers that are located within the required location. Therefore, in this paper, we use the X algorithm for measuring users influence on Twitter by ranking users based on followers context that is represented by number of elements. Each element is given a weight to prioritize elements based on client demand.

**Keywords:** Social influence measurement · Context
Twitter users influence

## 1 Introduction

Information propagation is an important process for many tasks of many sectors such as marketing, awareness, and news propagation. In order to ease the task of information propagation, social influence measurement becomes useful to provide us with the most influential nodes to be targeted by those who needs this information. To measure influence in social networks, users influential could be defined, and hence measured, differently considering different aspect. An Influential user can affect other users' actions [1], or change behavior, cause effect in online social networks [2]. Others focus on influential users in term of spread information. They see influential users as the most users who can spread information in the social network [1] and [3]. Furthermore, some went to classify influential users into many classification based on the context of influence, for

© ICST Institute for Computer Sciences, Social Informatics and Telecommunications Engineering 2019
Published by Springer Nature Switzerland AG 2019. All Rights Reserved
P. Cong Vinh and V. Alagar (Eds.): ICCASA 2018/ICTCC 2018, LNICST 266, pp. 136–149, 2019.
https://doi.org/10.1007/978-3-030-06152-4_12

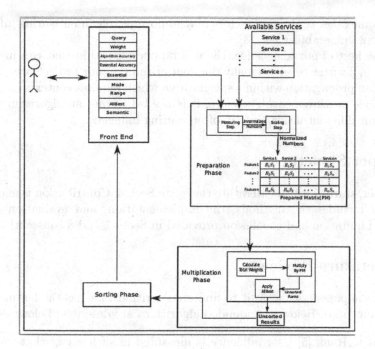

**Fig. 1.** XAlgorithm

example, opinion leaders, inventors (start new topics), celebrities, spreaders, disseminators, engager, connectors, etc [1]. This provides no agreed definition for influence in social networks.

Twitter is a social media tool that is used to propagate information through its users. Many work has been done to measure influence of Twitter users [1]. From this study, the social influence of Twitter's users is measured using different algorithms that consider all or some of the following elements:

- the number of followers
- number of tweets
- number of retweets
- Social influence is measured

In fact, the previous review gives intuitive idea that influence can be perceived from many different contexts.

## 2    Problem Definition

For twitter, usually deal with metrics that consider retweets, mentions, and number of followers [1]. However, the criteria for measuring influential users are as many as the growing number of techniques that rank influential users.

In fact, some other contextual factors play important role in measuring influence as location, vulnerability etc. [4].

To the best of our knowledge, there is no one algorithm that can measures influence in Twitter based on many different criteria. In our project, we consider information propagation within a specific area which requires contexts as criteria for influence measurement. Therefore, it is needed to find an algorithm that is able to suit different needs/criteria of measuring influence.

## 3   Paper Structure

This paper, starts with the literature review in Sect. 4. Contribution is explained in V. VI includes the methods, the implementation, and evaluation of our method. Limitation and conclusion provided in Sects. 7 and 8 consecutively.

## 4   Literature Review

Through the papers, we want it to find an algorithm that has the features that matches our need. Below, the founded algorithms are described below:

- textbfUserRank [5] User influence is measured in such a way that the more high ranked followers a user has, the higher user rank for this user. Hence the focus is more on the number of followers, however it has been shown that small number of followers is worth more than a large number of followers if the former are more active users [3]. Therefore, we can see that there is another metrics, which is activeness, could have been considered to give more accurate result. In fact, that emphasizes the need of consider many criteria when measure influential users in social networks
- textbfTrueTop [2] The algorithm of TrueTop, basically filters the list of users that are ranked as influential users to identify real users (non Sybil users) based on the incoming retweets, replies, and mentions each Twitter user has. Again this algorithm doesn't give the flexibility we are looking for because it has limited metrics to measure influence and doesn't prioritize them.
- textbfContent and Conversion [6] This method uses content and conversation metrics Based on number of tweets, mentions, retweets and replies and two Although it prioritize conversation and content by giving conversation more weight, considering it as more influential, but they only consider two concepts content and conversation.
- textbfThe X Algorithm [7] The X algorithm is a usercentric algorithm for ranking services Fig. 1. That is, the algorithm ranks services in the system based on the similarity of each service to the user query (requirement). The more similar the service is the higher rank it will get. The algorithm has a lot of features that motivated us to use it for our project, below are the most important features of the X algorithm:
  (1) Supporting different data type: Boolean, string, and numerical values.
  (2) The results manipulated with different modes such as Best/Exact Modes.

(3) Elements interpreted into different semantics: More is Better, Less is Better and Exact is Better semantics.
(4) Consistent outputs because it is based on provided requirements.
(5) X-Algorithm is not restricted to specific number of elements.
(6) Provide high performance.

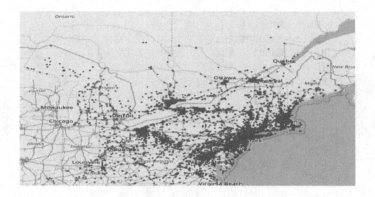

**Fig. 2.** Area of gathered data

```
type Tweet struct {
    TweetId             int64      `json:"tweet_id"`
    TweetFavoriteCount  int        `json:"tweet_favorite_count"`
    TweetRetweetCount   int        `json:"tweet_retweet_count"`
    TweetCoordinates    *geo.Point `json:"tweet_coordinates"`
    UserId              int64      `json:"user_id"`
}
```

**Fig. 3.** Data structure corresponding to a tweet

## 5  Contribution

In this project, we provide a new method for measuring influence with consideration to any number of elements with high efficiency. The method includes the ability to give a weight for each element depending on our priority.

Particularly, for our case we consider user's context that includes location, number of followers, and number of friends, as criteria for social influence measurement.

# 6  Proposed Solution

The solution goes through different phases that are described below:

## 6.1  Phase 1: Data Gathering

Gathering data has gone through six different steps described as follows:

```
type User struct {
    FollowersCount int      `json:"followers_count"`
    FriendsCount   int      `json:"friends_count"`
    ID             int64    `json:"id"`
    Location       string   `json:"location"`
    StatusesCount  int      `json:"statuses_count"`
}

type UserFollowers struct {
    User        *User     `json:"user"`
    FollowerIDs []int64   `json:"follower_ids"`
}
```

**Fig. 4.** Data structure corresponding to a user and its followers

(1) **Fetching tweets from the Twitter Stream API:** During two days of time, we fetched tweets from the Twitter Stream API, using a location filter parameter that restricted the area as in Fig. 2. The South West coordinates was set to 37.916, 82.182, while the North East coordinate is 49.774 69.700. During those two days 16,714 unique users tweeted a total of 41,403 tweets. All the data was gathered in JSON Lines files. JSON Lines format [8]. The JSON Lines format is essentially JSON Objects separated by new lines. It proved to be very beneficial, to work with the stream data, and to be able to do further operations on the files using basic Unix tools such as wc, split, tail, cut or head [9].

It is worth to note that we used a Golang library which is called go-twitter[10], to do all the operations with the Twitter API, the library offers a convenient client to interact with the Twitter API, and offers data structure to represents the different entities in Twitter Fig. 3.

(2) **Gathering User's Followes IDs:** Using the 16,714 followers, we go in the previous step, we gathered their followers IDs using the Twitter REST API. This was a very expensive operation. Twitter's API limits those call at 60 requests per hour, and it gives us only a maximum of 5000 IDs at a time. Therefore we decided to only make our analysis on users who have 5000 followers or less. This is of course, a great limitation, but can only alleviated with time.

However, we used Golang's builtin concurrency system to parallelize the API calls among 4 different accounts. At the end of this operation, we had 9,254,314 followers IDs, in a 4.3 GB file.

(3) **Accumulating user's information:** We needed the information of the followers to do our analysis, so we accumulated their own information using their ID that we gathered in the previous step Fig. 4. For this to be done, we made some batch HTTP request, Twitter is much more generous with this operation (1200 user per hour). It is worth noticing, that Twitter gives us much more information about the User, but for a storage purpose, we only kept the data with the most importance to this project [8,10].

(4) **Using Geocoding APIs to geocode User's location:** While Tweets have exact coordinates, as shown in Fig. 3, users only have a location represented as a string. This created another challenge: we needed to geocode the 9,254,314 Users [11,12]. For this purpose, we have used several APIs described in Table 1:

Once we had a sizable amount of geocoded location, we realized that some of the users had very similar locations, for example: "New York" "New York." "New York, NY "New York, NY" "New York NY!?" "NYC" As we can see, locations only differ by punctuations, or emojis. We therefore decided, to employ a Fuzzy Location Match, using Levenshtein distance. The program written in Golan ran on a Kubernetes Cluster on Google Cloud Platform with three nodes of type n1standard4. The program had to compare 6,500,000 UTF8 strings, with a set of 247,049 know location [13,16]. It ran for an entire day, at 100% CPU usage, and resulted in 490,340 new locations. To this date, we have a database of 1,190,068 unique locations, which covers 7,333,088 users.

(5) **Refetching the Tweets:**

One month after the tweets were tweeted, we refetched the tweets by ID, using another batch HTTP request (1200 tweets/hour). From there, we could see the number of retweets and the number of favorites the tweets got.

However, the numbers of retweets and favorites were really small. Over 14027 tweets, only 1297 tweets were retweeted and 5627 has a favorite count. The reason those numbers are really small is probably due to the very loose restrictions and filters on the tweets that we streamed in the first place. An improvement would been to filter tweets based on a minimum of retweets and favorites, then do the full analysis.

(6) **Calculate Distance:**

The remaining task was to compute the distance between the users and get the data ready for the XAlgorithm. The distance between two coordinates was computed using the Haversine distance. It is essentially, the great circle distance between two points on a sphere given their longitudes and latitudes. We also created an HTTP Client to make the request to the XAlgorithm HTTP Server. The only resource we had was a POST on /query with the following JSON body Fig. 5.

**Table 1.** Used geocoding APIs

| API | Number of account(s) | Limits |
| --- | --- | --- |
| Google geocoding [13] | 1 | 2,500 requests/day |
| Location IQ [14] | 2 | 10,000 requests/day |
| MapBox [11] | 1 | 5,000 requests/day |
| OpenCage [12] | 1 | 2,500 requests/day |
| MapQuest [15] | 3 | 15,000 requests/day |

## 6.2   Phase 2: Implementation

Before we go into the details of the implementation, it is important to understand how the X algorithm works Fig. 6. The X algorithm takes a query as an input that includes the required value and the weight (priority) for each field. Then, the algorithm based on the similarity between the items it has in the system to the given requirement will rank the items. The more similar, the higher rank is assigned. The X algorithm has two modes, one is the best mode and the other is the exact mode. The best mode provides the better items than the entered specifications. This mode is selected in our project because it does suit our requirement. The entered specification is the minimum specification that describes an influential for a local business case. Yet, time limit was a barrier for thorough study for logical and accurate justification. The attributes could be inter-operated in different semantics. There are two semantics considered in this project which are explained below:

```
{
    "prop_n": ["followers", "friends", "distance"],
    "rlp": ["followers"],
    "consumer_query": [5000, 100, 1],
    "consumer_rate": [0.005, 0.001, 0.004],
    "input": [[20.0, 5.0, 2.0], ......]
}
```

**Fig. 5.** JSON query to XAlgorithm server

- More is better (MB): is the attribute that is quality like. For example, if the required number of followers is 5000, then a user with 10000 followers is definitely better.

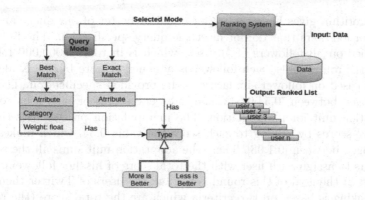

**Fig. 6.** Abstract XAlgorithm model

- Less is better (LB): is the attribute that is cost like. For example, if the maximum distance between a user and his/her follower is 10 Km then a user with 5 Km distance is better.

Each attribute is prioritized differently with weight element. The weight ranges from 1 to 5. 5 is the highest. The weight value depends on the priority you give for an attribute over another.

In this project, we used five attributes with different semantics and weight as explained in Tables 2 and 3. Hence, to measure influence of Twitter users within a specific area, the implemented program goes through two rounds to finish measurement Fig. 7. The explanation of both rounds are provided below:

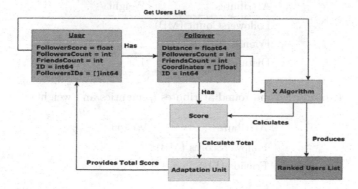

**Fig. 7.** UML context based algorithm for ranking influence measurement

- **Round 1:** the goal of this round is to provide a ranking score for each follower of all users of Twitter. The ranking score is based on three criteria, which are followers count, friends count, and distance. The semantics of each element provided in Table 2. The requirement (query) we provided for this round is: (number of followers maxFollowers, number of friends 100, and distance 1 km).

The algorithm gives higher score for equal or better of our query and lower score for followers that do not meet the query specification. The first round is applied on all followers of all users which is in total 9,000,000 followers. When the round ends, each follower is assigned a score by the X algorithm that is based on follower similarity to the provided specification. The scores are ranged between [0.54:0.54]. The followers' scores of each user go to the adaptation unit for manipulation. The manipulation process gets rid of all negative scores by adding to each score the value 0.54, which makes scores are ranged between [0:1.08]. Then, the adaptation unit sums all the scores of followers to assign each user with the total score of his/her followers.

- **Round 2:** the goal of this round is to rank the users of Twitter themselves. The ranking is based on two criteria which are the total score (the result of round 1) and the number of friends. The semantics of each of the elements provided in Table 3. The requirement (query) we provided for this round is: (FollowerScores = max(followerScore), and number of friends 100). The result of round 2 is a list that includes all users in our data ranked in order. We have 14000 user and their results illustrated in Fig. 8.

### 6.3    Phase3: Evaluation

There are three methods of evaluation that are applied, which are explained below:

**Table 2.** First round attributes (semantics and weight)

| Attributes | Weight |
| --- | --- |
| FollowersCount (MB) | 5 |
| Friends (LB) | 2 |
| Distance (LB) | 1 |

**Table 3.** Second round attributes (semantics and weight)

| Attribute | Weight |
| --- | --- |
| FollowerScores (MB) | 5 |
| Friends (LB) | 2 |

**Table 4.** Sample 1 for data evaluation

|  | User 1 | User 2 | User 3 |
| --- | --- | --- | --- |
| Follower 1 | 0.546000 | 0.552000 | 0.546976 |
| Follower 2 | 0.542933 | 0.549333 | 0.546329 |
| Follower 3 | 0.540266 | 0.546666 | 0.546044 |
| Rank result | Third | First | Second |

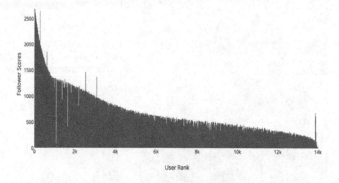

**Fig. 8.** 14000 ranked users

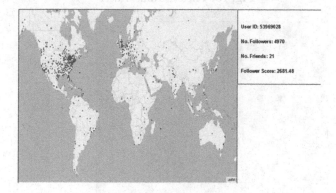

**Fig. 9.** First ranked user

- **Small Samples:** The algorithm is applied on predefined data to make sure it provides the expected results. In Table 4, we provided user 2 with the very good followers as they have high number of followers, low number of followers, and short distance according to the user's location. User 2 has high number

**Table 5.** Sample2 for data evaluation

|             | User 1   | User 2   | User 3   |
|-------------|----------|----------|----------|
| Follower 1  | 0.546000 | 0.552000 | 0.546976 |
| Follower 2  | 0.544494 | 0.549333 | 0.546329 |
| Follower 3  | 0.544444 | 0.546976 | 0.546044 |
| Follower 4  | 0.544255 | 0.546666 | 0.539110 |
| Follower 5  | 0.542933 | 0.546329 | 0.537855 |
| Follower 6  | 0.540266 | 0.546044 | 0.537636 |
| Rank result | Second   | First    | Third    |

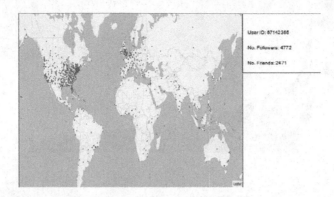

**Fig. 10.** Fiftieth ranked user

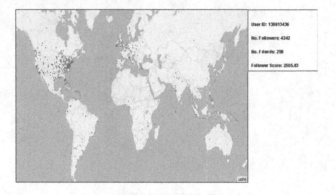

**Fig. 11.** Hundredth ranked user

of followers but all in far places and user 3 has lower number of followers compare to Users 1 and 2, yet, they live in close area to their user. The results showed what we have expected, as User 2 is considered more influential to our requirement than User1. In Table 5, we still keep User 2 as the optimal user. However, user 1 had the same number of good followers as User 3 but also has bad followers. User three has most of his followers good in terms of distance but not in terms of the number of followers. As we weight the number of followers more than the distance and as User 1 has the same number of good users as User 3, then the algorithm met our expectation by providing User 1 a higher rank than User 3.

- **Ranked User Illustration on Map:** In the following graph shows the geographical distribution of three different users ranked by aforementioned method. Each user is spotted on the map with his/her followers. In Fig. 9, the first ranked user is showing the most of his/her followers are surrounding him/her as most of them live close to the user which is matching our requirement. However, in Fig. 10, the 50th user is punished to be ranked in this position due to having high number of friends.

In Fig. 11, the user is ranked 100th because the specification of this user specially in terms of number of friends, followers and the total follower score do not match with the specification of this study, as a result this user gets a lower rank in general.

In Fig. 12, the three previous users are represented in one map. This is to show the difference User ranked 1, User ranked 50, and User ranked 100. It is obvious, the 50th user (blue color) his friends are scattered and not surrounding in his/her area. The 100th user (Green color) has fewer followers around himself/herself compared to the first ranked user (Red color)

- **Retweet and Favorites:** Keeping track of gathered tweets after one month shows 17% of retweets numbers just related to the first 1000 ranked user though this study method Fig. 13. To make it clearer, this population contains 7% of the whole gathered data user which means these ranked users' tweets has potential influence in term of being retweeted by their followers. User's tweet after one month, about 14000 users. Number of favorites of tweets released by the first 1000 ranked users consist of 16%. The density of the graphs for the first 1000 ranked users shows their potential influence Fig. 14.

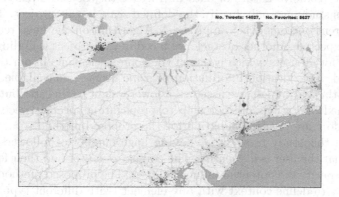

**Fig. 12.** Map includes the three ranked users (1, 50, and 100) (Color figure online)

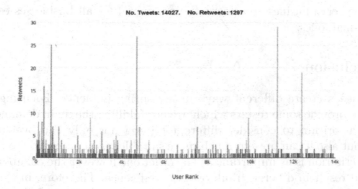

**Fig. 13.** Retweets of all users

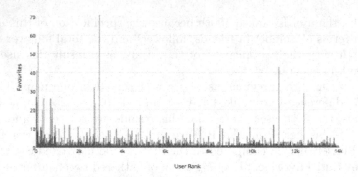

**Fig. 14.** Favorites of all users

# 7 Challenges and Limitations

Considering Twitter Laws and rules, our evaluation is limited to only users with at most 5000 followers since the accessibility to more than this is prevented. In addition, the recursive nature of data in Twitter to just two levels depth. The result of this study can only justify the defined scale in this project. Therefore, having different outcome when applying X-Algorithm on the huge real scale of Twitter is expected. Another obstacle we faced in this project is finding location information for all users, which is one of the context elements in our dataset. In the retrieved data, location information of some users is unavailable. To make the effect of this barrier less, we assigned a lower weight to this attribute. Having the mentioned limitations did not help to propagate a specific tweet in reality in order to do more precise evaluation for the proposed method.

However, this study proves that having huge number of followers does not guarantee that the user is influential. The context of a user and their followers is essential to specify the potential influential user. The proposed method provides the flexibility to define context with any element (with different type) with the ability to prioritize these elements using weight. Therefore, it is believed that this method can perfectly find those influential users that can be a profitable targets who serve business purposes. This is useful for all businesses especially local and small ones.

# 8 Conclusion

Different needs create different ways in measuring influence. Focusing on one context can provide some results which are not fulfilling the main demand. Using a flexible algorithm to consider different criteria not only can overcome this problem, but also it can present much more suitable result according to the need. Not every criterion is as important as the other one however the collaboration of them could result in different rank of user's influence. Therefore, in this paper, we provided a method that uses the XAlgorithm to rank users of Twitter based on the context of user's followers. The ranking results provided promising results as the retweet and the favorite evaluation method showed reasonable number of retweet and favorite for the first 1000 ranked users. With consideration to the dataset limitation we had, we believe that our method could be an effective method for influence measurement for different needs.

As a future work, many cases or needs could use our method for measuring influence not only on Twitter but any other social media tools. The method we provided is flexible enough to adapt to the needs of any organizations or businesses.

# References

1. Riquelme, F., González-Cantergiani, P.: Measuring user influence on twitter: a survey. Inf. Process. Manage. **52**(5), 949–975 (2016)
2. Zhang, J., Zhang, R., Sun, J., Zhang, Y., Zhang, C.: Truetop: a sybil-resilient system for user influence measurement on twitter. IEEE/ACM Trans. Netw. **24**(5), 2834–2846 (2016)
3. Anger, I., Kittl, C.: Measuring influence on twitter. In: Proceedings of the 11th International Conference on Knowledge Management and Knowledge Technologies, p. 31. ACM (2011)
4. Li, Y., Ding, Z., Zhang, X., Liu, B., Zhang, W.: Confirmatory analysis on influencing factors when mention users in twitter. In: Morishima, A., Chang, L., Fu, T.Z.J., Liu, K., Yang, X., Zhu, J., Zhang, R., Zhang, W., Zhang, Z. (eds.) APWeb 2016. LNCS, vol. 9865, pp. 112–121. Springer, Cham (2016). https://doi.org/10.1007/978-3-319-45835-9_10
5. Majer, T., Šimko, M.: Leveraging microblogs for resource ranking. In: Bieliková, M., Friedrich, G., Gottlob, G., Katzenbeisser, S., Turán, G. (eds.) SOFSEM 2012. LNCS, vol. 7147, pp. 518–529. Springer, Heidelberg (2012). https://doi.org/10.1007/978-3-642-27660-6_42
6. Hatcher, D., Bawa, G.S., de Ville, B.: How you can identify influencers in SAS® social media analysis (and why it matters). In: SAS Global Forum, pp. 4–7. Citeseer (2011)
7. Alsaig, A., Alagar, V., Mohammad, M., Alhalabi, W.: A user-centric semantic-based algorithm for ranking services: design and analysis. SOCA **11**(1), 101–120 (2017)
8. T.D. Team, dghubble/go-twitter (2017). https://github.com/dghubble/go-twitter
9. Jsonlines.org, Json lines (2017). http://jsonlines.org/
10. T.D. Team, Twitter api overview (2017). https://dev.twitter.com/overview/api
11. M.D. Team, Geocoding, mapbox (2017). https://www.mapbox.com/geocoding/
12. O. Geocoder, Easy, open, worldwide, affordable geocoding (2017). https://geocoder.opencagedata.com/
13. G. Developers, Developer's guide, Google maps geocoding api, Google developers (2017). https://developers.google.com/maps/documentation/geocoding/intro
14. Locationiq.org, Locationiq free and fast geocoding and reverse geocoding service from unwired labs (2017). https://locationiq.org/
15. M.A. Documentation, Geocoding api overview (2017). https://geocoder.opencagedata.com/
16. G.C. Platform, Machine types, compute engine documentation, Google cloud platform (2017). https://cloud.google.com/compute/docs/machine-types

# Context-Aware Recommendation
# with Objective Interestingness Measures

Nghi Mong Pham[1(✉)], Nghia Quoc Phan[2], Dang Van Dang[3],
and Hiep Xuan Huynh[4]

[1] Thapmuoi Vocational School, Dongthap 81000, Vietnam
phammongnghi1988@gmail.com
[2] Travinh University, Travinh City 87000, Vietnam
nghiatvnt@tvu.edu.vn
[3] Business Center VNPT Dongthap, Dongthap 81000, Vietnam
dangdv.dtp@vnpt.vn
[4] Cantho University, Cantho 900000, Vietnam
hxhiep@ctu.edu.vn

**Abstract.** Context-aware recommender systems researches now concentrate on adjusting recommendation results for situations specific context of the users. These studies suggest many ways to integrate user contextual information into the recommendation process such as using topic hierarchies with matrix factorization techniques to improve context-aware recommender systems, measuring frequency-based similarity for context-aware recommender systems, collecting data from social networking to support context-aware recommender systems, and so on. However, these studies mainly focus on the development of context-aware recommendation algorithms to propose items to users in a particular situation and do not care about the extent of contextual involvement in the recommendation process to make recommendation results. In this article, we propose a new approach for context-aware recommender systems based on objective interestingness measures to consider the contextual relationship of the users in the recommendation process. Based on the experimental results on two standard datasets, the proposed model is more accurate than the traditional models.

**Keywords:** Rating matrix · Context similarity matrix
Objective interestingness measures · Chi-square similarity kernel

## 1 Introduction

The recommender systems (RS) [1, 2] are a common solution used to suggest appropriate items for the user. This solution is widely used in many fields such as e-commerce, e-government, e-library, medicine, etc. In order to provide the information that usersneed to support, many recommender systems have been proposed such as collaborative filtering recommender systems, content-based recommender systems, demographic recommender systems, knowledge-based recommender systems, context-ware recommender systems (CARS). The CARS [5, 6] is the system that adjusts recommendation results for specific contextual situations of the users. In different

© ICST Institute for Computer Sciences, Social Informatics and Telecommunications Engineering 2019
Published by Springer Nature Switzerland AG 2019. All Rights Reserved
P. Cong Vinh and V. Alagar (Eds.): ICCASA 2018/ICTCC 2018, LNICST 266, pp. 150–162, 2019.
https://doi.org/10.1007/978-3-030-06152-4_13

situations, users can make different decisions, because users often change their preferences and decisions from one situation to another. For example, the user can choose a love movie to watch with his girlfriend or boyfriend, but if he or she goes out with children, the cartoon is suitable. Companion (girlfriend or child), in the example above is an influential context factor. Other examples of context can be time, location, weather, etc. Because the user's preferences and decisions vary depending on the situation, consider the context when making suggestions to the user. Thus, the integration of contextual information into the counseling system has become a topic that is becoming increasingly important in recommender systems research [12–14].

The results of the research on context-aware recommender systems in the past time are quite rich research such as doctoral dissertation: Providing Architectural Support for Building Context Aware Applications [7] provides a context definition and context awareness framework, builds and develops context-aware applications, another next in build the system found in context [13] proposes a solution to the development of a contextual recommender systems, which is applied to the travel suggestion, to suggest the most appropriate tourist destination travelers, frequency-based similarity measures for context-aware recommender systems [12] combine the information in the context to the user profile as an extra information through a new count method output, smart media-based context-aware recommender systems for learning [14] proposes a conceptual cognitive-based contextual intelligence system that can intelligently study the user's learning preferences as a context for making accurate and valid helpful recommendations. These studies mainly focus on the development of context-aware recommendation algorithms to propose items to users in a particular situation. However, current research on the recommender systems does not take into account the extent of contextual involvement in the recommendation process to make recommendations.

In this paper, we propose a new model for recommender systems, context-aware recommender model based on objective interestingness measures [8–10]. In this model, we are particularly interested in the degree of contextual similarity of users during the recommender process in order to provide items to users more accurate.

This article is organized into 6 sections. Section 1 presents introduction, Sect. 2 introduces the context-aware recommender systems, Sect. 3 describes objective interestingness measures, Sect. 4 determines the similarity context of two users, Sect. 5 presents a collaborative filtering model based on similarity context, and Sect. 6 discusses about the experimental results of the model and summarizes the results.

## 2 Context-Aware Recommender Systems

There are many studies on the context-aware recommender systems (CARS) since the original publication on this topic [5, 6]. Context-aware recommender systems (CARS) is a system that tries to adapt its proposals to contextual situations specific to the user [5, 6] because users often make different decisions in different situations. This approach has become commonplace in many areas and the application has recently been discovered in a number of sectors, such as tourism [18], trailers [19]. The traditional collaborative filtering [4] can be modeled as a two-dimensional (2D) prediction.

$$R : Users \times Items \; - > Ratings$$

In particular, the recommender systems will predict the user's rating values for items that users have not rated. Context-aware recommender systems attempt to incorporate more contextual information of users into the recommender process to estimate user preferences. This integration transforms the predictive function of the system from 2D space into a "multi dimensional" space.

$$R : Users \times Items \times Contexts \; - > Ratings$$

Where, R is the prediction function for items, Users are a set of users, Items are sets of items, Contexts are context of users and. Context is defined as "any information that can be used to characterize an entity" [7] such as time, location, weather.

The context-aware recommendation process can take one of the following three forms, based on how the contextual information is used, as follows: Contextual prefltering, Contextual postfltering, and contextual modeling.

- *Contextual pre-filtering* [5]: In this model, the contextual information of current user is used for selecting only the relevant set of data, and ratings are predicted using any traditional 2D recommender systems on the selected data.
- *Contextual post-filtering* [5]: In this model, the contextual information is initially ignored, and the ratings are predicted using any traditional 2D recommender systems on the entire data. Then, the resulting set of recommendations is adjusted (contextualized) for each user using the contextual information.
- *Contextual modeling* [5]: In this model, the contextual information is used directly in the modeling technique as part of the rating estimation.

## 3   Objective Interestingness Measures

Assume that we have a finite set T of transactions (for example, purchases from customers in a supermarket [9]. An association rule [9] is expressed as $X \rightarrow Y$ with X and Y are two separate sets of elements $(X \cap Y = \emptyset)$. Element set X (corresponding Y) is associated with a subset of transactions $t_X = T(X) = \{T \in T, X \subseteq T\}$ (corresponding $t_Y = T(Y)$). Element set $\overline{X}$ (corresponding $\overline{Y}$) be counted $t_{\overline{X}} = T(\overline{X}) = T - T(X) = \{T \in T, X \subseteq T\}$ (corresponding $t_{\overline{Y}} = T(\overline{Y})$). To confirm or negate the tendency to have Y when X occurs, so we will be interested in the number of elements $n_{X\overline{Y}}$ (negative examples, contra-examples) inability to support the formation of association rules. Each rule is described by four parameters: $n = |T|, n_X = |t_X|, n_Y = |t_Y|, n_{\overline{X}} = |t_{\overline{X}}|, n_{\overline{Y}} = |t_{\overline{Y}}|$ (See Fig. 1).

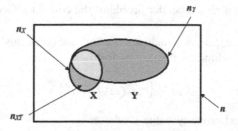

**Fig. 1.** The cardinality of an association rule X → Y [9].

The interestingness value of an association rules based on an objective interestingness measures (called interestingness measures for short) is computed based on four parameters of a rule $m(X \rightarrow Y) = f(n, n_X, n_Y, n_{X\overline{Y}})$.

Example: Given two sets of elements X = {Bread}, Y = {Milk, Diappers, Beer}. A association rules is formed in the form X → Y. With n = 500, $n_X$ = 150, $n_Y$ = 350, $n_{X\overline{Y}}$ = 10.

Objective interestingness measures to be used is Support Expectation is determined by the formula:

$$m(X \rightarrow Y) = f\left(n, n_X, n_Y, n_{X\overline{Y}}\right) = \frac{n_X\left(n_Y - n_X + n_{X\overline{Y}}\right)}{n(n - n_X)} \tag{1}$$

Thus the "interestingness value" of the association rule X → Y on the basis of the interestingness measures $m$ is defined as:

$$m(X \rightarrow Y) = \frac{150 * (350 - 150 + 10)}{500 * (500 - 150)} = 0.18$$

# 4   Context Similarity Between Two Users

## 4.1   Contextual Information of a User

Context information of users are the factors that directly influence the selection of items or services when users participate in the recommender systems. For example, when users want the systems support to booktours for their vacation, the contextual factors about time (season) and accompanying persons will be affected greatly to the users to choose the location for the trip. From the description above, we can see that the contextual information of the users depends on the particular problem. However, to model the context-based recommender problem, the context information of the user is defined as follows:

For a set $U = \{u_1, u_2, \ldots, u_n\}$ includes n users, the contextual information of each user $u_i$ defined in the k-dimension space as follows:

$$C_{ui} = \{c_{i,1}, c_{i,2}, \ldots, c_{i,k}\}$$

where $c_{i,k}$ is the context property value k of user $u_i$.

## 4.2   Context Similarity Between Two Users

Currently, there are several measures proposed to calculate the contextual similarity value between two users in the k-dimensional vector space. In this study, to calculate the contextual similarity between two users, we used Chi-Square Similarity Kernel [20] measures with the formula defined as follows:

Suppose that two users $u_i$ and $u_j$ have contextual information defined by two vectors in k-dimensional space with following values: $C_{ui} = \{c_{i,1}, c_{i,2}, \ldots, c_{i,k}\}$ and $C_{uj} = \{c_{j,1}, c_{j,2}, \ldots, c_{j,k}\}$, then the contextual similarity between the two users $u_i$ and $u_j$ are computed by the following formula [11]:

$$K(C_{ui}, C_{uj}) = \sum_{z=1}^{k} \frac{2c_{i,z}c_{j,z}}{c_{i,z} + c_{j,z}} \tag{2}$$

Where $K(C_{ui}, C_{uj})$ is contextual similarity value between users $u_i$ and $u_j$; k is the dimension of vector space (the number of user contextual properties); $c_{i,z}$ is the context similarity property value z of user $u_i$; $c_{j,z}$ is the context similarity property z of user $u_j$.

## 4.3   Context Similarity Matrix

Context similarity matrix between users is a symmetric matrix with structure: rows, columns of the matrix are users, cells of the matrix (intersection of rows and columns) are the context similarity value between two users on the corresponding row and column. For user set $U = \{u_1, u_2, \ldots, u_n\}$, the context information of each user is represented by a k-dimensional vector $C_{ui} = \{c_{i,1}, c_{i,2}, \ldots, c_{i,k}\}$, then, the context similarity matrix between the users is defined as follows:

$$Matrix_{sim}(C) = \begin{pmatrix} 1 & s_{12} & \cdots & s_{1n} \\ s_{21} & 1 & \cdots & s_{2n} \\ \vdots & & \ddots & \vdots \\ s_{n1} & s_{n2} & \cdots & 1 \end{pmatrix}$$

Where $s_{i,j}$ is the context similarity value between two users $u_i$ and $u_j$. This value is calculated by the formula (2).

# 5    Collaborative Filtering Model Based on Context Similarity

## 5.1    Model Definition

Collaborative filtering model based on context similarity (CUBCF) is defined as follows:

Suppose that $U = \{u_1, u_2, \ldots, u_n\}$ is a set of n users; $I = \{i_1, i_2, \ldots, i_m\}$ is a set of m items; $C_{uj} = \{c_{j,1}, c_{j,2}, \ldots, c_{j,k}\}$ is a vector that determines value for context information of user $u_j$; $R = \{r_{j,k}\}$ is rating matrix of nusers (U) for m items (I) in context information (C) with each row representing one user $u_j$ $(1 \leq j \leq n)$, each column represents one item $i_k$ $(1 \leq k \leq m)$, $r_{j,k}$ is the rating value of user $u_j$ for item $i_k$ in context $C_{uj}$, N is the number of items with the highest rating value and $u_a \in U$ is user who needs recommendation with contextual information $C_{ua} = \{c_{a,1}, c_{a,2}, \ldots, c_{a,k}\}$.

Collaborative filtering model based on context similarity is presented as follows:

Figure 2 presents a collaborative filtering model based on context similarity. In particular, In the first phase, the contextual information is used to construct a rating matrix by using two techniques: User splitting and item Splitting; In the nextphase, based on the context properties of users to build context similarity matrix between the users; Finalphase, the collaborative filtering model based on context similarity is built based on integration matrix between rating matrix and context similarity matrix.

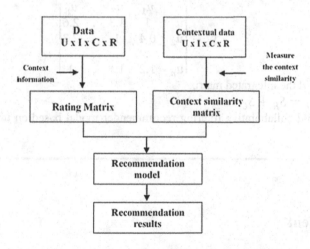

**Fig. 2.** Collaborative filtering model based on context similarity.

### 5.2    Collaborative Filtering Based on Context Similarity Algorithm

From the collaborative filtering model based on context similarity, we build a collaborative filtering algorithm based on context similarity that includes the following steps:

---

**Collaborative filtering based on context similarity algorithm**

Input: Transaction dataset (user set U, data set I, and context file C).
Output: N items with the highest rating value to recommend to user $u_a$.
**Begin**
**Step 1**: Build rating matrix ($S_R$).
    <Based on the context property values to douser splitting and item splitting>;
    For each user in set U do
        For each item in set I do

$$S_R = \begin{array}{c|cccc} & i_1 & i_2 & \dots & i_m \\ \hline u_1 & 0 & 3 & 2 & 5 \\ u_2 & 3 & 0 & 2 & 1 \\ . & 2 & 4 & 1 & 3 \\ u_n & 4 & 5 & 2 & 4 \end{array}$$

**Step 2**: Build a context similarity matrix based on the context properties ($S_C$).
    For each each user of set U do
        For each each user of set U do

$$S_C = \begin{array}{c|cccc} & u_1 & u_2 & . & u_n \\ \hline u_1 & 1 & 1.3 & . & 2.6 \\ u_2 & 0.4 & 1 & . & 2.3 \\ . & . & . & . & . \\ u_n & 1.2 & 1.4 & . & 1 \end{array}$$

**Step 3**: Build the integrated matrix
$$S_I = S_R + S_C$$
**Step 4**: Build collaborative filtering recommender model based on integrated matrix
End.

---

## 6    Experiment

### 6.1    Data Description

In this experiment, we used two different datasets to run the model on two different scenarios:

In scenario 1, we conducted experiments on DePaul_Movie dataset [17] is a collection of data collected from surveys from students, with 97 students required to rate 79 films in terms of context: time, place, and companions (5043 ratings from 1 to 5).

In scenario 2, we conducted experiments on InCarMusic dataset [16]. This dataset includes 43 users rated 139 music compositions with 8 different contextual conditions such as: driving style, lands cape, mood, natural phenomena, road type, sleepiness, traffic conditions, weather was organized into forms data frame with 4012 rows, 11 columns in that column Rating value is between 1 and 5.

## 6.2    Implementation Tools

In order to conduct experiment, we use tools ARQAT implemented on programming language R. This is a toolkit developed by our team from the foundation of the tool ARQAT [15]. This tool includes functions: data processing; calculating context similarity of two users; building and evaluating recommender models [3].

## 6.3    Scenario 1: Experiment on DePaul Movie Data Set

**Data Selecting and Processing.** DePaul_Movie dataset is stored as a data frame of properties UserID, ItemID, Rating, Time, Location, Companion. Where, the UserID has 97 values for 97 different users; The ItemID has 79 values with 79 decoded based on the context propertíe of 319 movies according to the movie criteria with the same movie name and different context properties (Time, Location, Companion); Rating values have five continuous values of 1 to 5 (with value 1 is 829; value 2 is 625; Value 3 is 1007; value 4 is 1.212; value 5 is 1.307). In particular, the majority of values ranged from 3 to 5 and 5 are the highest rated values. In order to clearly see the distribution of the rating values for the DePaul_Movie dataset, we use the heat chart to represent the user's rating values as shown in Fig. 3.

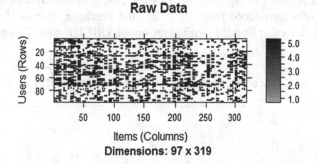

**Fig. 3.** The heat chart presents the distribution of user ratings on the DePaul Movie data set.

From the heat chart, we find that the distribution of the rating value of users for movies is relatively uniform. Although, there is a difference in assessed value in the two evaluation groups (1, 2) and (3, 4, 5) but the discrimination rate is not too far. So, we decided to select all the users who have ratings and all the films to build experimental data sets for the model. As such, the empirical data is full of 5043 lines with ratings from 1 to 5. In it, we divide the dataset into two subsets with training dataset and test dataset accounting for 80% and 20% respectively.

**Model Results.** With the goal of checking the model's accuracy on the dataset with some contextual similarities (3 properties). We conducted model training on a training dataset with 78 users and tested the results of the model on a test dataset with 19 users. The result of the model is exported in matrix format with structure $10 \times 19$ (each column is a user; each cell is a selected movie to recommend for the user in the corresponding column). Figure 4 presents the results of recommender model to the first 5 users; each of them selects the 10 highest rated movies.

```
         [,1]          [,2]          [,3]          [,4]          [,5]
 [1,]  "tt01111611"  "tt01111611"  "tt01111611"  "tt01111611"  "tt00887631"
 [2,]  "tt13756661"  "tt13756661"  "tt01098301"  "tt01098301"  "tt01330931"
 [3,]  "tt01111613"  "tt01143691"  "tt00887631"  "tt01103571"  "tt01098301"
 [4,]  "tt01111614"  "tt13756662"  "tt01330931"  "tt02325001"  "tt13756664"
 [5,]  "tt13756662"  "tt01143692"  "tt01098303"  "tt13756661"  "tt02665434"
 [6,]  "tt01111612"  "tt01103574"  "tt01143691"  "tt01111614"  "tt01111614"
 [7,]  "tt01103571"  "tt13756663"  "tt14783381"  "tt01098304"  "tt02665431"
 [8,]  "tt14783381"  "tt02665433"  "tt01111612"  "tt35100983"  "tt04417734"
 [9,]  "tt16573011"  "tt02665431"  "tt01111613"  "tt13756662"  "tt02665433"
[10,]  "tt01695471"  "tt02665432"  "tt01098304"  "tt35100981"  "tt00887633"
```

**Fig. 4.** Display the results of 5 users (each user is a column). In that, each user is advised 10 product codes.

**Model Evaluation.** To see the effect of the recommender model, we conducted a comparison of the accuracy of the proposed model with the accuracy of User-based collaborative filtering recommender model (UBCF) based on the k-fold assessment method with k = 5 and for two rating models run with the number of movies being introduced to the user increasing from 1 to 40. The comparison of the accuracy of the two models is shown in Fig. 5. This result shows the indicators Precision, Recall of the CUBCF model is higher or equal to those of the UBCF model. Specifically, when the number of movies introduced from 10 to 25, the Precision, Recall of the proposed model has a higher value than the two values on the UBCF model. This shows that the

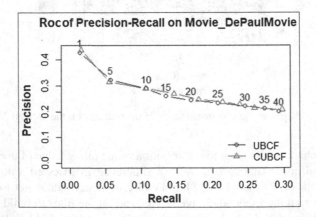

**Fig. 5.** Diagram showing the accuracy of two models on the DePaul_Movie dataset.

integration of contextual information of users based on objective interestingness measures to User-based collaborative filtering recommender model can improve the accuracy of the model.

## 6.4    Scenario 2: Experiment on InCarMusic Data Set

**Data Selecting and Processing.** The InCarMusic dataset includes the following properties: UserID, ItemID, Rating, DrivingStyle, Landscape, Mood, Natural Phenomena, RoadType, Sleepiness, Traffic Conditions, Weather. UserID has 43 values for 43 different users rated 139 music files broken down based on context properties to 43 UserID × 835 ItemID by the same User and Item criteria and 8 different context conditions for 4012 values. The rating is the same as the original dataset. This dataset has 37.09% users rated 1, 17.67% users rated 2, 16.40% users rated 3, 12.86% users rated 4 and 12.93% users rated 5 and only 3.04% users rated 0. Thus, the survey found that the number of music works rated by users at level 1 accounted for the largest number, while the ratings from 2 to 5 accounted for the average level and only a few user rated at 0. Therefore, we proceed to construct the dataset for the model in terms of selecting all the information in the dataset. After performing the selective operations, we have a data matrix for the experiment of size 43 × 835. Similar to scenario 1, the experimental data matrix is divided into two subsets: training dataset is 35 × 835 (80%), test dataset is 8 × 835 (20%) (Fig. 6).

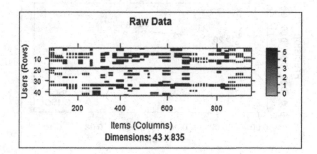

**Fig. 6.** The heat chart shows the distribution of the user's rating on the InCarsMusic dataset.

**Model Results.** With the goal of testing the accuracy of the model on datasets that have multiple contextual properties (8 properties), we conducted model training on a training dataset with 35 users and tested the results of the model on a test dataset with 8 users. The result of the model is exported in matrix format with structure 10 × 8 (each column is a user; each cell is a selected movie to recommend for the user in the corresponding column). Figure 7 shows the recommendation results for the first 5 users, with each user choosing the 10 highest rated music files.

**Model Evaluation.** Similar experimental scenario 1, In this empirical evaluation, we compared the accuracy of the CUBCF model with the accuracy of the UBCF model based on the methodology for constructing the assessment data K-fold with k = 5 and

| | [,1] | [,2] | [,3] | [,4] | [,5] |
|---|---|---|---|---|---|
| [1,] | "I29031" | "I29511" | "I26311" | "I68431" | "I25311" |
| [2,] | "I29521" | "I29031" | "I29511" | "I71921" | "I68911" |
| [3,] | "I29541" | "I29521" | "I26341" | "I25311" | "I74611" |
| [4,] | "I29531" | "I29541" | "I26321" | "I75411" | "I26311" |
| [5,] | "I74621" | "I28621" | "I26611" | "I68631" | "I26611" |
| [6,] | "I29511" | "I26331" | "I26331" | "I70431" | "I26341" |
| [7,] | "I70831" | "I26641" | "I29521" | "I70541" | "I26321" |
| [8,] | "I24811" | "I29531" | "I29531" | "I68441" | "I68941" |
| [9,] | "I24841" | "I26311" | "I29541" | "I69921" | "I74621" |
| [10,] | "I74641" | "I28321" | "I76031" | "I69941" | "I74641" |

**Fig. 7.** Present the recommended results on the InCarMusic file.

for two running models with the number of songs introduced to the user increasing from 1 to 40. The comparison of the accuracy of the two models is shown in Fig. 8. This result shows that the Precision, Recall of the CUBCF model is always higher than those values of the UBCF model. Specifically, when the number of songs introduced from 5 to 25, the Precision of the proposed model has a higher value than the UBCF model. This can again confirm that integrating user contextual information based on objective interestingness measures into the user-based collaborative filtering recommender model can dramatically improve accuracy of the model.

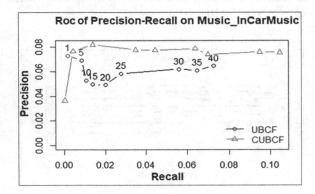

**Fig. 8.** The two model accuracy comparison charts on the InCarMusic dataset.

## 7  Conclusion

In this paper, we propose a new approach for context-aware recommender systems based on objective interestingness measures to consider the contextual relationship of the users in the recommendation process. In this model, we use the contextual information of the users to process the model's input data and integrate the contextual information of the users to build the context-aware recommender model based on context similarity. Based on the experimental results on the two data sets DePaul_-Movie and InCarMusic, our proposed model (CUBCF) is more accurate than the

UBCF model. This empirical result can confirm that the collaborative filtering model integrates user contextual information based on objective interestingness measures that can be applied in practice.

# References

1. Adomavicius, G., Tuzhilin, A.: Toward the next generation of recommender systems: a survey of the state-of-the-art and possible extensions. IEEE Trans. Knowl. Data Eng. (TKDE) **17**(6), 734–749 (2005)
2. Aggarwal, C.C.: Recommender Systems: The Textbook. Springer, New York (2016). https://doi.org/10.1007/978-3-319-29659-3
3. Hahsler, M.: recommenderlab: A Framework for Developing and Testing Recommendation Algorithms, Technical report - Southern Methodist University, pp. 1–27 (2015). https://cran.r-project.org/web/packages/recommenderlab/
4. Su, X., Khoshgoftaar, T.M.: A survey of collaborative filtering techniques. Adv. Artif. Intell. **2009**(4), 1–20 (2009)
5. Adomavicius, G., Tuzhilin, A.: Context-aware recommender systems. In: Ricci, F., Rokach, L., Shapira, B., Kantor, P.B. (eds.) Recommender Systems Handbook, pp. 217–253. Springer, Boston, MA (2011). https://doi.org/10.1007/978-0-387-85820-3_7
6. Ricci, F., Rokach, L., Shapira, B. (eds.): Recommender Systems Handbook. Springer, Boston (2015). https://doi.org/10.1007/978-1-4899-7637-6
7. Dey, K.A.: Providing architectural support for building context-aware applications. Doctoral dissertation, Georgia Institute of Technology (2000). ISBN 0-493-01246-X
8. Agrawal, R., Srikant, R.: Fast algorithms for mining association rules. In: Proceedings of the 20th International Conference on Very Large Data Bases, VLDB 1994, pp. 487–499 (1999)
9. Phan, P.L., Phan, Q.N., Phan, C.V., Huynh, H.H., Huynh, X.H., Fabrice, G.: Classification of objective interestingness measures. EAI Endorsed Trans. Context. Aware Syst. Appl. **3**(10), 1–13 (2016)
10. Huynh, X.H., Guillet, F., Blanchard, J., Kuntz, P., Gras, R., Briand, H.: A graph-based clustering approach to evaluate interestingness measures: a tool and a comparative study. In: Guillet, F.J., Hamilton, H.J. (eds.) Quality Measures in Data Mining, pp. 25–50. Springer, Heidelberg (2007). https://doi.org/10.1007/978-3-540-44918-8
11. Vedaldi, A., Zisserman, A.: Efficient additive kernels via explicit feature maps. IEEE Trans. Pattern Anal. Mach. Intell. **34**(3), 480–492 (2012)
12. Wasid, M., Kant, V., Ali, R.: Frequency-based similarity measure for context aware recommender systems. In: Proceedings of the IEEE International Conference on Advances in Computing, Communications and Informatics (ICACCI 2016), Jaipur, India, pp. 627–632 (2016)
13. Lu, T.T., Nguyen, T.N.: An approach in constructing a context-aware recommender system. In: Proceedings of the 8th National Conference on Basic Research and Application of Information Technology (FAIR 2015), pp. 486–494. Publishing house of natural sciences and technology (2015). [in Vietnamese]
14. Hassan, M., Hamada, M.: Smart media based context aware recommender systems for learning: A conceptual framework. In: Proceedings of the 16th IEEE Information Technology Based Higher Education and Training (ITHET 2017), Ohrid, Macedonia, pp. 1–4 (2017)

15. Phan, L.P., Phan, N.Q., Nguyen, K.M., Huynh, H.H., Huynh, H.X., Guillet, F.: Interestingnesslab: a framework for developing and using objective interestingness measures. In: Akagi, M., Nguyen, T.-T., Vu, D.-T., Phung, T.-N., Huynh, V.-N. (eds.) ICTA 2016. AISC, vol. 538, pp. 302–311. Springer, Cham (2017). https://doi.org/10.1007/978-3-319-49073-1_33
16. Baltrunas, L., et al.: InCarMusic: context-aware music recommendations in a car. In: Huemer, C., Setzer, T. (eds.) EC-Web 2011. LNBIP, vol. 85, pp. 89–100. Springer, Heidelberg (2011). https://doi.org/10.1007/978-3-642-23014-1_8
17. Zheng, Y., Mobasher, B., Burke, R.: CARSKit: A Java-based context-aware recommendation engine. In: Proceedings of the 15th IEEE International Conference on Data Mining Workshops (ICDMW 2015), pp. 1668–1671, Atlantic City (2015)
18. Dejo, A.E., Ngwira, M.S., Zuva, T.: A context aware proactive recommender system for tourist. In: Proceedings of the 2016 IEEE International Conference on Advances in Computing and Communication Engineering (ICACCE 2016), pp. 271–275, Durban, South Africa (2016)
19. Odić, A., Tkalčič, M., Tasič, J.F., Košir, A.: Predicting and detecting the relevant contextual information in a movie recommender system. Interact. Comput. **25**(1), 74–90 (2013)
20. Phan, N.Q., Dang, P.H., Huynh, H.X.: Similarity kernel for user-based collaborative filtering recommendation system. In: Proceedings of the 2016 IEEE International Conference on Computing & Communication Technologies (RIVF), vol. 2, pp. 40–46 (2016)

# Development of a Peer-Interaction Programming Learning System

Pham-Duc Tho[1,2(✉)], Nguyen-Hung Cuong[1,2], Hoang-Cong Kien[1], and Chih-Hung Lai[2]

[1] Hung Vuong University, Viet Tri, Vietnam
thopham@hvu.edu.vn
[2] National DongHwa University, Hualien County, Taiwan

**Abstract.** Computer programming is basic knowledge in the digital age and becoming an critical subject during recent years. However, learning to programme is not an easy topic as supported by many researchers. During the development of information technology, many online learning systems have been developed and proven their positive effect on students learning. However, few studies have geared toward supporting its use in programming courses with peer-interaction. Therefore, this study aimed to develop an online learning system named Peer-Interaction Programming Learning System. The system was developed and being used by many programming classes both in Vietnam and Taiwan. In this paper, we reported on the design of the system and its user interface, discussed our motivation and underlying teaching philosophy.

**Keywords:** Online learning system · Programming learning · Peer interaction

## 1 Introduction

Programming is a complex activity with some factors that could contribute to its difficulty. Jenkins [1] pointed out that the teaching methods employed by the instructor is the primary effect to students achievement during programming courses, but Matthíasdóttir [2] argue that the problematic nature of computer programming is the actual cause. Gomes and Mendes [3] in another research argue that some of the issues contributed to programming activity are the study methods, abilities and attitudes employed by the student, also the nature of the art of programming, the lack of prior knowledge of novice students, and the psychological influence that the student suffered from society [4].

From past studies, the learning benefits of online learning systems have been well recognized [5]. Allen and Seaman [6] reported that 77.1% of academic leaders in America agreed that online learning is critical to their long-term strategy. Increasing numbers of institutions have offered online courses to accommodate students' needs and also to reduce their budget [7]; however, online programming courses have been problematic for many students [8]. Students lack motivation and low self-efficacy for learning and may lead to lower completion rates than in face-to-face courses [9]. One of the possible reason is the lack of peer interaction and less immediate feedback from the instructor [10, 11].

© ICST Institute for Computer Sciences, Social Informatics and Telecommunications Engineering 2019
Published by Springer Nature Switzerland AG 2019. All Rights Reserved
P. Cong Vinh and V. Alagar (Eds.): ICCASA 2018/ICTCC 2018, LNICST 266, pp. 163–170, 2019.
https://doi.org/10.1007/978-3-030-06152-4_14

Little empirical research has been conducted in remedial online programming courses with regard to peer interaction. Law, Lee and Yu [12] suggest that social pressure and competition have a significant and positive relationship with efficacy during their research with online programming learning system named Programming Assignment aSsessment System (PASS). For decades, researchers have been building online learning systems to lower the barrier to programming learning [2, 9, 12–15]. For example, CodeWrite and StudySieve are systems created by Denny, Luxton-Reilly, Tempero and Hendrickx [16] which is aimed at helping students learning programming by using question posing and peer comment. Both CodeWrite and StudySieve have a significant effect in support students learn programming [16, 17] but only focus on free-response domain which limits students who wanted to create other types of questions. Also, only after the solution compiles and passes all the test cases are the solutions submitted by other students revealed [16] makes ordinary students harder to solve the intricate questions without any hints or supports. Although their research is helpful in improving students' achievement in programming courses, more empirical research is necessary for peer-interaction settings due to the explosion of social network nowa-days. Therefore, this study aimed to develop a programming learning system named Peer-Interaction Programming Learning System (PIPLS) to fulfill the gaps which remain in previous research.

## 2    Description of the System

PIPLS is a system first developed in 2015 in National Donghwa University, Taiwan, with the primary aim to assisting beginners in learning programming with the Student Question Generation (SQG) strategy [9]. It is now regularly used as an integrated part of many undergraduate courses related to computer programming.

PIPLS is designed aiming at fill some gaps which are remains from previous systems:

- Allow students to choose to use their real name, their nickname or anonymous.
- Support more question types: multiple choice, short answer, true-false, fill-in-the-blank, coding and essay with an automatic judge or semi-automatic which is significant benefit for staff.
- Make the peer-interactive process more accurate and accessible for students whom nowadays familiar with many social networking sites.
- Allow learning content to be integrated into courses.

PIPLS supports student-generated multiple types of questions, included free-response, multiple-choices, fill in the blanks, and true-false questions. In this system, the students can discuss with each other by asking and answering the questions. The teachers can set questions, share the resources of learning and develop the effectiveness of class management.

After logging in, via the home page (Fig. 1), students can find some quick statistic information about their progress: courses they are following, contributed questions, answered questions, unanswered questions, and exercises with grade.

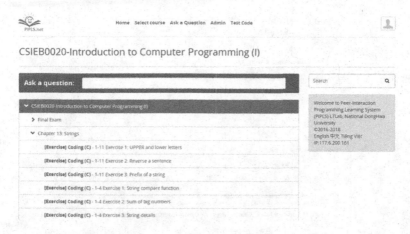

**Fig. 1.** The main page of PIPLS

Besides those sections, there are many features and functions that we developed to help students and teachers. The system was developed on the basis of the Question2Answer system, so it has inherited all features of Question2Answer [18]. Due to the limit of this paper, the role of some of these sections is described next.

### 2.1 Composing a Question

This section (Fig. 2) allows a student to compose a question. The student was asked to choose the type of question before they can reach this section. The student can post open question to Discussion board or post regular question as an exercise to their classmates. PIPLS is designed to support multiple question types, including free-response, multiple-choices, fill in the blanks, and true-false questions.

Inherited from Question2Answer [18], the question title must be provided with detailed information and embed multimedia, links, ... To help students find and organize relevant questions, the questions may be tagged with appropriate topics by the author.

Original Question2Answer only provided free-response question so we developed additional fields applied for different types of question. Figure 2 illustrates how a coding question is defined.

Besides important information come with types of question, we also developed available time for the question, anonymous feature, mark question as exercise specifically for teacher, and the maximum answer per user allowed for the question.

### 2.2 Answering Questions and Peer Interactions

In PIPLS, answers are revealed according to course setting. Teacher can allow student to view others answer by default, after deadline or only after the student submitted the correct answer for automatically judged questions, or the answer for an essay question.

**Fig. 2.** Composing a new question in PIPLS

We enhanced PIPLS by including many functions of traditional online learning systems, include "call for help" function. When student cannot figure out the answer, they don't need to give up or require help by giving some comment and wait. They can keep thinking straight without losing time by "call for help". This function will allow student reading the answers from other classmates without knowing which answer is correct. Then the student need to decide which answer is correct and complete their own answer.

According to peer-interaction features, students also have the opportunity to write formative feedback to the question author, thanks to the comment feature of original Question2Answer which is visible to all users, and can agree or disagree with other feedback provided by their peers by voting feature. When the others' answer is visible, students can give comment and also voting in others' answer (Fig. 3).

**Fig. 3.** Students and TAs comments to a question

All the notifications in PIPLS will be sent to students by Facebook Messenger, students also able to post question to discussion board or reply to another's comment via Facebook Messenger (Fig. 4).

## 2.3 Evaluating Questions and Answer

PIPLS support multiple-choice, true/false, fill in the blanks, and coding questions so it can automatically generate feedback for students who answer questions, by reporting whether the answer is correct (by percentage) or not. The student needs to submit the correct answer in order to see other answers. And numbers of answer are limited by author (or not) in the question composing interface (Fig. 5).

**Fig. 4.** Facebook Messenger notification

**Fig. 5.** Answer a Coding question in PIPLS

**Fig. 6.** Immediate feedback after student submit answer

In the PIPLS, we have two types of free-response question: essay questions and coding question. Essay questions needs author or teacher to examine but other type of questions are automatically judged. PIPLS now supporting C, C++, Java, Pascal, Python, JavaScript and PHP in auto-judge function (Fig. 6).

Coding questions are not only judged automatically, teacher also can re-judge the answer in case the machine cannot or if teacher want to give some bonus points for the good solution.

## 3  Conclusion and Future Work

We developed the system based on previous research and focused on supporting students to learn Programming. We also extended the type of question generation (multiple-choice, true/false, fill in the blanks, essay, and coding) and developed many additional features. We hope to give more support to students when compared with other systems which also support programming learning.

In the future, we will plan to enhance the existed systems' functions and evaluate the impact of the tool on students' performance. We also intend to study the nature and quality of the artifacts (questions, answers, and feedback) produced by students.

# References

1. Jenkins, T.: On the Difficulty of Learning to Program. Citeseer (2002)
2. Matthíasdóttir, Á.: How to teach programming languages to novice students? Lecturing or not. In: International Conference on Computer Systems and Technologies-CompSysTech (2006)
3. Gomes, A., Mendes, A.J.: Learning to program-difficulties and solutions (2007)
4. Jenkins, T.: On the difficulty of learning to program. In: Proceedings of the 3rd Annual HEA Conference for the ICS Learning and Teaching Support Network, pp. 1–8 (2002)
5. Gökçearslan, Ş., Alper, A.: The effect of locus of control on learners' sense of community and academic success in the context of online learning communities. Int. Higher Educ. **27**, 64–73 (2015)
6. Allen, I.E., Seaman, J.: Online Report Card: Tracking Online Education in the United States. Babson Survey Research Group (2016)
7. El Said, G.R.: Understanding how learners use massive open online courses and why they drop out: thematic analysis of an interview study in a developing country. J. Educ. Comput. Res. **55**, 724–752 (2017)
8. Dolgopolovas, V., Jevsikova, T., Dagiene, V.: From Android games to coding in C—An approach to motivate novice engineering students to learn programming: a case study. Comput. Appl. Eng. Educ. **26**, 75–90 (2018)
9. Lai, C.H., Tho, P.D., Liang, J.S.: Design and evaluation of question-generated programming learning system. In: 2017 6th IIAI International Congress on Advanced Applied Informatics (IIAI-AAI), pp. 573–578 (2017)
10. Echeverría, L., Cobos, R., Machuca, L., Claros, I.: Using collaborative learning scenarios to teach programming to non-CS majors. Comput. Appl. Eng. Educ. **25**, 719–731 (2017)
11. Lu, O.H.T., Huang, J.C.H., Huang, A.Y.Q., Yang, S.J.H.: Applying learning analytics for improving students engagement and learning outcomes in an MOOCs enabled collaborative programming course. Interact. Learn. Environ. **25**, 220–234 (2017)
12. Law, K.M.Y., Lee, V.C.S., Yu, Y.T.: Learning motivation in e-learning facilitated computer programming courses. Comput. Educ. **55**, 218–228 (2010)
13. Thomas, L., Ratcliffe, M., Woodbury, J., Jarman, E.: Learning styles and performance in the introductory programming sequence. SIGCSE Bull. **34**, 33–37 (2002)
14. Bergin, S., Reilly, R.: Programming: factors that influence success. SIGCSE Bull. **37**, 411–415 (2005)
15. Funabiki, N., Korenaga, Y., Nakanishi, T., Watanabe, K.: An extension of fill-in-the-blank problem function in Java programming learning assistant system. In: 2013 IEEE Region 10 Humanitarian Technology Conference (R10-HTC), pp. 85–90 (2013)
16. Denny, P., Luxton-Reilly, A., Tempero, E., Hendrickx, J.: CodeWrite: supporting student-driven practice of java. In: Proceedings of the 42nd ACM Technical Symposium on Computer Science Education, pp. 471–476. ACM, Dallas (2011)
17. Luxton-Reilly, A., Denny, P., Plimmer, B., Bertinshaw, D.: Supporting student-generated free-response questions. In: Proceedings of the 16th Annual Joint Conference on Innovation and Technology in Computer Science Education, pp. 153–157. ACM, Darmstadt (2011)
18. Greenspan, G., Contributors: Question2Answer (2016)

# Dynamic Measurement for Detecting the Road of an Autonomous Vehicle Using the Proximity Sensor

Thang Hoang[1], Hoai Nguyen[2(✉)], Thanh Le Chau Nguyen[2],
Khoa Xuan Le[3], and Tung Minh Phung[2]

[1] National Taipei University of Technology, 1, Sec. 3,
Zhongxiao E. Rd., Taipei 10608, Taiwan, R.O.C.
[2] University of Technology and Education, The University of Danang,
48 Cao Thang Street, Hai Chau District, Da Nang City, Viet Nam
nhoai@ute.udn.vn
[3] Centre for Sustainable Technologies, University of Ulster,
Newtownabbey, Co Antrim BT37 0GY, UK

**Abstract.** The majority of sensors have played a vital role in the autonomous vehicle area. In this research, a dynamic model for measuring a characteristic of the analog sensor is developed, the shape of the output signal is a critical factor in road identification of autonomous vehicles. By hand-made testing system is built successfully, a number of alloys and non-magnetic metals (Aluminium and Copper) are considered in every aspect of them. In addition, the comparison experimental outcomes between various dynamic models prove that, with the same metal size (50 × 20), and sensing distance (6 mm), the shape of the output signal of measuring is similar. These results are distinguished clearly with alloys. Signal interference will also be minimized due to the control of the movement speed of the sensor. This is an integral element for approaching road of mobile devices with different obstacles.

**Keywords:** Dynamic performance · Analog proximity sensor
Autonomous vehicle · Identification · Sensing distance

## 1 Introduction

### 1.1 Proximity Sensor and Autonomous Vehicle

Proximity sensors are used for metal detection in long-term periods [1]. Whether to detect a stainless-steel object on a line or a copper tape on a machine, these sensors were one of the first implemented in the area and remain popular these days.

Ferrous and nonferrous metals influence on proximity sensors in different manners which are sensed by identifying their operation range depending on the object being detected. The standard sensing range of proximity sensors is determined by its response to a one-millimeter thick square piece of mild steel [2]. In fact, the sensors must be adjusted to the sensing distance per metal respectively. The more conductive the metal, the less the sensor's range.

© ICST Institute for Computer Sciences, Social Informatics and Telecommunications Engineering 2019
Published by Springer Nature Switzerland AG 2019. All Rights Reserved
P. Cong Vinh and V. Alagar (Eds.): ICCASA 2018/ICTCC 2018, LNICST 266, pp. 171–179, 2019.
https://doi.org/10.1007/978-3-030-06152-4_15

Conventional inductive proximity sensors are designed for non-contact detection of metal objects [3]. In addition, they also identify the properties of various metals. Generally, a sensor includes a coil and ferrite core arrangement, an oscillator and detector circuit, and a solid-state output as shown in Fig. 1. They operate with a high-frequency electromagnetic field created by LC-resonance circuit with a ferrite core and a single coil which is encircled the ferrite core [4]. When a metal object (target) gets into the high-frequency field, eddy currents are induced on the surface of the target resulting in a loss of energy in the oscillator and creating a signal which turns the solid-state output to 'ON' or 'OFF' [5]. When the target leaves the sensing area the oscillator regenerates, allowing the sensor to return to its original state.

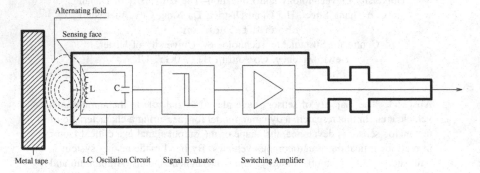

**Fig. 1.** Schematic of the analog proximity sensor

Cameras and sensors are highly important to the self-operation of autonomous vehicles. While cameras can be used for the purposes of navigation and object iden-tification [6], processing the captured images is often difficult and time-consuming as it requires modern algorithms such as machine learning etc. Alternatively, proximity sensors can be utilized to facilitate cameras' tasks with simple and fast object identi-fication. Therefore, this paper investigates how proximity sensors perform to identify objects, which in turn can be used to track the road for autonomous vehicles.

## 1.2    Principles of Operation of Eddy Current Testing

Eddy currents are a phenomenon generated by a changing magnetic flux intersecting a conductor wire [7]. Simultaneously, it also triggers a circulating stream of electrons or current within the conductor. In addition, the skin effect in conductors carrying alter-nating current is the outcome of establishing eddy current. Eddy currents move in a plane which is 3 parallel to the coil or metal surface and are reduced in phase with depth. The principles of electromagnetic induction may inspect eddy current working. And it is shown in Fig. 2.

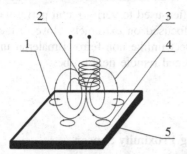

1- Eddy current
2- Coil
3- Coil's magnetic field
4- Eddy current's magnetic field
5- Conductive material

**Fig. 2.** Eddy current in a metal tapes

Eddy currents can be used for measuring metals for the difference in composition, structure, hardness, and for detecting and testing surface [8]. They can also be applied to measuring changes in dimensions of rods and tubes and of the metal plate thickness and coatings of non-metallic on metal substrates or coatings of metal on non-metallic substrates.

In calculating, Z0 is the impedance parameter which characterizes every coil. This parameter is defined by the voltage-current ratio (V0/I0). The relationship between them has pointed out Eq. (1). Impedance Z0 has a magnitude |Z| and a phase $\varphi$:

$$Z_0 = \frac{V_0}{I_0} = R_0 + jX_0 = R_0 + j2\pi f\, L_0 = \underset{\varphi = atan2\left(\frac{X_0}{R_0}\right)}{\sqrt{R_0^2 + X_0^2}} = |Z|\varphi \qquad (1)$$

When an alternating current is generated within a coil, it also creates a time-varying magnetic field. The magnetic streams of flux tend to be focused on the center of the coil. Faraday's electromagnetic induction law inspects eddy current as shown in Eq. (2). Faraday found out that a time-varying magnetic induction flux density causes on currents in an electrical conductor. The electromotive force $\varepsilon$ is proportional to the time-rate change of the magnetic induction flux density $\Phi_B$:

$$\varepsilon = -\frac{d\phi_B}{dt} \qquad (2)$$

In [9] proved that non-ferrous metal accuracy may be tested with results better than 1%, in the kHz or even MHz range. The measurement of the ferrous metal is more complex and challenging. Additionally, an extra problem to be solved is separating of an effect of the magnetic permeability and electrical conductivity of the metal under test onto the eddy current measurement outcomes. The technique for simultaneous distance and thickness testing of zinc-aluminum coating is shown in [10]. In order to enhance of this research direction, NASA Langley Research Center developed a flux-focusing eddy current probe by using a ferromagnetic material between the drive and pickup coils [11]. A range of non-ferrous metal is conductive materials. Therefore, eddy current testing uses the principle of electromagnetic induction to detect flaws has a critical role. For nonferrous materials such as aluminum and copper, eddy current electrical conductivity measurements are often used to verify metal performance [12]. For ferrous metal, the eddy current flow focused on extremely close to the surface, making sub-surface defects difficult to detect unlike non-ferrous material unless you strongly magnetize the materials or use special remote field probes.

## 2　Methodology

### 2.1　Experimental Set-up for an Analog Proximity Sensor

Schematic of the measurement set-up is shown in Fig. 3. A test panel (12) has a rectangular shape, which located on all laboratory instruments. Using rod (9) to fix analog proximity sensor (10). In the testing process, in order to change sensing distance between sensor and metal tape, stepper motor (4) is used. The smooth motion of the sensor is achieved by the lead screw (7). Using support (2) in order to fix this lead screw. In addition, to guide the straight motion of the screw, the navigation rod (3) is fixed. In order to observe the change of the output signal from the sensor, the sensor slider (11) will control the sensor along the test surface. The navigation rod will also be used in this case to facilitate the slide frame to straight.

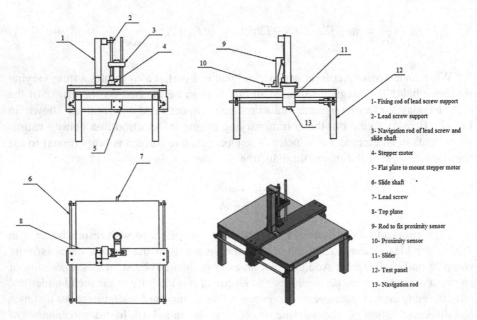

1- Fixing rod of lead screw support
2- Lead screw support
3- Navigation rod of lead screw and slide shaft
4- Stepper motor
5- Flat plate to mount stepper motor
6- Slide shaft
7- Lead screw
8- Top plane
9- Rod to fix proximity sensor
10- Proximity sensor
11- Slider
12- Test panel
13- Navigation rod

**Fig. 3.** Testing set-up of the measurement system

## 2.2    Diagram and Operating Principle of the Dynamic Measurement System

This is an analog proximity sensor which operates at 12.04 V used for identifying the metallic performance. It includes 4 wires consisting of red (positive wire), black (ground wire or negative wire), a white wire and blue wire. The out wire is the output of the sensor which is taken as the acquiring signal to the LabVIEW software by interfacing with MyRIO hardware. It is connected as the 4th pin to the Proximity Sensor with My-RIO Toolkit Using LabVIEW an analog output of the MyRIO hardware as the acquiring signal, which sends a signal to the program indicating the detection or non-detection of the type of metallic. Achievement results are shown in Fig. 4.

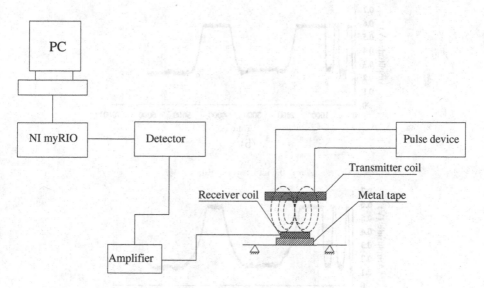

**Fig. 4.** Diagram of the measurement system of the analog proximity sensor

With this method of measurement, the analog sensor is mounted on a mobile device which may control the speed. Firstly, let it pass through each of the metal tapes of the same size (non-ferrous metals and alloys) on the flat table. Then, in turn, change the sensing distance to observe the signal received on the computer screen. Simultaneously, compare the results obtained with previous studies to draw conclusions.

Firstly, stick non-ferrous metals and an alloy have the same size on the test table surface, respectively. In addition, the stepper motor is controlled in order to the sensor passes through the center of the metal tape, the signal received on the computer screen specifies the difference in amplitude of the signal which is well illustrated in Fig. 5.

Secondly, the sensing distance (h) is changed correspondingly on the material. From there, the distinction of the output signal shape from the analog sensor is also determined precisely. In this case, the movement speed of the sensor is kept at a constant merit. The experimental result is shown in Fig. 6.

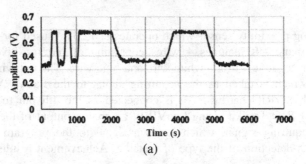

(a)

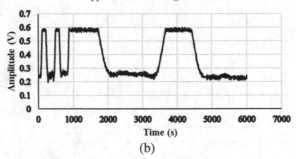

(b)

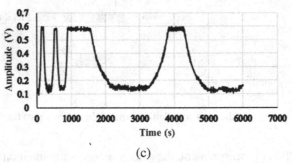

(c)

**Fig. 5.** Shape of output signal when testing various metal

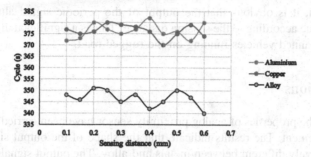

**Fig. 6.** The relationship between output signal and sensing distance

## 3   Results and Discussions

Overall, it is clear that there are differences in terms of the shape of the output signal when identifying non-ferrous and alloys. Since the velocity of the stepper motor is not too fast, the received signal is less noise than the result in [13]. This causes the electromagnetic of the sensor to sweep through the metal is relatively stable. From there, it improves the accuracy of metal identification in practice.

### 3.1   The Shape of the Output Signal on Various Metal

At the same sensing distance, the amplitude of the signal received when testing the alloy is greatest almost 0.6 V, while the amplitude of the signal from aluminum is the smallest approximately 0.3 V. This is explained by the difference in static properties when the identification of proximity switch with various metals has been studied in [14]. Nevertheless, the identification range of the proximity sensor for aluminum is larger than copper and alloys. This is a key element for aluminum applications in the research of mobile robot devices.

Experimental results on Fig. 5a–c prove that it takes about 360 s for the amplitude of output signal to reach a peak for the first time when testing aluminum tape. Meanwhile, the height of signal peaked for the initial time at almost 150 s when identifying copper metal. Conductive properties between various non-ferrous metal have trigged of this phenomenon.

### 3.2   The Relationship Between the Output Signal and Sensing Distance on Various Metal

Line graph illustrates the change oscillation cycle of the signal by sensing distance. It is also noticeable that the shape of the signal when the copper and aluminum identification is the same. This is distinguished from the measurement of the alloy. This is explained by the similarity of static characteristics between the two metals which are also mentioned in [14]. This result also demonstrates that non-ferrous metal is easier than alloys to detect and identify road. This is also similar to the results which found in [15].

In addition, it is obvious that the output of the periodic signal almost does not change the value according to the sensing distance. This is a significant direction for the design of unmanned vehicles running on the rugged road.

# 4 Conclusions

In this study, the properties of analog proximity sensor have been carried out by means of lab measurement. The results indicate that the shape of the output signal from the sensor is relatively different between metals and alloy. The output signals in this study are less interfered because the measurement system is carefully set up.

Specifically, the shape of the signal almost does not depend on the distance of the sensor in the same material. In addition, the comparison of the average oscillation period between each material also demonstrates that the use of mobile devices to detect metals is easier than the alloy.

On the other hand, aluminum has some special properties between various metals. Due to its properties, a mobile robot may detect road or identify easily. This is a critical element to research and control of devices in autonomous vehicles.

# References

1. Crosby, R.J., Everson Jr., H.W.: Proximity sensor having a non-ferrous metal shield for enhanced sensing range. U.S. Patent, No. 5 (1998)
2. Davenport, G.C.: Remote sensing applications in forensic investigations. Hist. Archaeol. 35, 87–100 (2001)
3. Woolsey, K., Lamping, J., Marler, J., Burreson, B., Knudson, S.: Inductive proximity sensor for detecting ferromagnetic, non-permeable or magnet targets. U.S. Patent No. 6 (2002)
4. Luo, R.C.: Sensor technologies and microsensor issues for mechatronics systems. IEEE/ASME Trans. Mechatron. 1, 39–49 (1996)
5. Ben-Ari, M., Mondada, F.: Element of Robotic. Springer (2017)
6. Bertozzi, M., Broggi, A., Fascioli, A.: Vision-based intelligent vehicles: State of the art and perspectives. Robot. Auton. Syst. 32, 1–16 (2000)
7. García-Martín, J., Gómez-Gil, J., Vázquez-Sánchez, E.: Non-destructive techniques based on eddy current testing. Sensors 11, 2525–2565 (2011)
8. Mercier, D., Lesage, J., Decoopman, X., Chicot, D.: Eddy currents and hardness testing for evaluation of steel decarburizing. NDT E Int. 39, 652–660 (2006)
9. Neikov, O.D., Yefimov, N.V., Naboychenko, S.: Handbook of non-ferrous metal powders: technologies and applications. Elsevier (2009)
10. Kamanalu, S.S.: Proximity and Thickness Estimation of Aluminum 3003 Alloy Metal Sheets Using Multi-Frequency Eddy Current Sensor. Diss. Wright State University (2010)
11. Wincheski, B., et al.: Characteristics of Ferromagnetic Flux Focusing Lens in the Development of Surface/Subsurface Flaw Detector (1993)
12. Bowler, N., Huang, Y.: Electrical conductivity measurement of metal plates using broadband eddy-current and four-point methods. Meas. Sci. Technol. 16 (2005)

13. Tsing, T.-T., Hoai, N.: Dynamic performance measurement of proximity sensors for a mobile robot. Key Eng. Mater. **625** (2014)
14. Tsung, Tsing-Tshih, Hoai, Nguyen: Measurement of static performance of inductive proximity switch for a mobile robot. Appl. Mech. Mater. **404**, 502–507 (2013)
15. Nguyen, H.: Identification Performance of Proximity Sensor for a Mobile Robot. Final thesis, Chinese Culture University (2015)

# ICTCC 2018

# Post-quantum Cryptoschemes: New Finite Non-commutative Algebras for Defining Hidden Logarithm Problem

Hieu Minh Nguyen[1]($\boxtimes$), Nikolay Andreevich Moldovyan[2],
Alexandr Andreevich Moldovyan[2], Nam Hai Nguyen[1], Cong Manh Tran[3],
and Ngoc Han Phieu[1]

[1] Academy of Cryptography Techniques, 141 Chien Thang Street, Hanoi, Vietnam
hieuminhmta@gmail.com, nnhaivn61@gmail.com, phieungochan@gmail.com
[2] St. Petersburg Institute for Informatics and Automation of Russian
Academy of Sciences, 14-th line 39, 199178 St. Petersburg, Russia
nmold@mail.ru, maa1305@yandex.ru
[3] Le Quy Don Technical University, No 236 Hoang Quoc Viet Road, Hanoi, Vietnam
manhtc@gmail.com

**Abstract.** In the article we present some properties of non-commutative finite algebras of four-dimension vectors with parameterized multiplication operation characterized in that different modifications of the multiplication operation are mutually associative. One of the introduced finite algebras represents ring. Other algebra contains no global unit element, its elements are invertible locally, and is characterized in that the multiplication operation possess compression property. Regarding the investigated ring, the detailed attention is paid to properties of the set of non-invertible elements of the ring. Formulas for zero-divisors and unit elements of different types are derived. The introduced finite algebras represent interest to define over them the hidden discrete logarithm problem that is a promising cryptographic primitive for post-quantum cryptography.

**Keywords:** Finite algebra · Ring · Galois field · Vector
Local left unit element · Bi-side unit element
Associative multiplication · Parameterized multiplication
Cryptoscheme

## 1 Introduction

Cryptographic algorithms and protocols [1,2], including cryptosystems with public key, based on the computational difficulty of the factorization problem for numbers of a special type [3] and the discrete logarithm problem (DLP) [4] have found a wide practical application for solving problems of providing information-safe modern computer technologies. The security of cryptosystems based on

© ICST Institute for Computer Sciences, Social Informatics and Telecommunications Engineering 2019
Published by Springer Nature Switzerland AG 2019. All Rights Reserved
P. Cong Vinh and V. Alagar (Eds.): ICCASA 2018/ICTCC 2018, LNICST 266, pp. 183–194, 2019.
https://doi.org/10.1007/978-3-030-06152-4_16

these problems is determined by the fact that the most effective algorithms for solving these problems, known at the present time and implemented with the use of existing computer technology, have a subexponential (factorization and DLP in finite fields) or exponential complexity (DLP on an elliptic curve). In connection with the significant progress in the development of quantum computations [5,6], interest in estimating the complexity of discrete logarithmic and factorization in solving these problems on a quantum computer has arisen. It was shown that both of these problems have a polynomial complexity in the model of quantum computations [7,8]. These results and the expectation of the appearance of practically functioning quantum computers capable of effectively solving the problem of cracking existing cryptoschemes based on the DLP and the factorization problem, raises the problem of creating an arsenal of the electronic digital signature, public key distribution, and public encryption protocols, which would be convenient for practical use and resistant to attacks using quantum computers. Algorithms of cryptography with a secret key, for example block ciphers, according to experts will remain resistant to cryptanalysis using quantum computers. However, to ensure sufficient security of the public key cryptoschemes it is required to put into their basis computationally difficult problems of another type whose computational complexity of solution would be of superpolynomial complexity when using both conventional and quantum computers. The response to this challenge was the announcement by the National Institute of Standards and Technology (NIST) of the competition but the post-quantum two-key cryptograms development [9] and the appearance of regularly held thematic conference [10].

Finite non-commutative rings (FNRs) are interesting for designing public-key cryptoschemes based on the discrete logarithm problem in hidden commutative subgroup [11–14] that represents interest as potential primitive of the post-quantum cryptography. Earlier, for the development of post-quantum cryptosystems based on the computational difficulty of the hidden discrete logarithm problem, the finite algebra of quaternions was applied [12,13]. However, realizing the potential of this computationally difficult problem as a primitive of the post-quantum cryptography requires significantly expanding the class of its carriers [14]. Present paper introduces two novel carriers of the hidden discrete logarithm problem and discusses their properties. Different FNR can be constructed in the form of associative finite algebras (AFAs), defining multiplication operation of vectors in some finite vector space.

Suppose $\mathbf{e}, \mathbf{i}, \mathbf{j}, \mathbf{k}$ be some formal basis vectors and $a, b, c, d \in GF(p)$, where prime $p \geq 3$, are coordinates. The vectors are denoted as $a\mathbf{e} + b\mathbf{i} + c\mathbf{j} + d\mathbf{k}$ or as $(a, b, c, d)$. The terms $\tau\mathbf{v}$, where $\tau \in GF(p)$ and $\mathbf{v} \in \{\mathbf{e}, \mathbf{i}, \mathbf{j}, \mathbf{k}\}$, are called components of the vector.

The operation of addition of two vectors $(a, b, c, d)$ and $(x, y, z, v)$ is defined via addition of the corresponding coordinates according to the following formula: $(a, b, c, d) + (x, y, z, v) = (a + x, b + y, c + z, d + v)$.

The multiplication of two vectors $a\mathbf{e} + b\mathbf{i} + c\mathbf{j} + d\mathbf{k}$ and $x\mathbf{e} + y\mathbf{i} + z\mathbf{j} + v\mathbf{k}$ is defined with the following formula:

$$(a\mathbf{e} + b\mathbf{i} + c\mathbf{j} + d\mathbf{k}) \circ (x\mathbf{e} + y\mathbf{i} + z\mathbf{j} + v\mathbf{k})$$
$$= ax\mathbf{e} \circ \mathbf{e} + bx\mathbf{i} \circ \mathbf{e} + cx\mathbf{j} \circ \mathbf{e} + dx\mathbf{k} \circ ... \circ \mathbf{j} + av\mathbf{e} \circ \mathbf{k} + bv\mathbf{i} \circ \mathbf{k} + cv\mathbf{j} \circ \mathbf{k} + dv\mathbf{k} \circ \mathbf{k},$$

where $\circ$ denotes the vector multiplication operation and each product of two basis vectors is to be replaced by some basis vector or by a one-component vector in accordance with the basis-vector multiplication table (BVMT) defining associative and non-commutative multiplication. In this paper there are introduced two novel BVMTs that define parameterized multiplication operations, different modifications of which are mutually associative. The proposed BVMTs are shown in Tables 1 and 2, where $\mu \in GF(p)$ and $\tau \in GF(p)$ are structural coefficients. In the last formula it is assumed that in every product of two basis vectors the left (right) operant indicates the row (column) of the BVMT and the intersection of the indicated row and column defines the cell of the BVMT in which it is given the value of the product. The AFA defined with Table 2 is characterized in that the multiplication operation possesses property of compression, i.e. multiplication of arbitrary two non-zero elements of the AFA gives as the result a vector $(a, b, c, d)$ satisfying the condition $ac = bd$.

**Table 1.** The basis-vector multiplication table defining a finite ring

| $\circ$ | $\vec{e}$ | $\vec{i}$ | $\vec{j}$ | $\vec{k}$ |
|---|---|---|---|---|
| $\vec{e}$ | e | $\mu$k | $\mu$e | k |
| $\vec{i}$ | $\tau$j | i | j | $\tau$i |
| $\vec{j}$ | j | $\mu$i | $\mu$j | i |
| $\vec{k}$ | $\tau$e | k | e | $\tau$k |

**Table 2.** The basis-vector multiplication table defining a finite algebra with compressing multiplication operation

| $\circ$ | $\vec{e}$ | $\vec{i}$ | $\vec{j}$ | $\vec{k}$ |
|---|---|---|---|---|
| $\vec{e}$ | $\mu$e | $\mu$i | $\mu$i | $\mu$e |
| $\vec{i}$ | $\tau$e | $\tau$i | $\tau$i | $\tau$e |
| $\vec{j}$ | $\tau$k | $\tau$j | $\tau$j | $\tau$k |
| $\vec{k}$ | $\mu$k | $\mu$j | $\mu$j | $\mu$k |

The paper is organized as follows: Sect. 2 describes the properties of the introduced FNR, Sect. 3 describes briefly properties of the introduced AFA, Sect. 4 presents a homomorphic map of the non-invertible vectors of the FNR for defining the discrete logarithm problem in hidden cyclic group, and Sect. 5 concludes the paper.

## 2   Properties of the Introduced Ring

**Lemma 1.** *Suppose* $\circ$ *and* $\star$ *are two arbitrary modifications of the vector multiplication operation, which correspond to different pairs of structural coefficients* $(\mu_1, \tau_1)$ *and* $(\mu_2, \tau_2) \neq (\mu_1, \tau_1)$. *Then for arbitrary three vectors* $A$, $B$, *and* $C$ *the following formula* $(A \circ B) \star C = A \circ (B \star C)$ *holds.*

Proof of this lemma consists in straightforward using the definition of the multiplication operation and Table 1.

To find the unit element of the considered ring one can solve the following vector equation:

$$(a\mathbf{e} + b\mathbf{i} + c\mathbf{j} + d\mathbf{k}) \circ (x\mathbf{e} + y\mathbf{i} + z\mathbf{j} + w\mathbf{k}) = (a\mathbf{e} + b\mathbf{i} + c\mathbf{j} + d\mathbf{k}), \qquad (1)$$

where $V = (a\mathbf{e} + b\mathbf{i} + c\mathbf{j} + d\mathbf{k})$ is an arbitrary vector and $X = (x\mathbf{e} + y\mathbf{i} + z\mathbf{j} + w\mathbf{k})$ is the unknown.

Equation (1) can be reduced to solving the following two systems of linear equations:

$$\begin{cases} (a + d\tau)x + (a\mu + d)z = a \\ (c + b\tau)x + (c\mu + b)z = c \end{cases} \qquad (2)$$

and

$$\begin{cases} (b + c\mu)y + (b\tau + c)w = b \\ (a\mu + d)y + (a + d\tau)w = d. \end{cases} \qquad (3)$$

Each of the systems has the same main determinant

$$\Delta = ab(1 - \mu\tau) + dc(\mu\tau - 1) = (\mu\tau - 1)(dc - ab)$$

and the same auxiliary determinants

$$\Delta_x = ab - cd; \Delta_z = \tau(cd - ab); \Delta_y = ab - cd; \Delta_w = \mu(cd - ab).$$

For the case $dc - ab \neq 0$ there exists the unique solution of each of the systems:

$$x = \frac{\Delta_x}{\Delta} = \frac{1}{1 - \mu\tau}; y = \frac{\Delta_y}{\Delta} = \frac{1}{1 - \mu\tau};$$
$$z = \frac{\Delta_z}{\Delta} = \frac{\tau}{\mu\tau - 1}; w = \frac{\Delta_w}{\Delta} = \frac{\tau}{\mu\tau - 1}. \qquad (4)$$

The vector $E = (\frac{1}{1-\mu\tau}, \frac{1}{1-\mu\tau}, \frac{\tau}{\mu\tau-1}, \frac{\tau}{\mu\tau-1})$ has been computed as the right unit element of the ring.

Considering the vector equation

$$X \circ V = V \qquad (5)$$

gives the same solution $X = E$ as the left unit element.

For the case $dc - ab = 0$ there exists $p$ different solutions of each of the systems (2) and (3), which include the solution (4). Thus we have come to the following lemma:

**Lemma 2.** *The vector* $E = \left( \frac{1}{1-\mu\tau}, \frac{1}{1-\mu\tau}, \frac{\tau}{\mu\tau-1}, \frac{\mu}{\mu\tau-1} \right)$ *is the (global) unit element of the considered ring, i.e. for arbitrary vector* $V$ *the following equations* $V \circ E = E \circ V = V$ *hold.*

The examination of the vector equation $V \circ X = E$ leads to the following

**Lemma 3.** *Vectors* $V = (a, b, c, d)$, *where* $ab \neq cd$, *are invertible.*

Calculating number of the vectors satisfying condition $ab \neq cd$ one can get

**Lemma 4.** *The order* $\Omega$ *of the multiplicative group of the considered ring is equal to* $\Omega = p(p-1)(p^2 - 1)$.

Examination of the vector Eqs. (1) and (5) for the case $ab = cd$ leads to the following two lemmas:

**Lemma 5.** *For an arbitrary vector* $N = (a, b, c, d)$ *such that* $ab = cd$ *and* $a\tau + c \neq 0$, *each of the vectors*

$$E_l = \left( x, \frac{c}{a\tau + c} - \frac{a + c\mu}{a\tau + c} z, z, \frac{a}{a\tau + c} - \frac{a + c\mu}{a\tau + c} x \right),$$

*where* $x, y \in GF(p)$ *acts as the left local unit element on all elements of the set* $N^i$, *where* $i$ *is an arbitrary natural number, i.e., equalities* $E_l \circ N^i = N^i$ *hold true.*

**Lemma 6.** *For an arbitrary vector* $N = (a, b, c, d)$ *such that* $ab = cd$ *and* $a\mu + d \neq 0$, *each of the vectors*

$$E_r = \left( x, \frac{d}{a\mu + d} - \frac{a + d\tau}{a\mu + d} w, \frac{a}{a\mu + d} - \frac{a + d\tau}{a\mu + d} x, w \right),$$

*where* $x, w \in GF(p)$ *acts as the right local unit element on all elements of the set* $N^i$, *where* $i$ *is a natural number, i.e., equalities* $N^i \circ E_r = N^i$ *hold true.*

The sets of left and right local unit elements contain invertible and non-invertible vectors $(a', b', c', d')$.

It is of interest to consider subsets of non-invertible vectors. Imposing the condition $(a'b' = c'd')$ on the coordinates of the local unit elements leads to the following two formulas describing subsets of non-invertible local unit elements:

$$E_l^* = \left( x; \frac{c}{a\tau + c} - \frac{a + c\mu}{a\tau + c} \cdot \frac{c}{a} x; \frac{c}{a} x; \frac{a}{a\tau + c} - \frac{a + c\mu}{a\tau + c} x \right). \tag{6}$$

$$E_r^* = \left( x; \frac{d}{a\mu + d} - \frac{a + d\tau}{a\mu + d} \cdot \frac{d}{a} x; \frac{a}{a\mu + d} - \frac{a + d\tau}{a\mu + d} x; \frac{d}{a} x \right). \tag{7}$$

The elements included simultaneously in the sets (6) and (7) represent bi-side local unit elements of the vector $(a, b, c, d)$. From condition $E_l^* = E_r^*$ one has four equations with the unknown value $x$ which are satisfied simultaneously at some unique value $x = x_0$:

**Lemma 7.** *The local bi-side unit element $E'$ is described with the following formula* $E' = \left( x_0, \frac{d}{a\mu+d} - \frac{a+d\tau}{a\mu+d} \cdot \frac{d}{a} x_0, \frac{d}{a\mu+d} - \frac{a+d\tau}{a\mu+d} x_0, \frac{d}{a} x_0 \right)$,
*where* $x_0 = \frac{a^2}{ca\mu+cd+a^2+ad\tau} = \frac{a}{c\mu+b+a+d\tau}$.

Proof of this statement is performed substituting the value $x_0$ in the formulas describing all possible values $E_l^*$ and $E_r^*$.

It is evident that

$$(E' \circ N = N \circ E' = N) \Rightarrow (E' \circ N^i = N^i \circ E' = N^i)$$

for all integers $i$. Let us consider the sequence $N, N^2, ..., N^i$ (for $i = 1, 2, 3, ...$). If the vector $N$ is not a zero-divisor relatively some its power (formulas describing zero-divisors are presented below), then for some two integers $h$ and $k > h$ we have $N^k = N^h$ and $N^k = N^{k-h} \circ N^h = N^h \circ N^{k-h} = N^{k-h} \circ N^h$. Thus, we have the following:

**Lemma 8.** *Suppose $N = (a, b, c, d)$ be a non-invertible vector, i.e. $ab = cd$, such that there exists no integer $k$ for which the condition $N^k = (0, 0, 0, 0)$ holds true. Then the sequence $N, N^2, ..., N^i, ...$, where $i = 1, 2, ...$, is periodic and for some integer $\omega$ we have $N^\omega = E'$, where $E'$ is the local unit element such that $N \circ E' = E' \circ N = N$.*

If for some integer $\omega$ (that can be called order of the non-invertible vector $N$) $N^\omega = E'$ holds true, then the bi-side local unit element corresponding to the vector $N$ can be computed as a power of $N$.

The following computational example illustrates this fact:

for $p = 241740125706839$ and $\mu = 1; \tau = 1$

$$N = (a, b, c, d) = \tag{8}$$
$$(235252752952, 124252511124, 855846652525, 52660042235214).$$

Computation of the value $E'$ as $E' = N^{p^2-1}$ and with using formula from Lemma 7 gives the same result:

$$E' = (152632284483677, 212707439691227, 72220177461588, 45920349777187). \tag{9}$$

Product of some two non-invertible vectors can be equal to zero $(0, 0, 0, 0)$ of the ring. Such vectors are called zero-divisors. For some non-invertible vector $N = (a, b, c, d)$ there exit sets of the left and right zero-divisors $D$ such that the following equalities hold: $N \circ D = (0, 0, 0, 0)$ and $D \circ N = (0, 0, 0, 0)$.

For the first case, finding vectors $D$ is connected with solving the systems of two linear Eqs. (2) and (3) with the right part equal to zero of the field $GF(p)$.

Considering such modified systems of equations it is sufficiently easy to derive the following formula describing the set of the right zero-divisors

$$D_r = \left( x; y; -\frac{a+d\tau}{a\mu+d}x; -\frac{a\mu+d}{a+d\tau}y \right), \tag{10}$$

where $x$ and $y$ take on all values in the field $GF(p)$. Thus, for arbitrary given non-invertible vector such that $a\mu+d \neq 0$ and $a+d\tau \neq 0$ there exist $p^2$ different zero-divisors including the trivial one $(0,0,0,0)$. The analogous consideration of the left zero-divisors leads to the following formula

$$D_l = \left( x; y; -\frac{a\tau+c}{a+c\mu}y; -\frac{a+c\mu}{a\tau+c}x \right). \tag{11}$$

It is easy to see that sets of the right and left divisors include only non-invertible vectors. Let us find intersection of these two sets. The intersection corresponds to the pairs of the values $(x,y)$ at which we have the following two equalities:

$$-\frac{a+d\tau}{a\mu+d}x = -\frac{a\tau+c}{a+c\mu}y; \; -\frac{a\mu+d}{a+d\tau}y = -\frac{a+c\mu}{a\tau+c}x.$$

Each of the following two equations gives the following:

$$(a\mu+d)(a\tau+c)x = (a+c\mu)(a+d\tau)y \Rightarrow$$
$$a^2(\mu\tau-1)x = cd(\mu\tau-1)y \Rightarrow y = \frac{a^2}{cd}x = \frac{a}{b}x. \tag{12}$$

Thus, for the case $\mu\tau-1 \neq 1$ and $cd \neq 0$ all bi-side zero-divisors of the vector $N$ are described with the formula

$$D' = \left( x; \frac{a}{b}x; -\frac{a\tau+c}{a+c\mu} \cdot \frac{a}{b}x; -\frac{a+c\mu}{a\tau+c}x \right), \tag{13}$$

where $x$ is an arbitrary element of the field $GF(p)$.

It is of interest to get formula describing square roots from zero of the ring, i.e., solutions of the vector equation

$$D \circ D = (0,0,0,0). \tag{14}$$

In the case $ab = cd$ the last equation defines the following system of linear equations:

$$\begin{cases} a(a+b+c\mu+d\tau) = 0 \\ b(a+b+c\mu+d\tau) = 0 \\ c(a+b+c\mu+d\tau) = 0 \\ d(a+b+c\mu+d\tau) = 0, \end{cases} \tag{15}$$

where $D = (a, b, c, d)$ is the unknown. From system (15) we have the following:

**Lemma 9.** *Square roots from the vector* $(0,0,0,0)$ *are non-invertible vectors* $N = (a, b, c, d)$, *the coordinates of which satisfy the condition* $a + b + \mu c + \tau d = 0$.

Comparing Lemmas 7 and 9 one can see that for the non-invertible vectors that are square roots from the zero vector there exist no local bi-side unity elements. Taking into account this relation one can put forward the following hypothesis:

**Lemma 10.** *If the coordinates of the non-invertible vectors* $N = (a, b, c, d)$ *satisfy the condition* $a + b + \mu c + \tau d \neq 0$, *then the bi-side local unity element can be computed as* $E' = N^\omega$ *at some integer* $\omega$.

Lemmas 5 to 8 show that the set of non-invertible vectors includes different cyclic groups with different bi-side local unit elements.

## 3    Finite Non-commutative Associative Algebra with Compressing Multiplication Operation

**Lemma 11.** *Lemma 1 is valid for the AFA defined over the field* $GF(p)$ *with Table 2 as the BVMT.*

**Lemma 12.** *Result of multiplying two arbitrary non-zero elements of the AFA represents a vector* $(a, b, c, d)$ *satisfying condition* $ac = bd$.

Proof of this lemma includes straightforward using the definition of the multiplication operation and Table 2. Naturally, squaring maps set of $p^2 - 1$ non-zero elements of the AFA into the subset of the four-dimension vectors $(a, b, c, d)$ such that $ac = bd$ number of which is equal to $p^3 + p^2 - p$. Thus, on the average there exists approximately $p$ different square roots from some element of the last subset.

**Lemma 13.** *The local right-side unit elements exist for vectors* $(a, b, c, d)$ *such that* $ac = bd$, $\mu a + \tau b \neq 0$, $\mu d + \tau c \neq 0$ *and the set of the right-side units of the non-zero vector* $(a, b, c, d)$ *is described with the following formula*

$$E_r = \left( x, y, \frac{b}{\mu a + \tau b} - y, \frac{a}{\mu a + \tau b} - x \right),$$

*where* $x, y \in GF(p)$.

**Lemma 14.** *The local left-side unit elements exist for vectors* $(a, b, c, d)$ *such that* $ac = bd$, $a + d \neq 0$, $b + c \neq 0$ *and the set of the left-side units of some non-zero vector* $(a, b, c, d)$ *is described with the following formula*

$$E_l = \left( x, \frac{a}{\tau(a + d)} - \frac{\mu}{\tau}x, z, \frac{d}{\tau(a + d)} - \frac{\tau}{\mu}z \right),$$

*where* $x, z \in GF(p)$.

**Lemma 15.** *The local bi-side unit elements of the non-zero vector $(a, b, c, d)$ such that $ac = bd$, $\mu a + \tau b \neq 0$, $\mu d + \tau c \neq 0$, $a + d \neq 0$, and $b + c \neq 0$ is described with the following formula*

$$E' = \left( x, \frac{a}{\tau(a+d)} - \frac{\mu}{\tau}x, \frac{b}{\mu a + \tau b} - \frac{a}{\tau(a+d)} + \frac{\mu}{\tau}x, \frac{a}{\tau(a+d)} - x \right),$$

*where $x \in GF(p)$.*

**Lemma 16.** *For some non-zero vector $(a, b, c, d)$ such that $ac = bd$, $\mu a + \tau b \neq 0$, $\mu d + \tau c \neq 0$, $a + d \neq 0$, and $b + c \neq 0$ there exists exactly one local bi-side unit element $E' = (a', b', c', d')$ such that $a'c' = b'd'$. The local bi-side unit $E'$ can be computed using formula from Lemma 15 and substituting the value $x = x_0$, where*

$$x_0 = \frac{a^2}{(a+d)(\mu a + \tau b)}.$$

In the considered AFA the left, the right, and bi-side zero-divisors are global, i.e. they acts on each element of the AFA. The following three lemmas describes the sets of the mentioned three types of the zero-divisors.

**Lemma 17.** *The set of the right-side zero-divisors is described with the following formula*

$$D_r = (x, y, -y, -x),$$

*where $x, y \in GF(p)$.*

**Lemma 18.** *The set of the left-side zero-divisors is described with the following formula*

$$D_l = \left( x, -\frac{\mu}{\tau}x, z, -\frac{\tau}{\mu}z \right),$$

*where $x, z \in GF(p)$.*

**Lemma 19.** *The set of the bi-side zero-divisors is described with the following formula*

$$D' = \left( x, -\frac{\mu}{\tau}x, \frac{\mu}{\tau}x, -x \right),$$

*where $x \in GF(p)$.*

**Lemma 20.** *Suppose the non-zero vector $V = (a, b, c, d)$ and local bi-side unit $E' = (a', b', c', d')$ corresponding to $(a, b, c, d)$ are such that $ac = bd$, $\mu a + \tau b \neq 0$, $\mu d + \tau c \neq 0$, $a + d \neq 0$, $b + c \neq 0$, and $a'c' = b'd'$. Then the local bi-side unit $E'$ can be computed as $E' = V^\omega$ at some integer $\omega$.*

Lemma 15 shows that the considered AFA includes different subsets of four-dimension vectors that represent cyclic groups the units of which are different in general case.

## 4    Discussion of the Potential Application

Designing different BVMTs for defining the multiplication operation in finite four-dimension vector space one can get different types of AFA, for example, finite rings, non-commutative [12] and commutative ones [15]. As a particular case of the lasts it is possible to define finite fields [15].

In accordance with the well-known Representation Theorem an $m$-dimension AFA over $GF(p)$ is isomorphic to an subalgebra of the $m \times m$ matrix algebra over $GF(p)$ (see, for example [16]).

In the case $m = 4$ one has the following illustration. For arbitrary given four-dimension AFA multiplication of all elements of the four-dimension vector space over $GF(p)$ by some fixed four-dimension vector $V$ defines a map $\varphi_V(X) : X \to \varphi_V(X)$ of the vector space into itself (in particular cases, when the fixed vector is an invertible element of the AFA, such map represents linear transformation of the vector space). Indeed, from the definition of the multiplication operation in the AFA one can see that the result of multiplication of the vector $X$ by $V$ represents multiplication of the vector $X$ by some $4 \times 4$ matrix $M_V$ elements of which are defined by coordinates of the vector $V$ and by the BVMT. Thus, it can be written the following:

$$\varphi_V(X) = X \circ V = X * M_V,$$

where $M_V = f(V)$ and $*$ denotes the matrix multiplication. Considering maps defined by two different vectors $V_1$ and $V_2$ we have

$$\varphi_{V_2}\left(\varphi_{V_1}(X)\right) = X \circ V_1 \circ V_2 = X \circ (V_1 \circ V_2) = \varphi_{V_1 \circ V_2}(X).$$

Considering the same two maps defined by the matrices $M_{V_1} = f(V_1)$ and $M_{V_2} = f(V_2)$ we get

$$\varphi_{M_{V_2}}\left(\varphi_{M_{V_1}}(X)\right) = X * M_{V_1} * M_{V_2} = X * (M_{V_1} * M_{V_2}) =$$
$$\varphi_{M_{V_1} * M_{V_2}}(X) = \varphi_{V_1 \circ V_2}(X) = \varphi_{f(V_1 \circ V_2)}(X).$$

Thus, we have

$$f(V_1 \circ V_2) = f(V_1) * f(V_2).$$

In analogous way it is easy to show the following

$$f(V_1 + V_2) = f(V_1) + f(V_2).$$

The last two formulas show that between any four-dimension AFA over $GF(p)$ and some subset of the $4 \times 4$ matrices there exists isomorphism, i.e. the results described in Sects. 2 and 3 relates to some subsets of the $4 \times 4$ matrices over $GF(p)$.

A characteristic feature of the ring considered in Sect. 2 and of the AFA considered in Sect. 3 is mutual associativity of different modifications of the parameterized multiplication operation. Such property is of interest for applications concerning the design of the cryptoschemes using the key-dependent operations.

It is also interesting to consider potential cryptographic applications concerning the definition of the hidden conjugacy search problem (it can be called alternatively the discrete logarithm problem in a hidden cyclic subgroup) over subset of the non-invertible vectors.

Suppose $N$ be some non-invertible vector in the considered FNR (or element in the considered AFA) such that for some prime number $q$ we have $N^q = E'$. Using the local unit element $E'$ one can define the following homomorphism $\varphi_t$ over set of non-invertible vectors $V_{E'}$, where $V_{E'} = V \circ E'$ and $V$ takes on all values in the considered ring of the four-dimension vectors.

Like standard automorphisms $\psi_W$ of the finite non-commutative ring described by the formula $\psi_W(V) = W^{-1} \circ V \circ W$, where $W$ is an invertible element of the ring, the homomorphism $\varphi_t$ is defined as follows:

$$\varphi_t(V_{E'}) = N^{q-t} \circ V_{E'} \circ N^t. \tag{16}$$

Actually, the last formula defines homomorphism since with evidence the following holds true:

$$\varphi_t\left(V'_{E'} \circ V''_{E'}\right) = \\ \varphi_t\left(V'_{E'}\right) \circ \varphi_t\left(V''_{E'}\right), \tag{17}$$

$$\varphi_t\left(V'_{E'} + V''_{E'}\right) = \\ \varphi_t\left(V'_{E'}\right) + \varphi_t\left(V''_{E'}\right). \tag{18}$$

To define public-key cryptoschemes, like that described in [11], one can select some invertible vector $G$ having sufficiently large prime order $g$, which satisfies the condition $G \circ N \neq N \circ G$, and use the formula $Y = N^{q-t} \circ (G \circ E')^x \circ N^t$, where $Y$ is public key and the pair of numbers $(t, x)$ is private key (the integers $t < q$ and $x < g$ are to be selected at random).

## 5    Conclusion

In this paper, two new BVMTs have been introduced to define the parameterized non-commutative multiplication operation in finite space of four-dimension vectors defined over the field $GF(p)$.

The BVMTs are characterized that each of them defines mutual associativity of all possible modifications of the multiplication of the vectors. The first BVMT defines an AFA that represents a FNR. Formula for the order of the multiplicative group of the considered finite non-commutative ring of the four-dimension vectors has been got and some properties of the subset of the non-invertible vectors have been investigated.

The second BVMT defines an AFA with multiplication operation possessing compression property. The AFA contains no global unit, it contains many different subsets in frame of which local bi-side unit exists.

Using formula (16) and selecting different values $t$ and different non-invertible vectors $N$ it is possible to define a variety of homomorphic maps.

Like in papers [12, 13], one can construct public-key crypto-schemes using the homomorphisms in the considered finite ring of four dimension vectors.

Future research in frame of the concerned topic is related with proving Statement 10, finding new BVMT defining other types of finite algebras of four-dimension vectors, consideration of the case of defining finite non-commutative algebras of the vectors having dimension $m > 4$.

# References

1. Sirwan, A., Majeed, N.: New algorithm for wireless network communication security. Int. J. Cryptogr. Inf. Secur. **6**(3/4), 1–8 (2016)
2. Feng, Y., Yang, G., Liu, J.K.: A new public remote integrity checking scheme with user and data privacy. Int. J. Appl. Cryptogr. **3**(3), 196–209 (2017)
3. Chiou, S.Y.: Novel digital signature schemes based on factoring and discrete logarithms. Int. J. Secur. Appl. **10**(3), 295–310 (2016)
4. Poulakis, D.: A variant of digital signature algorithm. Des. Codes Cryptogr. **51**(1), 99–104 (2009)
5. Yan, S.Y.: Quantum Computational Number Theory, 1st edn. Springer, Cham (2015). https://doi.org/10.1007/978-3-319-25823-2
6. Yan, S.Y.: Quantum Attacks on Public-Key Cryptosystems, 1st edn. Springer, Boston (2013). https://doi.org/10.1007/978-1-4419-7722-9
7. Shor, P.W.: Polynomial-time algorithms for prime factorization and discrete logarithms on quantum computer. SIAM J. Comput. **26**, 1484–1509 (1997)
8. Smolin, J.A., Smith, G., Vargo, A.: Oversimplifying quantum factoring. Nature **499**(7457), 163–165 (2013)
9. Federal Register: Announcing Request for Nominations for Public-Key Post-Quantum Cryptographic Algorithms. The Daily journal of the United States Government. https://www.gpo.gov/fdsys/pkg/FR-2016-12-20/pdf/2016-30615.pdf. Accessed 6 June 2018
10. Takagi, T. (ed.): PQCrypto 2016. LNCS, vol. 9606. Springer, Cham (2016). https://doi.org/10.1007/978-3-319-29360-8
11. Sakalauskas, E., Tvarijonas, P., Raulynaitis, A.: Key Agreement Protocol (KAP) using conjugacy and discrete logarithm problems in group representation level. Informatica **18**(1), 115–124 (2007)
12. Moldovyan, D.N.: Non-commutative finite groups as primitive of public-key cryptoschemes. Quasigroups Relat. Syst. **18**(2), 165–176 (2010)
13. Moldovyan, D.N., Moldovyan, N.A.: Cryptoschemes over hidden conjugacy search problem and attacks using homomorphisms. Quasigroups Relat. Syst. **18**(2), 177–186 (2010)
14. Kuz'min, A.S., Markov, V.T., Mikhalev, A.A., Mikhalev, A.V., Nechaev, A.A.: Cryptographical algorithms on groups and algebras. J. Math. Sci. **223**(5), 629–641 (2017)
15. Moldovyan, N.A., Moldovyanu, P.A.: Vector form of the finite fields $GF(p^m)$. Bul. Acad. Ştiinţe Repub. Mold. Mat. **3**(61), 1–7 (2009)
16. Ronyai, L.: Computing the structure of finite algebras. J. Symb. Comput. **9**, 355–373 (1990)

# Simulating the Irrigation Operations
# with Cellular Automata

Hiep Xuan Huynh[1(✉)], Nha Thanh Huynh[2], Toan Phung Huynh[1],
Son Van Tran[3], and Linh Thuy Thi Nguyen[1]

[1] Cantho University, Cantho City 94000, Vietnam
{hxhiep, hptoan, nttlinh}@ctu.edu.vn
[2] TMA Solutions, Hochiminh City 70000, Vietnam
nhathanh36@gmail.com
[3] Kiengiang Medical College, Kiengiang Province 91000, Vietnam
tvsonkl3@gmail.com

**Abstract.** In this paper, we propose a new simulation approach based on a cellular automata to predict the closing or opening of irrigation culvert. To solve this problem, water quality parameters such as salinity, temperature, pH, dissolved oxygen, etc. were measured at culverts. Then, opening or closing the culverts depending on the quality of the water there is considered. However, due to the large number of culverts, it is very time consuming to carry out manual measurements of all culverts. It is important to have a measure to help predict the water quality at culverts so as to reduce the amount of effort and time spent by farmers, meanwhile it helps farmers to feel secure to do the production (The simulations are based on data on water quality collected at culverts in subregion X - South Ca Mau, Ca Mau province, Vietnam).

**Keywords:** Water quality · Irrigation culverts · Simulation · Cellular automata

## 1 Introduction

The irrigation culvert (Fig. 1) is an irrigation structure to control the water level and regulate the flow. The culvert is one of the irrigation works belonging to the technical infrastructure, carrying out irrigation activities including water storage, water supply, drainage and salinity prevention. When irrigation activities are implemented, they must be organized, managed and operated closely, effectively and sustainably to meet the requirements of the task; give priority to protecting and meeting the requirements of direct service to people; ensure national food security.

In the recent years, there were a number of research projects on cellular automata integrating GIS and automotive technologies to simulate a demonstration pattern of wildfire activity with a flexible and user-friendly interface based on parameters such as wind speed, topography, fire propagation direction [19]; or constructed a model of macro cellular automata to simulate the biological treatment of contaminated soils [9]. This model is a hierarchical model, made up of a fluid dynamics class, a solubility class and a biological class, or proposed a cellular autoclave model for flood routing - simulating the flow of floods based on terrain elevation parameters [4]. However, these

© ICST Institute for Computer Sciences, Social Informatics and Telecommunications Engineering 2019
Published by Springer Nature Switzerland AG 2019. All Rights Reserved

P. Cong Vinh and V. Alagar (Eds.): ICCASA 2018/ICTCC 2018, LNICST 266, pp. 195–210, 2019.
https://doi.org/10.1007/978-3-030-06152-4_17

**Fig. 1.** A typical irrigation culvert (https://www.tienphong.vn/dia-oc/cong-song-kien-niem-mo-uoc-cua-nguoi-dan-khu-vuc-tu-giac-long-xuyen-999807.tpo).

studies have not applied the culvert cellular automata model into the simulation of the closing and opening of culverts based on the criteria of water quality.

Drainage culverts aim to prevent saltwater intrusion and to store fresh water for local agricultural and aquaculture (for short, agriculture instead of agriculture and aquaculture) production. In addition, drainage culverts also provide water (saline or sweet) for agricultural production as well as drainage as needed. For example, when people have a need for water, the water needs to be freshened, so the drainage canals near the estuary should be closed to avoid seawater intrusion. For drainage culverts on rivers or canals, it is advisable to store for sweet storage if people need fresh water for production such as growing rice or stocking for aquaculture. Or when people need fresh water and the water is salty, the nearby culvert should suggest opening to reduce salinity. As a result, the quality of water is very important to the opening or closing of culverts. Therefore, it is necessary to supervise and monitor the water quality periodically so that it is possible to predict the opening of culverts at the most unnoticed sites.

In this paper, a new simulation approach is proposed based on the model of cellular automata to predict the closing or opening of culverts. Simulation of the opening and closing of culverts is based on the existing drainage culverts system. The paper focuses on analyzing, proposing a cellular automata model and modeling rules, and installing tools to illustrate the closure and opening of culverts. The purpose is to contribute to support the prediction of the opening and closing of culverts based on water quality in order to reduce the time and effort of the person performing the measurement of water quality at culverts. This is where people can use water to meet their farming needs.

The article is organized into 6 sections: Sect. 1 presents introduction, Sect. 2 introduces culvert closing/opening model, Sect. 3 presents experimental data; Sect. 4 describes empirical tools and experiments and Sect. 5 discusses the experimental results and summarizes the results.

## 2   Irrigation Culvert Model

### 2.1   Culvert Cellular Automata

Irrigation culvert model based on cellular automata model [5, 10] is a model of a system of "culverts" with the following characteristics: (i) A culvert (or a cell) is located in a grid and (ii) each culvert has an adjacent area (neighborhood - Fig. 2). This can be defined in many ways, but it is usually a list of adjacent culverts. (iii) Each cell has a state. The number of possible states of cells is usually finite. The simplest example is that there are two possible states of 0 and 1 (or "on" and "off" or "open" and "closing"). (iv) The transition rules determine the change in the state of each cell.

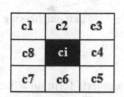  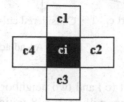

a. Moore adjacent area      b. von Neumann adjacent area

**Fig. 2.** Two types of adjacent area. In (a) the cell $c_i$ has an adjacent area with 8 cells and in (b) the cell $c_i$ has an adjacent area with 4 cells.

The adjacent area of the culvert is a group of culverts surrounding an existing culvert, defining an affected area, the state of the culvert, and its adjacent area during the time t affects the state of the culvert at time t + 1. Supposing that $x_{ij}$ is the culvert/cell at position (i, j), then S $(x_{ij})$ t is the state of the culvert $x_{ij}$ at time t. S $(x_{ij})$ (t + 1) is the state at time t + 1, which is defined as: $S_{x_{ij}}^{t+1} = f(S_{x_{ij}}^{t}, S_{\Omega_{x_{ij}}}^{t})$.

Inside, $\Omega_{x_{ij}}$ is the set of culverts in the neighborhood of the adjacent area of the culvert/cell $x_{ij}$, $S_{\Omega_{x_{ij}}}^{t}$ t is the set of states of the culverts $\Omega_{x_{ij}}$ at time t and f is a function represented by a set of transition rules.

The function f representing the set of transition rules will assume the values of: the state of the culvert at time t and the states of the neighboring states at time t to determine the state of the culvert under consideration time t + 1.

## 2.2   A Simple Culvert Cellular Automata

Simple culvert cellular automata model is a one-way culvert model [15]. The model include a culvert grid as a stream of culverts (Fig. 3), a set of states with of two states 0 or 1 (Fig. 4), an adjacent area includes considered culvert/cell ($c_i$) and two neighboring culverts: one left and one right (Fig. 5).

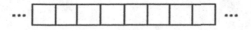

**Fig. 3.** An irrigation culvert grid.

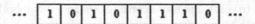

**Fig. 4.** A set of irrigation culvert states.

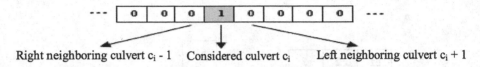

Right neighboring culvert $c_i - 1$    Considered culvert $c_i$    Left neighboring culvert $c_i + 1$

**Fig. 5.** An adjacent area.

A considered culvert ($c_i$) and two neighboring culverts form an adjacent area with three culverts. Thus, there will be $2^3 = 8$ initial states (Fig. 6).

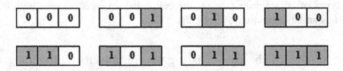

**Fig. 6.** A set of initial states.

Assuming that the state of a neighborhood at time $t = 0$ is known, the state of the remaining $t = 0$ can be determined. Based on the state at $t = 0$ and the rules of change it is determined the state of the culvert at the next $t = 1$, $t = 2$, $t = 3$,... (Figure 7).

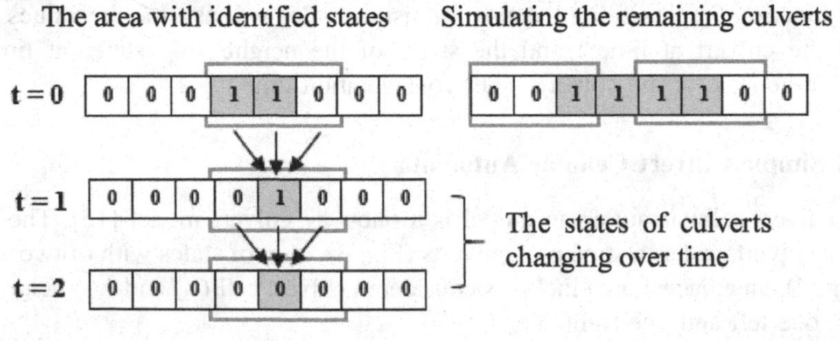

The area with identified states    Simulating the remaining culverts

| t = 0 | 0 | 0 | 0 | 1 | 1 | 0 | 0 | 0 |

| t = 1 | 0 | 0 | 0 | 0 | 1 | 0 | 0 | 0 |

| t = 2 | 0 | 0 | 0 | 0 | 0 | 0 | 0 | 0 |

The states of culverts changing over time

**Fig. 7.** The simulation of culvert states changing over time.

## 2.3 Culvert States

Each culvert in the network is seen as a cell in a cellular automata (CA) system [5, 10] and has a certain state corresponding to the open or closed state of the culvert and the direction of water at the culvert is flowing in or out, specifically, open, flowing states;

open, flowing; closed, flowing; closed, outflow and no data (Table 1). The water inlet or outlet is determined by the following principle: the direction of water flowing from the culvert to the inlet will be determined to be outflow and vice versa. The state set of a culvert is defined as $S = \{s_1, s_2, s_3, s_4, s_5\}$.

**Table 1.** The culvert states.

| States | Descriptions | Typical colors |
|--------|--------------|----------------|
| 1 | Open, inlet (flow in) | |
| 2 | Open, outlet (flow out) | |
| 3 | Closed, inlet | |
| 4 | Closed, outlet | |
| 5 | No data | |

## 2.4 Culvert Neighborhood

The network of culverts is considered as a graph G(V, E), where: V is the set of vertices, E is the set of edges. The set V is equivalent to the set of culverts $V = \{v_1, v_2, ..., v_n\}$. When considering a vertex and its neighbor, the Euclidean distance between two vertices (from the vertex looking at the remaining vertices), the smallest distance is considered and then the vertex will be the neighbor of the vertex considered. This is considered until the appropriate number of neighbors have been identified (up to 8 neighbors). Thus, each irrigation culvert will in fact be a cell in the cellular automata model and each cell will have a maximum of 8 neighbors (Figs. 8 and 9).

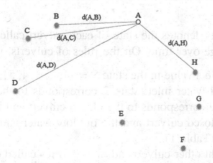

**Fig. 8.** Selecting culvert neighbors based on the Euclidean distance with a set of culverts {A, B, C, D, E, F, G, H}.

| | | Vam Dinh | May Doc | Cay Gia | Ba Chu | Tu Ta | Bao Chau | Kenh Cung | So Dua Nho | Lung Bon1 | Xeo Xay | Cai Chim | Cay Duong 9 | Que Hai | Ca Dai | Xeo Xu | Xeo Thang | Ma Tam | Muoi Ho | So Dua Lon | Ca Nay | Xeo Dop | Lung Bon2 | Lung Tram | Bo De |
|---|---|---|---|---|---|---|---|---|---|---|---|---|---|---|---|---|---|---|---|---|---|---|---|---|---|
| | | 1 | 2 | 3 | 4 | 5 | 6 | 7 | 8 | 9 | 10 | 11 | 12 | 13 | 14 | 15 | 16 | 17 | 18 | 19 | 20 | 21 | 22 | 23 | 24 |
| Vam Dinh | 1 | | 2 | | | | | | | 7 | 1 | 3 | 5 | | | | | | | | 8 | | 4 | 6 | |
| May Doc | 2 | 1 | | | | | | | | 7 | 3 | 2 | 4 | | | | | | | | 8 | | 6 | 5 | |
| Cay Gia | 3 | | | | 2 | | | | | | | | 1 | | | | | | | | | | | | |
| Ba Chu | 4 | 8 | 7 | 2 | | 6 | | | | | | 4 | 3 | 1 | 5 | | | | | | | | | | |
| Tu Ta | 5 | | | | 4 | | 2 | | | | | 8 | 5 | 3 | 1 | | | 6 | 7 | | | | | | |
| Bao Chau | 6 | | | | 5 | 1 | | | 8 | | | | 4 | 3 | 2 | | | 6 | 7 | | | | | | |
| Kenh Cung | 7 | | | | | | | | 2 | | | | | | | | | | 1 | | | | | | |
| So Dua Nho | 8 | | | | | | 5 | 2 | | | | | | 8 | | | | 4 | 3 | 1 | 6 | 7 | | | |
| Lung Bon 1 | 9 | 3 | 5 | | | | | | | | 4 | | | | | | | | | | 8 | 6 | 7 | 2 | 1 |
| Xeo Xay | 10 | 1 | 2 | | | | | 6 | | | | 7 | 8 | | | | | | | | | | 5 | 4 | 3 |
| Cai Chim | 11 | 3 | 1 | | 5 | | | | | | 4 | | | 2 | 6 | 7 | | | | | | | | 8 | |
| Cay Duong | 12 | 8 | 3 | 1 | 5 | 7 | | | | | | 2 | | 4 | 6 | | | | | | | | | | |
| Que Hai | 13 | | 7 | 4 | 1 | 3 | 8 | | | | | 6 | 5 | | 2 | | | | | | | | | | |
| Ca Dai | 14 | | 8 | | 3 | 2 | 4 | | | | | 6 | 5 | 1 | | | | 7 | | | | | | | |
| Xeo Xu | 15 | | | | 7 | 3 | 2 | | 8 | | | | 6 | 4 | | 1 | 5 | | | | | | | | |
| Xeo Thang | 16 | | | | | | | | | | | | | 1 | | | 2 | | | | | | | | |
| Ma Tam | 17 | | | | 7 | 5 | | | 3 | | | | 6 | | | 1 | | 2 | | | 4 | 8 | | | |
| Muoi Ho | 18 | | | | 8 | 4 | 2 | 3 | | | | | 6 | | | 1 | | | | | 5 | 7 | | | |
| So Dua Lon | 19 | | | | | 6 | | 1 | | | | | 8 | | | | | 4 | 3 | | 2 | 5 | 7 | | |
| Ca Nay | 20 | | | | 8 | | | | 6 | | | | | | 7 | | | 4 | 5 | 2 | | 1 | 3 | | |

**Fig. 9.** An example of culvert neighbor matrix with 20 culverts. Each culvert will in fact be a cell in the culvert pattern and each culvert will have a maximum of 8 neighbors. Neighbor matrix after selection (matrix 18x24 with the place name in Ca Mau province):

Based on the culvert cellular automata model to update the opening/closing status of the culverts, we have set of culverts (Fig. 10):

| | 16 | | | | |
|---|---|---|---|---|---|
| 21 | 19 | 17 | 3 | 4 | |
| 15 | 20 | 2 | 11 | 24 | 7 |
| 18 | 23 | 1 | 10 | 13 | 8 |
| | 9 | 22 | 12 | 14 | 6 |
| | | | | 5 | |

**Fig. 10.** Set of cells/culverts in irrigation culvert cellular automata model.

A set of cells/culverts denotes the state of each culvert called a configuration. This configuration will change over time. On the rules of culverts, we have:

- Each culvert will have a value in the state $S = \{1, 2, 3, 4, 5\}$. State 1 corresponds to the open culvert and water inlet, state 2 corresponds to the open culvert and the outflow water, state 3 corresponds to the closed culvert and incoming water, state 4 corresponds to the closed culvert and the outflow water and state 5 corresponds to the absence of data (Table 1).
- Each culvert has eight other culverts adjoining to it - called eight adjacent culverts.
- The state of a culvert current at time $t + 1$ will be determined based on the state of the neighboring 8 wells and their state at time t.

– The change of culvert will follow a principle defined in the rules of culverts, which apply equally to each culvert and do not change over time (Fig. 11).

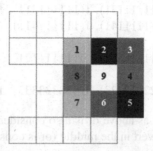

**Fig. 11.** An example of the states of adjacent culverts and the current considered culvert.

In Fig. 5, the culverts under consideration (9) have no data (5), there are 8 adjacent culverts, of which 2 open and outlet (2), 2 culverts are closed, inlet (3) and 2 open, outlets (1). Over time, the state of the cell under consideration will change, the change in the state of the cells under consideration follows a set of rules in the culvert cellular automata rules.

## 3   Irrigation Culvert Rules

### 3.1   Transition Rules

A rule that determines how a culvert changes state based on the neighbors around is called a transition rule with a mapping function f: $S^9 \rightarrow S$. A rule in the rule set shows the changing rules of the central culverts based on neighboring culverts, each of which has 5 states of 1, 2, 3, 4 or 5. There are $5^9$ different patterns. For each set of 9 culverts, each sample will be mapped to 1, 2, 3, 4 or 5 for the centered/considered state, i.e. we have $5^9 = 1\,953\,125$ rules for a set of rules. So the input of a 9 bit rule is the state of the culvert and the neighbors are arranged in the order shown in Fig. 12.

| S1 | S2 | S3 |
|----|----|----|
| S8 | S9 | S4 |
| S7 | S6 | S5 |

**Fig. 12.** The order of culvert put in the rule set.

Thus, the rule set includes:

f(111111111),
f(111111112), f(111111121), f(111111211), f(111112111),...
f(111111113), f(111111131), f(111111311), f(111113111),...
f(111111114), f(111111141), f(111111411), f(111114111),...
...
f(1111111122), f(111111221), f(111111212), f(111111221),...
...
f(111111111), f(222222222), f(333333333), f(444444444).

where f is a function mapped as above or is also considered to be a rule to update the $9^{th}$ bit, i.e. the state of the culvert in the middle (or is considered). Each rule in the rule set will be of the form:

$$f(S1, S2, S3, S4, S5, S6, S7, S8, S9) \rightarrow 1$$
$$\text{or} \quad f(S1, S2, S3, S4, S5, S6, S7, S8, S9) \rightarrow 2$$
$$\text{or} \quad f(S1, S2, S3, S4, S5, S6, S7, S8, S9) \rightarrow 3$$
$$\text{or} \quad f(S1, S2, S3, S4, S5, S6, S7, S8, S9) \rightarrow 4$$

Example:

Rule f(111223345) → 1

Rule f(222222222) → 3|

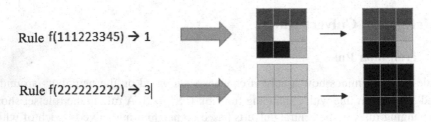

**Fig. 13.** An example of the rule set.

## 3.2  Constructing a Transition Rule Set

**The Considered Culvert Only Knows an Adjacent Culvert Status.** A rule proposed as the state of the culvert considered is equal to the state of a nearby culvert. There are 8 culverts with 5 states so the rule of this state is: 8 x 5 = 40 (Fig. 14), where 8 are the same rules when the corresponding state is 5 (Fig. 13).

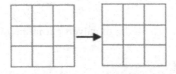

**Fig. 14.** The rule when an adjacent culvert status is recognized.

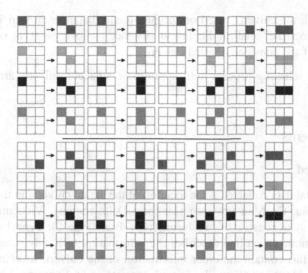

**Fig. 15.** The rule set when an adjacent culvert status is recognized.

**The Considered Culvert Knowing more than Two Adjacent Culverts Status.** A rule proposed as the state of the culvert considered the integer value of the neighboring culvert whose state is known. The number of rules is: $5^8 = 390\ 625$ (Fig. 15).=

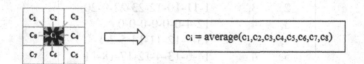

**Fig. 16.** The rule when knowing more than two adjacent culvert status

The proposed rule formula is based on data available in selected provinces of the X-subregion of the Mekong Delta region (Soc Trang and Kien Giang provinces), Vietnam. In addition, the correctness of the rule will be tested and commented by experts to ensure that the simulation is more reliable and can be easily applied to practice (Fig. 16).

## 4  Neighbor Selecting Algorithm

Based on the graph G(V, E), in which V is the set of culverts and E is the set of distances, we have developed a neighbor selecting algorithm with a view to finding the adjacent culverts of a tested culvert by calculating its Euclidean distance from itself to the rest of culverts. The algorithm includes the following steps:

Step 1: List all the current culverts, in turn calculate the Euclidean distance from a considered/tested culvert to the rest of culverts.

Step 2: Rank the culverts based on the just-found distances in step 1

Step 3: Select the smallest Euclidean distance, whose point is considered the adjacency of the considered/tested culvert.

Repeat this selecting process until appropriate adjacent culverts are identified (8 adjacencies).

## 5   Experiments

### 5.1   Data Used

The experimental data collected is the location of the actual culverts in the subregion X - South Ca Mau, Ca Mau province (Mekong Delta region), Vietnam. Information structure of the data consists of two forms (type 1 and type 2). Type 1 consists of 25 lines and 3 columns, each line describes the information of a culvert and 1 headline. The three columns contain the order information of the culvert, its state, and its corresponding neighborhood (Fig. 17). Type 2 consists of 24 lines and 3 columns, lines containing information about culverts and the 3 columns correspond to information about coordinates, names and status of culverts. (Figure 18).

| No, On/Off (0,1,2,..), In/Out (0,1,2,..) | | |
|---|---|---|
| 1,  | 2,  | 10-2-11-22-12-23-9-20 |
| 2,  | 3,  | 1-11-10-12-23-22-9-20 |
| 3,  | 4,  | 12-4-0-0-0-0-0-0 |
| 4,  | 1,  | 13-3-12-11-14-5-2-1 |
| 5,  | 4,  | 14-6-13-4-12-17-18-11 |
| 6,  | 2,  | 5-15-14-13-4-17-18-8 |
| 7,  | 3,  | 18-8-0-0-0-0-0-0 |
| 8,  | 4,  | 19-7-18-17-6-20-21-14 |
| 9,  | 1,  | 23-22-1-10-2-20-21-19 |
| 10, | 2,  | 1-2-24-23-22-9-11-12 |
| 11, | 0,  | 2-12-1-10-4-13-14-23 |
| 12, | 0,  | 3-11-2-13-4-14-5-1 |
| 13, | 0,  | 4-14-5-3-12-11-2-6 |
| 14, | 0,  | 13-5-4-6-12-11-17-2 |
| 15, | 0,  | 16-6-5-14-17-13-4-8 |
| 16, | 0,  | 15-17-0-0-0-0-0-0 |
| ... | | |
| ... | | |

**Fig. 17.**  List of culverts examined.

The rule set of the culvert cellular automata model is stored in text with each line as a sequence of input states of the transition rule (Fig. 19).

| Coordinates | Names | Status |
|---|---|---|
| 200@102, | Vam Dinh, | 2 |
| 236@70, | May Doc, | 3 |
| 564@30, | Cay Gia, | 4 |
| 612@109, | Ba Chu, | 1 |
| 596@434, | Bao Chau, | 2 |
| 346@550, | Kenh Cung, | 3 |
| 321@446, | So Dua Nho, | 4 |
| 46@340, | Lung Bon, | 1 |
| 86@134, | Xeo Xay, | 2 |
| 367@55, | Cai Chim, | 0 |
| 529@36, | Cay Duong, | 0 |
| 612@146, | Que Hai, | 0 |
| 621@237, | Ca Dai, | 0 |
| 462@535, | Xeo Su, | 0 |
| 435@548, | Xeo Thang, | 0 |
| 415@549, | Ma Tam, | 0 |
| ...... | | |
| ..... | | |

**Fig. 18.** Coordinates, names and status of culverts.

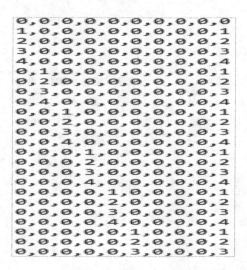

```
0,0,0,0,0,0,0,0,0,0
1,0,0,0,0,0,0,0,0,1
2,0,0,0,0,0,0,0,0,2
3,0,0,0,0,0,0,0,0,3
4,0,0,0,0,0,0,0,0,4
0,1,0,0,0,0,0,0,0,1
0,2,0,0,0,0,0,0,0,2
0,3,0,0,0,0,0,0,0,3
0,4,0,0,0,0,0,0,0,4
0,0,1,0,0,0,0,0,0,1
0,0,2,0,0,0,0,0,0,2
0,0,3,0,0,0,0,0,0,3
0,0,4,0,0,0,0,0,0,4
0,0,0,1,0,0,0,0,0,1
0,0,0,2,0,0,0,0,0,2
0,0,0,3,0,0,0,0,0,3
0,0,0,4,0,0,0,0,0,4
0,0,0,0,1,0,0,0,0,1
0,0,0,0,2,0,0,0,0,2
0,0,0,0,3,0,0,0,0,3
0,0,0,0,4,0,0,0,0,4
0,0,0,0,0,1,0,0,0,1
0,0,0,0,0,2,0,0,0,2
0,0,0,0,0,3,0,0,0,3
```

**Fig. 19.** Rule set content.

## 5.2    Used Tool

The experimental tool is based on the Netgen platform [14] - a multilingual support platform, including the Smalltalk language [7], developed by our cooperation with Brest University - France. This tool has the following main functions: map display (Google Map, Open Street Map), displaying the points to be simulated and points where the data has a certain coordinates on the map, performing status change for the drainage cellular automata model, displaying Google Map maps with previously saved images based on the NetGen toolkit - QuickMap and PickCell developed by UBO (Université de Bretagne Occidentale).

*Description:* Display the location of the points to be simulated and points where the data is available on the map.

*Input:* A txt file containing geographic coordinates of points in the form of longitude @ latitude or x @ y (coordinates defined on the tool), the data is stored in the tool.

*Results:* The tool calculates and displays the location of points on the map based on stored data.

### Perform Status Change for the Culvert Cellular Automata Model

*Description:* Apply the rule set of the culvert cellular automata model to convert the state of the culverts to be simulated (based on the drainage status of the data) so that the state of the culverts to be simulated has their status different from 5 - no data yet.

*Input:* The txt file contains the rules

*Results:* The cellular automata model with the culvert to be simulated had definite states.

### Tool Interface
(See Fig. 20)

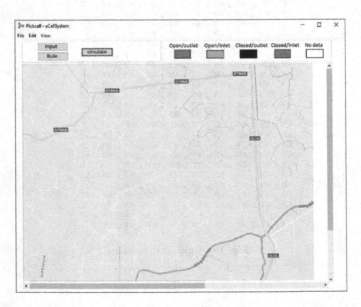

**Fig. 20.** Experiment tool.

### 5.3    Scenario 1: Transforms the State of the Culverts When They Only Know the State of a Nearby Neighbor

In this case, we consider culverts with the condition that they only know the information of a single neighbor. The tool will perform the conversion of the state of the culvert points based on the model of the built-in cellular automata culvert. The initial configuration (Fig. 19) of the model is generated by the input data set, data on the status of known culverts.

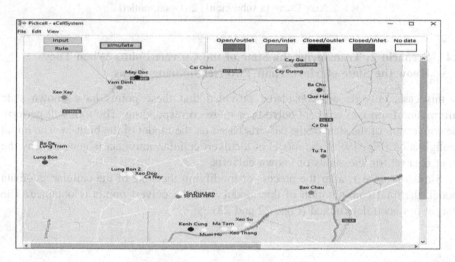

**Fig. 21.** The initial configuration.

After the state modification of the culvert cellular automata model is implemented, it is possible to obtain the final configuration of the model with the identified culverts (Fig. 21).

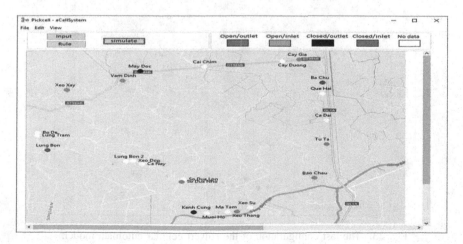

**Fig. 22.** The last configuration.

In the last configuration of the model, the status of the culvert named Xeo Thang has been changed from status 5 - data not available to status 2 - open/outlet. The results obtained after experiment with case 1 on the data of culvert point of the subregion X - South Ca Mau are as follows (Table 2):

**Table 2.** The results.

| No | Culvert | Status |
|----|---------|--------|
| 1 | Xeo Thang (a subregion) | 2 (Open, outlet) |

### 5.4    Scenario 2: Transforms the State of the Culvert Points When They Know the State of More Than Two Neighboring Areas

In this case, culverts are considered provided that these points have known state information from two adjacent culverts or more corresponding. The tool will perform the conversion of the state of the culverts based on the model of the built-in. The initial configuration (Fig. 19) of the model of a culvert cellular automata is generated by the input data set, on the status of known culverts.

Similar to case 1, after the process of modifying the state of the cellular automata model, the final configuration of this model with the culvert points is obtained. The margin has been determined (Figs. 22 and 23).

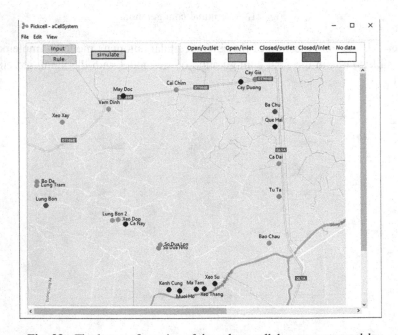

**Fig. 23.** The last configuration of the culvert cellular automata model.

In the final configuration of the model, the state of the 14 culverts to be simulated has been determined by the known data of the neighboring culvert lines.

The results obtained after experiment with case 2 on the data of culvert point of the subregion X - South Ca Mau, Ca Mau province, Vietnam are as follows (Table 3):

**Table 3.** The results

| No | Culvert points (culverts at selected subregions) | Status |
|----|---------------------------------------------------|-----------------|
| 1  | Cai Chim     | 2 (Open, outlet) |
| 2  | Cay Duong    | 3 (Closed, inlet) |
| 3  | Que Hai      | 3 (Closed, inlet) |
| 4  | Ca Đai       | 2 (Open, outlet) |
| 5  | Xeo Su       | 3 (Closed, inlet) |
| 6  | Xeo Thang    | 3 (Closed, inlet) |
| 7  | Ma Tam       | 3 (Closed, inlet) |
| 8  | Muoi Ho      | 3 (Closed, inlet) |
| 9  | Big So Dua   | 2 (Open, outlet) |
| 10 | Ca Nay       | 3 (Closed, inlet) |
| 11 | Xeo Dop      | 2 (Open, outlet) |
| 12 | Lung Bon 2   | 2 (Open, outlet) |
| 13 | Lung Tram    | 2 (Open, outlet) |
| 14 | Bo De        | 2 (Open, outlet) |

# 6  Conclusion

In this paper, a new approach is presented based on a culvert cellular automata model to simulate the opening and closing of irrigation systems based on the approach of autoclave theory. We have built a model of automobile and culvert irrigation and proposed the law for the model of automobile cooled culvert. The simulations are verified on data of water quality collected at the culverts in sub-area South of Ca Mau, Ca Mau province, Vietnam. This proposal will help support the prediction of opening and closing water-based culverts in order to reduce the time and effort of the person performing the measurement of water quality at culverts, based on which people can use water according to their agricultural production needs.

# References

1. Averill, M.L., Kelton, D.W.: Simulation Modeling and Analysis. Mcgraw-Hill Inc, Singapore (1991)
2. Bandini, S.: Guest editorial - cellular automata. Futur. Gener. Comput. Syst. **18**, v–vi (2002)
3. Burks, A.W.: Essays on Cellular Automata. University of Illinois Press, Urbana (1970)
4. Cai, X., Li, Y., Guo, X., Wu, W.: Mathematical model for flood routing based on cellular automaton. Water Sci. Eng. **7**(2), 133–142 (2014)

5. Chaudhuri, P.P., Chowdhury, D.R., Nandi, S., Chatterjee, S.: Additive Cellular Automata – Theory and Applications, vol. 1. IEEE Computer Society Press, CA (1997). ISBN 0-8186-7717-1
6. Gardner, M.: Mathematical games - the fantastic combinations of john conway's new solitaire game 'life'. Sci. Am. **223**, 120–123 (1970)
7. Goldberg, A., Robson, D.: Smalltalk-80: The Language and its Implementation. Addison-Wesley, Boston (1983). ISBN 0-201-11371-6
8. Gordon, G.: System Simulation. Prentice Hall of India Private Limited, Delhi (1989)
9. Gregorio, S.D., Serra, R., Villani, M.: Applying cellular automata to complex environmental problems: The simulation of the bioremediation of contaminated soils. Theoret. Comput. Sci. **217**, 131–156 (1999)
10. Kari, J.: Theory of cellular automata: a survey. Theoret. Comput. Sci. **334**, 3–33 (2005)
11. Langton, C.G.: Self-reproduction in cellular automata. Physica D **10**, 134–144 (1984)
12. Mitchell, M., Hraber, P.T., Crutchfield, J.P.: Revisiting the edge of chaos: evolving cellular automata to perform computations. Complex Syst. **7**, 89–130 (1993)
13. Nguyen, C.H., Nguyen, P.T.A.: Modeling System and Simulation. Hanoi University of Science and Technology, Vietnam (2006)
14. Pottier, P., Lucas, P.Y.: Dynamic networks "Netgen: objectives, installation, use and programming". Université de Bretagne Occidentale (2015). https://github.com/NetGen Project. Accessed 03 Oct 2018
15. Shiffman, D., Shannon, F., Zannah, M.,: Cellular automata. In: The nature of Code: Simulating Natural Systems with Processing, Chap. 7, pp. 323–354. Springer, Heidelberg (2012). ISBN-13: 9780985930806
16. Wolfram, S.: A New Kind of Science, 1280 pages. Wolfram Media, Champaign (2002)
17. Wolfram, S.: Cellular Automata and Complexity. World Scientific, Singapore (1994). ISBN 9971-50-124-4 pbk
18. Wolfram, S.: Theory and Applications of Cellular Automata. World Scientific, Singapore (1986). ISBN 9971-50-124-4 pbk
19. Yassemi, S., Dragícevíc, S., Schmidt, M.: Design and implementation of an integrated GIS-based cellular automata model to characterize forest fire behaviour. Ecol. Model. **210**, 71–84 (2008)
20. Yu, J., Chen, Y., Wu, J.P.: Cellular automata and GIS based land use suitability simulation for irrigated agriculture. In: 18th World IMACS/MODSIM Congress, Cairns, Australia, 13–17 July 2009
21. Yu, J., Chen, Y., Wu, J., Khane, S.: Cellular automata-based spatial multi-criteria land suitability simulation for irrigated agriculture. Int. J. Geogr. Inf. Sci. **25**, 131–148 (2011)

# Modeling with Words Based on Hedge Algebra

Nguyen Van Han[1]($\boxtimes$) and Phan Cong Vinh[2]

[1] Faculty of Information Technology, College of Science, Hue University,
77 Nguyen Hue street, Phu Nhuan ward, Hue city, Vietnam
nvhan@fit-hitu.edu.vn
[2] Faculty of Information Technology, Nguyen Tat Thanh University,
300A Nguyen Tat Thanh street, Ward 13 District 4, Ho Chi Minh city, Vietnam
pcvinh@ntt.edu.vn

**Abstract.** In this paper, we introduce a method for modeling with words based on hedge algebra using fuzzy cognitive map. Our model, called linguistic cognitive map, consists of set of vertices and edges with value to be linguistic variables. We figure out relationship between the length of linguistic variables for fuzzifying data and a number of partition from unit interval. We also prove finite properties of state space, generating from linguistic cognitive map.

**Keywords:** Fuzzy logics · Linguistic variable · Hedge algebra
Fuzzy cognitive map

## 1 Introduction

In everyday life, people use natural language (NL) for analysing, reasoning, and finally, make their decisions. Computing with words (CWW) [5] is a mathematical solution of computational problems stated in an NL. CWW based on fuzzy set and fuzzy logic, introduced by L.A. Zadeh is an approximate method on interval [0,1]. In linguistic domain, linguistic hedges play an important role for generating set of linguistic variables. A well known application of fuzzy logic (FL) is fuzzy cognitive map (FCM), introduced by Kosko [1], combined fuzzy logic with neural network. FCM has a lots of applications in both modeling and reasoning fuzzy knowledge [3,4] on interval [0,1] but not in linguistic values, However, many applications cannot model in numerical domain [5], for example, linguistic summarization problems [6]. To solve this problem, in the paper, we use an abstract algebra, called hedge algebra (HA) as a tool for computing with words.

The remainder of paper is organized as follows. Section 2 reviews some main concepts of computing with words based on HA in Subsect. 2.1 and describes several primary concepts for FCM in Subsect. 2.2. In Sect. 3, we introduce an approach technique to modeling with words using HA. Sect. 4 outlines discussion and future work. Section 5 concludes the paper.

© ICST Institute for Computer Sciences, Social Informatics and Telecommunications Engineering 2019
Published by Springer Nature Switzerland AG 2019. All Rights Reserved
P. Cong Vinh and V. Alagar (Eds.): ICCASA 2018/ICTCC 2018, LNICST 266, pp. 211–217, 2019.
https://doi.org/10.1007/978-3-030-06152-4_18

## 2　Preliminaries

This section presents basic concepts of HA and FCM used in the paper.

### 2.1　Hedge Algebra

In this section, we review some HA knowledges related to our research paper and give basic definitions. First definition of a HA is specified by 3-Tuple $HA = (X, H, \leq)$ in [7]. In [8] to easily simulate fuzzy knowledge, two terms $G$ and $C$ are inserted to 3-Tuple so $HA = (X, G, C, H, \leq)$ where $H \neq \emptyset$, $G = \{c^+, c^-\}$, $C = \{0, W, 1\}$. Domain of X is $L = Dom(X) = \{\delta c \mid c \in G, \delta \in H^*(\text{hedge string over H})\}$, $\{L, \leq\}$ is a POSET (partial order set) and $x = h_n h_{n-1} \ldots h_1 c$ is said to be a canonical string of linguistic variable $x$.

**Example 1.** Fuzzy subset $X$ is Age, $G = \{c^+ = young; c^- = old\}$, $H = \{less; more; very\}$ so term-set of linguistic variable Age X is $L(X)$ or $L$ for short: $L = \{very\ less\ young\ ;\ less\ young\ ;\ young\ ;\ more\ young\ ;\ very\ young\ ;\ very\ very\ young \ldots\}$

Fuzziness properties of elements in HA, specified by $fm$ (fuzziness measure) [8] as follows:

**Definition 2.1.** A mapping $fm : L \rightarrow [0, 1]$ is said to be the fuzziness measure of $L$ if:

1. $\sum_{c \in \{c^+, c^-\}} fm(c) = 1$, $fm(0) = fm(w) = fm(1) = 0$.
2. $\sum_{h_i \in H} fm(h_i x) = fm(x)$, $x = h_n h_{n-1} \ldots h_1 c$, the canonical form.
3. $fm(h_n h_{n-1} \ldots h_1 c) = \prod_{i=1}^{n} fm(h_i) \times \mu(x)$.

### 2.2　Fuzzy Cognitive Map

Fuzzy cognitive map (FCM) is feedback dynamical system for modeling fuzzy causal knowledge, introduced by Kosko [1]. FCM is a set of nodes, which present concepts and a set of directed edges to link nodes. The edges represent the causal links between these concepts. Mathematically, a FCM bis defined by.

**Definition 2.2.** A FCM is a 4-Tuple:

$$FCM = \{C, E, \mathcal{C}, f\} \tag{1}$$

In which:

1. $C = \{C_1, C_2, \ldots, C_n\}$ is the set of N concepts forming the nodes of a graph.

2. $E : (C_i, C_j) \longrightarrow e_{ij} \in \{-1, 0, 1\}$ is a function associating $e_{ij}$ with a pair of concepts $(C_i, C_j)$, so that $e_{ij}$ = "weight of edge directed from $C_i$ to $C_j$. The connection matrix $E(N \times N) = \{e_{ij}\}_{N \times N}$

3. The map: $\mathcal{C} : C_i \longrightarrow C_i(t) \in [0, 1], t \in N$

4. With $C(0) = [C_1(0, C_2(0), \ldots, C_n(0)] \in [0, 1]^N$ is the initial vector, recurring transformation function $f$ defined as:

$$C_j(t + 1) = f(\sum_{i=1}^{N} e_{ij} C_i(t)) \tag{2}$$

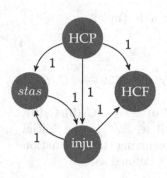

**Example 2.** Fig.1 shows a medical problem from expert domain of strokes and blood clotting involving. Concepts C={blood stasis (stas), endothelial injury ( inju), hypercoagulation factors (HCP and HCF)} [2]. The conection matrix is:

$$E = (e_{ij})_{4\times4} = \begin{pmatrix} 0 & 1 & 1 & 1 \\ 0 & 0 & 1 & 0 \\ 0 & 1 & 0 & 1 \\ 0 & 0 & 0 & 0 \end{pmatrix}$$

**Fig. 1.** A simple FCM

FCMs have played a vital role in the applications of scientific areas, including expert system, robotics, medicine, education, information technology, prediction, etc. [3,4] (Fig. 1).

## 3  Modeling with Words

Our model, based on linguistic variables, is constructed from linguistic hedge of HA. The following are definitions in our research paper.

**Definition 3.1** (Linguistic lattice). With $\mathbb{L}$ as in the Sect. 2.1, set $\{\wedge, \vee\}$ are logical operators, defined in [7,8], a linguistic lattice $\mathcal{L}$ is a tuple:

$$\mathcal{L} = (\mathbb{L}, \vee, \wedge, 0, 1) \tag{3}$$

**Property 3.1.** *The following are some properties for $\mathcal{L}$:*

1. *$\mathcal{L}$ is a linguistic-bounded lattice.*
2. *$(\mathbb{L}, \vee)$ and $(\mathbb{L}, \wedge)$ are semigroups.*

*Proof.* Without loss of generality, let $\mathbb{L} = \{\rho\, c^+ | \rho \in (H^+)^* \wedge c^+ \in G\}$. W is the neutral element in HA, we have:

1. $0 < w < c^+ < 1$ and for $\forall\, \rho \in (H^+)^*$ : $\rho 0 < \rho w < \rho c^+ < \rho 1$. Because $\rho 0 = 0$; $\rho w = w$; $\rho 1 = 1$. This is equivalent to: $0 < \rho c^+ < 1$ or $\mathcal{L}$ is bounded
2. Let $\circ = \wedge$ or $\circ = \vee$ be operators in HA and $\{p, q, r\} \in X$. Applying definitions of operators $\wedge$ and $\vee$ from [9]:
   $p \circ (q \circ r) \wedge (\circ = \vee) = max\{p, max\{q, r\}\} = max\{p, q, r\} = (p \circ q) \circ r \wedge (\circ = \vee)$

$\square$

**Definition 3.2.** A linguistic cognitive map (LCM) is a 4- Tuple:

$$LCM = \{C, E, \mathcal{C}, f\} \tag{4}$$

In which:

1. $C = \{C_1, C_2, \ldots, C_n\}$ is the set of N concepts forming the nodes of a graph.
2. $E : (C_i, C_j) \longrightarrow e_{ij} \in \mathbb{L}; e_{ij} =$ "weight of edge directed from $C_i$ to $C_j$. The connection matrix $E(N \times N) = \{e_{ij}\}_{N \times N} \in \mathbb{L}^{N \times N}$

3. The map: $\mathcal{C} : C_i \longrightarrow C_i(t) \in \mathbb{L}, t \in N$
4. With $C(0) = [C_1(0), C_2(0), \ldots, C_n(0)] \in \mathbb{L}^N$ is the initial vector, recurring transformation function $f$ defined as:

$$C_j(t+1) = f(\sum_{i=1}^{N} e_{ij}C_i(t)) \in \mathbb{L} \tag{5}$$

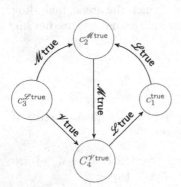

**Example 3.** Fig. 2 shows a simple LCM. Let

$$\mathbb{HA} = <\mathcal{X} = \text{truth}; c^+ = \text{true}; \mathcal{H} = \{\mathscr{L}, \mathscr{M}, \mathscr{V}\}> \tag{6}$$

be a HA with order as $\mathscr{L} < \mathscr{M} < \mathscr{V}$ ( $\mathscr{L}$ for less, $\mathscr{M}$ for more and $\mathscr{V}$ for very are hedges ). $C = \{c_1, c_2, c_3, c_4\}$ is the set of 4 concepts with corresponding values $\mathcal{C} = \{\text{true}, \mathscr{M}\text{true}, \mathscr{L}\text{true}, \mathscr{V}\text{true}\}$

**Fig. 2.** A simple LCM

Square matrix:

$$M = (m_{ij} \in \mathbb{L})_{4\times 4} = \begin{vmatrix} 0 & \mathscr{L}\text{true} & 0 & 0 \\ 0 & 0 & 0 & \mathscr{M}\text{true} \\ 0 & \mathscr{M}\text{true} & 0 & \mathscr{V}\text{true} \\ \mathscr{L}\text{true} & 0 & 0 & 0 \end{vmatrix}.$$

is the adjacency matrix of LCM. Causal relation between $c_i$ and $c_j$ is $m_{ij}$, for example if $i = 1, j = 2$ then causal relation between $c_1$ and $c_2$ is: "*if $c_1$ is true then $c_2$ is $\mathscr{M}$true is $\mathscr{L}$true* "or let $\mathcal{P}=$" if $c_1$ is true then $c_2$ is $\mathscr{M}$true" be a proposition then truth($\mathcal{P}$) = $\mathscr{L}$true (Fig. 2).

To have well fuzzify unit interval $\mathbb{I} = [0, 1]$ with $\mathbb{L}$, we need a number of hedges large enough. Assume $\hbar c = h_n h_{n-1} \ldots h_1 c$, accuracy in presenting interval $\mathbb{I}$ must be proportion to $length(h)$. Set $|\hbar| = \text{length}(\hbar)$, a question is what is the $|\hbar|$ value to be good enough for fuzzifying without increasing complexity. The following theorem clarifies this question.

**Theorem 3.1.** *Linguistic representations for unit interval*

- *Let sequences $\{\mathbb{I}_j\}_{j=1}^k$ be $k$ partitions of $\mathbb{I}$, $I$ is index set, for $\forall j, l \in I \wedge j \neq l$*

$$\mathbb{I} = \cup_{j=1}^k \mathbb{I}_j; \mathbb{I}_j \cap \mathbb{I}_l = \emptyset \tag{7}$$

- *Let*

$$\hbar c = h_n h_{n-1} \ldots h_1 c \tag{8}$$

*be a linguistic variable, $\hbar c \in \mathbb{L}$, $\bigvee$ for max operator, $H$ is a set of hedges $h_i, i \in I$.*

*Then:*

$$|\hbar| < \frac{\log(\frac{k-1}{k})}{\log(\bigvee_{h_i \in H} fm(h_i))} \tag{9}$$

*Proof.*

$$\mathbb{I} = \{\mathbb{I}_1, \mathbb{I}_2, \ldots, \mathbb{I}_k\}$$
$$= \{(0, \frac{1}{k}], (\frac{1}{k}, \frac{2}{k}], \ldots, (\frac{k-2}{k}, \frac{k-1}{k}], (\frac{k-1}{k}, 1)\}$$

Let $\hbar_k c = h_n h_{n-1} \ldots h_1 c \in \mathbb{L}$ to represent a point in $\mathbb{I}_k$, then

$$fm(\hbar_k c) = \prod_{h_i \in H}^n fm(h_i) \times \mu(c)$$
$$\leq (\bigvee_{h_i \in H} fm(h_i))^n \times \mu(c) < (\bigvee_{h_i \in H} fm(h_i))^n. \text{ because } \mu(c) < 1$$
$$so, \exists n \in \mathbb{N} : \frac{k-1}{k} < (\bigvee_{h_i \in H} fm(h_i))^n < 1$$
$$And : \log(\frac{k-1}{k}) < \log((\bigvee_{h_i \in H} fm(h_i))^n) < \log(1)$$
$$Therefore : \frac{\log(\frac{k-1}{k})}{\log(\bigvee_{h_i \in H} fm(h_i))} > n > 0$$

$\square$

Theorem 3.1 is important in limiting the length of linguistic variables for fuzzifying knowledge. On the other hand, knowing $|\hbar|$ value, the complexity of computations will be decreased

From Eq. (5), let $\mathcal{C}^n = \{C(i)\}_{i=1}^n = \{C(0), C(1), \ldots, C(n)\}$ be a set of state space, we want to know whether $\mathcal{C}^n$ finite or infinite. Finding $\mathcal{C}^n$ helps to limit searching space in many cases. Size of $\mathcal{C}^n$, say $|\mathcal{C}^n|$, proportions to $|\hbar|$ and size of vertices $|C|$ in LCM.

**Theorem 3.2.** *State space $\mathcal{C}^n$, generating by* $\mathbb{LCM}$ *with* $\mathbb{N}$ *vertices, using* $\hbar$
*hedges is:*

$$|\mathcal{C}^n| = |\hbar|^{\mathbb{N} \times |\hbar|} \tag{10}$$

*Proof.* It is straightforward to prove Theorem 3.2 by using combinatory algebra.
$\hbar$ hedges produce $|\hbar|^{|\hbar|}$ combinations which are hedges string with length $= |\hbar|$.
$\mathbb{LCM}$ has $\mathbb{N}$ vertices, $|\hbar|^{|\hbar|}$ cases for each vertex, apply the rule of product, we
have $\overbrace{|\hbar|^{|\hbar|} \times |\hbar|^{|\hbar|} \times \ldots \times |\hbar|^{|\hbar|}}^{\mathbb{N} \ times} = |\hbar|^{\mathbb{N} \times |\hbar|}$. $\qquad\square$

## 4   Discussion and Future Work

We have introduced a new graphical model for representing fuzzy knowledge
using linguistic variables from $\mathbb{HA}$. Our model, called $\mathbb{LCM}$, extended from $\mathbb{FCM}$,
is a dynamical system with two properties: static and dynamic. Static proper-
ties allow forward or what-if inferencing between concepts on linguistic domain.
Especially, we indicate inverse proportion relationship between length of hedges
string and a number of partitions in representing fuzzy knowledge.

Dynamic behaviors are transformation states in state space $\mathcal{C}^n = \{\mathcal{C}\}_0^n = \{\mathcal{C}(0), \mathcal{C}(1), \ldots, \mathcal{C}(n)\}$, where $\mathcal{C}(i) = \{C_1(i), C_2(i), \ldots, C_{\mathbb{N}}(i)\}, i = \overline{0, n}$. We also
prove the theorem about the number of states in state space is $|\mathcal{C}^n| = |\hbar|^{\mathbb{N} \times |\hbar|}$,
this is the important theorem to decide whether or not installable computer
programs.

Our next study is as follow: Let $A = \{\hbar^n : \hbar^n = h_n h_{n-1} \ldots h_1 h_0$ with $h_i \in
H, i = \overline{0, n}\}$ be a string of hedges. Assume $I = \mathcal{C}(0), T = \mathcal{C}(n)$ and $\mathcal{T} \subset \mathcal{C} \times A \times \mathcal{C}$
in order are initial, final and transition states. We will prove that $\mathbb{LCM}$ actions
are fuzzy linguistic automata $\mathcal{A} = <A, \mathcal{C}, I, \mathcal{T}, T>$.

## 5   Conclusion

A new visual method for modeling with words representations of fuzzy knowledge
based on $\mathbb{HA}$ has been proposed in this reseach paper. Our model has been shown
easily reading, understanding and presenting of human. Theorem on limiting
the hedges string length is clearly proved to reduce complexity in representing
method and counting on the number of states in state space of fuzzy $\mathbb{LCM}$ is
demonstrated with certainty.

## References

1. Kosko, B.: Fuzzy cognitive maps. Int. J. Man Mach. Stud. **24**, 65–75 (1986)
2. Osoba, O.A., Kosko, B.: Fuzzy cognitive maps of public support for insurgency and
   terrorism. J. Defense Model. Simul. Appl. Methodol. **14**(I), 17–32 (2017)
3. Glykas, M.: Fuzzy Cognitive Maps, Advances in Theory Tools and Applications.
   Springer, Heidelberg (2010). https://doi.org/10.1007/978-3-642-03220-2

4. Papageorgiou, E.I.: Fuzzy Cognitive Maps for Applied Science and Engineering From Fundamentals to Extensions and Learning Algorithms. Springer, Heidelberg (2014). https://doi.org/10.1007/978-3-642-39739-4
5. Zadeh, L.A.: Computing with words - Principal Concepts and Ideas. Studies in Fuzziness and Soft Computing. Springer, Heidelberg (2012). https://doi.org/10.1007/978-3-642-27473-2
6. Kacprzyk, J., Wilbik, A., Zadrożny, S.: Linguistic summarization of trends: a fuzzy logic based approach. In: The 11th International Conference Information Processing and Management of Uncertainty in Knowledge-based Systems, pp. 2166–2172 (2006)
7. Ho, N.C., Wechler, W.: Hedge algebras: an algebraic approach to structure of sets of linguistic truth values. Fuzzy Sets Syst. **35**, 281–293 (1990)
8. Ho, N.C., Van Long, N.: Fuzziness measure on complete hedge algebras and quantifying semantics of terms in linear hedge algebras. Fuzzy Sets Syst. **158**(4), 452–471 (2007)
9. Phuong, L.A., Khang, T.D.: Generalized if... then... else... inference rules with linguistic modifiers for approximate reasoning. Int. J. Comput. Sci. Issues (IJCSI) **9**(6), 184–190 (2012). No 3

# A Variable Neighborhood Search Algorithm for Solving the Steiner Minimal Tree Problem

Tran Viet Chuong[1(✉)] and Ha Hai Nam[2]

[1] The Center for Information Technology and Communication,
284 Tran Hung Dao Street, Ca Mau City, Vietnam
chuongtv@camau.gov.vn
[2] Research Institute of Posts and Telecommunications (RIPT),
122 Hoang Quoc Viet Street, Ha Noi City, Vietnam
namhh@ptit.edu.vn

**Abstract.** Steiner Minimal Tree (SMT) is a complex optimization problem that has many important applications in science and technology; This is a NP-hard problem. Much research has been carried out to solve the SMT problem using approximate algorithms. This paper presents a variable neighborhood search (VNS) algorithm for solving the SMT problem; The proposed algorithm has been tested on sparse graphs in a standardized experimental data system, and it yields better results than some other heuristic algorithms.

**Keywords:** Minimal tree · Sparse graph
Variable neighborhood search algorithm · Metaheuristic algorithm
Steiner minimal tree

## 1 Introduction

### 1.1 Definitions

This section presents several definitions and properties associated with the Steiner minimal tree problem.

**Definition 1.** *Steiner tree* [2]

Let's assume that $G = (V(G), E(G))$ is a simple undirected connected graph with non-negative weight on the edge; V (G) is the set of $n$ vertices, E (G) is a set of $m$ edges, $w(e)$ is the weight of edge $e$, $e \in E(G)$. Assume that $L$ is a subset of vertices of $V(G)$; *Tree T* passing through all vertices in $L$ is called *Steiner tree's L.*

The set $L$ is called the *terminal* set, the vertices in the set $L$ are called the *terminal* vertices; the vertices in the $T$ trees that are not in the set $L$ are called the Steiner vertices. Unlike most common spanning tree problems, the Steiner tree just passes through all the vertices in the terminal set $L$ and some other vertices in the set $V(G)$.

**Definition 2.** *Cost of Steiner tree* [2]

Let $T = (V(T), E(T))$ is a Steiner tree of graph $G$, cost of the tree $T$, denoted by $C(T)$, is the total weight of the edges of the tree $T$, i.e. $C(T) = \sum\limits_{e \in E(T)} w(e)$.

© ICST Institute for Computer Sciences, Social Informatics and Telecommunications Engineering 2019
Published by Springer Nature Switzerland AG 2019. All Rights Reserved
P. Cong Vinh and V. Alagar (Eds.): ICCASA 2018/ICTCC 2018, LNICST 266, pp. 218–225, 2019.
https://doi.org/10.1007/978-3-030-06152-4_19

**Definition 3.** *Steiner Minimal Tree* [2]

Given the graph *G*, the problem of finding Steiner Trees with Minimal Cost is defined as the Steiner Minimal Tree problem – SMT or more concisely as Steiner Tree Problem.

In this paper, the word *graph* is used to described a connected undirected graph with the non-negative weights.

## 1.2    Application of SMT Problem

The *SMT* problem has important applications in different fields of science and technology. For example, it has applications in network design, circuit layout...SMT problem is *NP-hard* [6, 7], and hence its applications shall be considered in two different perspectives: design and execution. Design problems favor the quality of the solution while running time is more prioritized for execution problems [1, 3, 8, 11].

## 1.3    Related Work

The *SMT* problem has attracted the academic attention of many scientists in the world over the past decades; There have been different algorithms for solving *SMT* problem that can be divided into the following approaches:

*The first approach* is the algorithms for finding the correct solution. Algorithms of this class are dynamic programming, augmented Lagrangian-based algorithms, Branch and Bound Algorithm, etc. One of the advantages of this approach is that correct solutions can be found. However, this class of algorithms is only suitable for the small-sized problems. The algorithms with correct solutions can be used for benchmarking the accuracy of approximation algorithms. Finding a correct solution to the *SMT* problem is a big challenge in combinatorial optimization theory [4, 6].

*The second approach* is the class of heuristic algorithms. Heuristic algorithms make use of individual experiences for finding solutions to a particular optimization problem. Heuristic algorithms yield acceptable solutions, which might not be the best solution, in the permissible time. Optimal running time can be achieved with this class of algorithms [9–11].

*The third approach* is of metaheuristic algorithms. The metaheuristic algorithms use a variety of heuristic algorithms in combination with auxiliary techniques to exploit the search space; The metaheuristic algorithm belongs to the class of optimal search algorithms. There have been already a number of different projects employed the metaheuristic algorithms for solving the SMT problem such as local search algorithms, Tabu search algorithms, genetic algorithms, parallel genetic algorithms, etc. Up to the present, the metaheuristic approach provides high quality solutions among approximation algorithms [13, 14]; However, the execution time of the metaheuristic algorithms is much slower than that of the heuristic algorithms.

This paper presents a metaheuristic approximation algorithm that is specifically a VNS algorithm for solving the *SMT* problem.

# 2   VNS Algorithm for Solving *SMT* Problem

## 2.1   Using the Variable Neighborhood Search Node-Base (Node-Based) [12]

**Input:** Let $G=(V(G),E(G))$ be an undirected graph with $V$ - a set of vertices, $E$ - a set of edges; $L \subseteq V$ - a set of terminal vertices.

**Output:** A minimum Steiner tree $T$

Use Like Prim's algorithm to search a spanning tree in the graph, T is a tree;

Remove redundant edges of T, then T is a Steiner tree, proceed as follows: With each Steiner tree $T$, browse all pendant vertices $u \in T$, if $u \notin L$, delete edge containing vertex $u$ from $E(T)$, delete vertex $u$ in $V(T)$ and update the vertex's degree which is adjacent to vertex $u$ in $T$. Repeat this procedure until $T$ is unchanged.

while (stop condition is not satisfied)
{

Let $T_1=T$;

Select random vertex $u \in T_1$; the vertex $u$ which doesn't belong to a set of terminal vertices $L$; then, remove the edges related to the vertex $u$ in $T_1$; when $T_1$ is divided into more connected parts; that graph is $T_2$.

Arrange the edges of the G – graph by ascendant weights, add the edges in the order sorted in $G$ to the graph $T_2$ until $T_2$ is a tree;

Remove redundant edges in $T_2$;

If the tree $T_2$ is lighter weight than $T$, replace $T$ by $T_2$; vice versa, if the tree $T_2$ is not created, let $T$ be $T_1$;
}

## 2.2   Path-Based Variable Neighborhood Search (Path-Based) [13]

A *key-node* is a *Steiner* node with *degree* of 3 at the lowest.

A key-path is one with all intermediate vertices (not be terminal vertex) with degree 2, the first and the last vertex of that path or belong to a set of terminal vertices or become a key-node.

Searching a random key-path proceeds as follows: Select a random edge in T; if the first and the last vertex are ones with degree 2 and they and Steiner vertices, add the next adjacent edge of that vertex until the first and the last vertex have degree not equal to 2 and they are not Steiner vertices, check if the path is a key-path or not. Stop if stop condition is met.

Using Like Prim's algorithm to search the Steiner of tree, T is a tree;

Remove redundant edges of T, then T is a Steiner tree;

while (stop condition is not satisfied)
{

Let $T_1=T$;

Suppose that $p$ is a random key-path; proceed removing $p$; then $T$ is divided into two components $T_a$ and $T_b$;

Select the minimum-weight edge which connects two components $T_a$ and $T_b$; suppose we have a new tree $T_2$.

If the tree $T_2$ is lighter weight than $T$, replace $T$ by $T_2$; vice versa, if $T_2$ doesn't exist, let $T$ be $T_1$;
}

## 2.3    Using VNS Algorithm to Solve SMT Problem

**Stop condition:** Stop condition is considered to be met if the best solution cannot be improved by after a predefined number of iterations t.

**Initial condition:** Each spanning tree is created by using Prim's algorithm described as: initialize a tree with a single vertex chosen arbitrarily from the graph. the algorithm will be iterated for n–1 times. In each iteration, grow the tree by adding a vertex that is adjacent to at least one vertex of the spanning tree without consideration of its weight and its connected edges to the spanning tree. This algorithm is named as *Like Prim's* algorithm.

*Like Prim (V,E)*
**Input**: Graph G = (V(G),E(G))
**Output**: Return a random spanning tree T = (V(T),E(T))
    1. Choose a vertex $u \in V(G)$;
    2. $V(T) = \{u\}$;
    3. $E(T) = \emptyset$;
    4. **while** $(|V(T)| < n)$ {
    5. Choose a vertex $v \in V(G) - V(T)$ v is an adjacent vertex of a vertex $z \in V(T)$;
    6.   $V(T) = V(T) \cup \{v\}$;
    7.   $E(T) = E(T) \cup \{(v, z)\}$;
    8. }
    9. **return** spanning tree *T*;


Run the Like Prim's algorithm separately for each connected component and/or connected components of the graph or to find the minimum spanning forest in heuristic and metaheuristic algorithm to solve SMT problem. The advantage of Like Prim's algorithm in comparison with heuristic algorithms in providing an initial solution is the variety of edges of the spanning tree. The quality of the initial population created by Like Prim's algorithm is not so good as that of the initial population created by heuristic algorithms. However, after the evolutionary process, spanning trees created by Like Prim's algorithm usually provide better quality solutions.

**Step – form of VNS algorithm to solve SMT problem**:

T is a spanning tree which is formed by Like Prim algorithm.

Remove redundant edges.

Get the Steiner tree by removing redundant edges in T;

While (The stop condition is not true)

{

    - Execute 2 variable neighborhood search Node-based and Path-based one by one;

    - Record the better solution;

    - While executing VNS algorithm, if a better solution is found, execute VNS algorithm from the beginning (after while loop) and vice versa, continue to the next VNS algorithm;

    - VNS algorithm stops when stop condition is met. The stop condition in this particularly algorithm is the number of iterations, which is 10*n in this case, n is the number of vertex in the graph.

}

Return to the best solution.

## 3    Experiments Experimental Environment

### 3.1    Experimental Data

Experiment has been conducted to evaluate related algorithms. 40 sets of data has been selected from the standard experimental database for benchmarking algorithms for solving the Steiner tree problem. The data set can be found at URL http://people.brunel. ac.uk/~mastjjb/jeb/orlib/steininfo.html [5]. 20 graphs are from group *steinc* and the other 20 graphs come from *steind*.

### 3.2    Experimental Environment

The Node-Base algorithm, Path-Based algorithm and VNS algorithm are implemented in C++, DEV C++ 5.9.2; experimented on a Virtual Server Windows server 2008 R2 Enterprise, 64bit, Intel(R) Xeon (R) CPU E5-2660 0 @ 2.20 GHz, RAM 4 GB.

### 3.3    Experimental Results and Evaluation

Experimental results of algorithms are given in Tables 1 and 2. The tables are structured as follows: The first column (Test) is the name of the data sets in the experimental data system; number of vertices (n), number of edges (m) and number of vertices in the terminal vertices ($|L|$) of each graph; The next column records the Steiner tree's cost value corresponding to the Node-based, Path-based and Variable Neighborhood Search algorithm (VNS).

With 20 sets of data in *steinc* group, the VNS algorithm offers better solution quality at 5%, equivalent quality at 95% in comparison with Node-based algorithm. The VNS algorithm offers better the solution quality at 20%, equivalent quality at 80% in comparison to Path-based algorithm.

With 20 sets of data in *steind* group, the VNS algorithm offers better solution quality at 10%, equivalent quality at 75% and worse quality at 15% in comparison with Node-based algorithm. The VNS algorithm offers better the solution quality at 35%, equivalent quality at 60% and worse quality at 5% in comparison to Path-based algorithm.

**Table 1.** Experimental algorithm results on the *steinc* graph group.

| Test | n | m | |L| | Node-based | Path-based | VNS |
|------|---|---|-----|------------|------------|-----|
| steinc1.txt | 500 | 625 | 5 | 85 | 85 | 85 |
| steinc2.txt | 500 | 625 | 10 | 144 | 144 | 144 |
| steinc3.txt | 500 | 625 | 83 | 754 | 754 | 754 |
| steinc4.txt | 500 | 625 | 125 | 1079 | 1079 | 1079 |
| steinc5.txt | 500 | 625 | 250 | 1579 | 1579 | 1579 |
| steinc6.txt | 500 | 1000 | 5 | 55 | 55 | 55 |
| steinc7.txt | 500 | 1000 | 10 | 102 | 103 | 102 |
| steinc8.txt | 500 | 1000 | 83 | 509 | 509 | 509 |
| steinc9.txt | 500 | 1000 | 125 | 707 | 707 | 707 |
| steinc10.txt | 500 | 1000 | 250 | 1093 | 1093 | 1093 |
| steinc11.txt | 500 | 2500 | 5 | 32 | 33 | 32 |
| steinc12.txt | 500 | 2500 | 10 | 46 | 46 | 46 |
| steinc13.txt | 500 | 2500 | 83 | 258 | 258 | 258 |
| steinc14.txt | 500 | 2500 | 125 | 323 | 323 | 323 |
| steinc15.txt | 500 | 2500 | 250 | 556 | 556 | 556 |
| steinc16.txt | 500 | 12500 | 5 | 11 | 11 | 11 |
| steinc17.txt | 500 | 12500 | 10 | 18 | 18 | 18 |
| steinc18.txt | 500 | 12500 | 83 | 116 | 116 | 115 |
| steinc19.txt | 500 | 12500 | 125 | 147 | 147 | 147 |
| steinc20.txt | 500 | 12500 | 250 | 267 | 268 | 267 |

**Table 2.** Experimental algorithm results on the *steind* graph group.

| Test | n | m | |L| | Node-based | Path-based | VNS |
|------|---|---|-----|------------|------------|-----|
| steind1.txt | 1000 | 1250 | 5 | 106 | 106 | 106 |
| steind2.txt | 1000 | 1250 | 10 | 220 | 220 | 220 |
| steind3.txt | 1000 | 1250 | 167 | 1565 | 1565 | 1565 |
| steind4.txt | 1000 | 1250 | 250 | 1935 | 1935 | 1935 |
| steind5.txt | 1000 | 1250 | 500 | 3250 | 3254 | 3250 |

*(continued)*

**Table 2.** (*continued*)

| Test | $n$ | $m$ | $|L|$ | Node-based | Path-based | VNS |
|------|-----|-----|-------|------------|------------|-----|
| steind6.txt | 1000 | 2000 | 5 | 68 | 70 | 67 |
| steind7.txt | 1000 | 2000 | 10 | 103 | 103 | 103 |
| steind8.txt | 1000 | 2000 | 167 | 1072 | 1077 | 1073 |
| steind9.txt | 1000 | 2000 | 250 | 1448 | 1449 | 1448 |
| steind10.txt | 1000 | 2000 | 500 | 2110 | 2111 | 2110 |
| steind11.txt | 1000 | 5000 | 5 | 29 | 29 | 29 |
| steind12.txt | 1000 | 5000 | 10 | 42 | 42 | 42 |
| steind13.txt | 1000 | 5000 | 167 | 501 | 502 | 501 |
| steind14.txt | 1000 | 5000 | 250 | 669 | 667 | 669 |
| steind15.txt | 1000 | 5000 | 500 | 1117 | 1120 | 1116 |
| steind16.txt | 1000 | 25000 | 5 | 13 | 13 | 13 |
| steind17.txt | 1000 | 25000 | 10 | 23 | 23 | 23 |
| steind18.txt | 1000 | 25000 | 167 | 228 | 228 | 228 |
| steind19.txt | 1000 | 25000 | 250 | 313 | 317 | 317 |
| steind20.txt | 1000 | 25000 | 500 | 537 | 539 | 539 |

## 4   Conclusions

In this paper, the VNS algorithm has been proposed to solve SMT problem; The proposed algorithm has been experimentally implemented and evaluated using 40 sets of data as sparse graphs in the standard experimental datasets. The experiment outcomes show promising results in which the solution quality provided by the proposed algorithm is significantly improved compared to Node-based and Path-based algorithm.

## References

1. Koster, A., Munoz, X.: Graphs and Algorithms in Communication Networks. Springer, Heidelberg (2010)
2. Wu, B.Y., Chao, K.: Spanning Trees and Optimization Problems. Chapman & Hall/CRC, Boca Raton (2004). pp. 158–165
3. Lu, C.L., Tang, C.Y.: The Full Steiner Tree Problem. Elsevier (2003). pp. 55–67
4. Una, D.D., Gange, G., Schachte, P., Stuckey, P.J.: Steiner tree problems with side constraints using constraint programming. In: Proceedings of the Thirtieth AAAI Conference on Artificial Intelligence (2016)
5. Beasley, J.E.: OR-Library: http://people.brunel.ac.uk/~mastjjb/jeb/orlib/steininfo.html. Accessed 2018
6. Laarhoven, J.W.V.: Exact and heuristic algorithms for the Euclidean Steiner tree problem. University of Iowa, Doctoral thesis (2010)
7. Caleffi, M., Akyildiz, I.F., Paura, L.: On the solution of the steiner tree NP-Hard Problem via Physarum BioNetwork, pp. 1092–1106. IEEE (2015)
8. Hauptmann, M., Karpinski, M.: A compendium on steiner tree problems, pp. 1–36 (2015)

9. Hougardy, S., Silvanus, J., Vygen, J.: Dijkstra meets Steiner: a fast exact goal-oriented Steiner tree algorithm. University of Bonn (2015)
10. Bosman, T.: A Solution Merging Heuristic for the Steiner Problem in Graphs Using Tree Decompositions, pp. 1–12. VU University Amsterdam, Netherlands (2015)
11. Cheng, X., Du, D.Z.: Steiner Trees in Industry, vol. 5, pp. 193–216. Kluwer Academic Publishers (2004)
12. Martins, S.L., Resende, M.G.C., Ribeiro, C.C., Pardalos, P.M.: A parallel grasp for the steiner tree problem in graphs using a hybrid local search strategy (1999)
13. Uchoa, E., Werneck, R.F.: Fast Local Search for Steiner Trees in Graphs (2010)
14. Ribeiro, C.C., Mauricio, C., Souza, D.: Tabu search for the steiner problem in graphs. Networks **36**, 138–146 (2000)

# Handling Missing Values for the CN2 Algorithm

Cuong Duc Nguyen$^{(\boxtimes)}$ ⓘ, Phuong-Tuan Tran ⓘ, and Thi-Thanh-Thao Thai ⓘ

HCMC University of Foreign Languages - Information Technology,
Ho Chi Minh City, Viet Nam
{cuong.nd,tuantranphuong,thao.ttt}@huflit.edu.vn

**Abstract.** Missing values are existed in several practical data sets. Machine Learning algorithms, such as CN2, require missing values in a data set be pre-processed. The estimated values of a missing value can be provided by Data Imputation methods. However, the data imputation can introduce unexpected information to the data set so that it can reduce the accuracy of Rule Induction algorithms. If missing values can be directly processed in Rule Induction algorithms, the overall performance can be improved. The paper studied the CN2 algorithm to propose a modified version, CN2MV, which is able to directly process missing values without preprocessing. Testing on 17 benchmarking data sets from the UCI Machine Learning Repository, CN2MV outperforms the original algorithm using data imputations.

**Keywords:** CN2 · Missing value · Rule induction · Data imputation

## 1 Introduction

Several practical data sets from research and industry have missing values (MV). MVs can be from non-response fields in surveys. Users can intentionally skip sensitive items, unintentionally bypass some difficult fields or be too busy to fill the full survey. MVs can also come from technical errors due to machine malfunction. Human errors in data inputting can also cause MVs.

The majority of Machine Learning and Data Mining classification algorithms can only process a complete data set, in which, a missing value has to be preprocessed by filling with a value, such as a mean, a pre-defined constant or a imputed value based on other available values. A research question is the difference in the criteria of missing-value preprocessing technique and the criteria of the main learning algorithm can decrease the overall performance. If the missing-value processing is integrated into the main learning algorithm, the whole efficiency may be improved.

This paper focuses on supporting CN2, a popular Rule Induction algorithm, with the capability of processing missing values during the learning process. In Sect. 2, techniques of processing missing values in data sets have been reviewed.

© ICST Institute for Computer Sciences, Social Informatics and Telecommunications Engineering 2019
Published by Springer Nature Switzerland AG 2019. All Rights Reserved
P. Cong Vinh and V. Alagar (Eds.): ICCASA 2018/ICTCC 2018, LNICST 266, pp. 226–234, 2019.
https://doi.org/10.1007/978-3-030-06152-4_20

CN2 is also reviewed in Sect. 2. Section 3 represents the CN2MV algorithm, the modified version of CN2. CN2MV will be tested with benchmarking data sets and compared with the CN2 in Sect. 4. Section 5 is the conclusion.

## 2  Related Work

### 2.1  Processing Missing Values by Data Imputations

Data Imputation (DI) is the well known technique to calculate an estimated value to replace for a MV. Several Machine Learning algorithms cannot process MVs directly so that DI are used to replace MVs in the pre-processing phase. The estimated value can be a constant, a mean or mode of an attribute, or the result from an estimation model. A deep review of DIs can be seen in Little and Roben's book [10].

The MV existence and the applying of DI methods has bold effects on the performance of Machine Learning algorithms. Incomplete data in either the training/test set or in both sets affects on the prediction accuracy of learned classifiers [3]. Wohlrab, Lars and Fürnkranz [16] studied possible strategies for handling missing values in separate-and-conquer rule learning algorithms, and compared them experimentally on a large number of datasets. The correlation between the data imputation methods and the classification algorithms are experimentally examined by Luengo et al. [11]. That study studies the impact of fourteen data imputation methods on three groups of classification algorithms: rule induction, approximate models and lazy learning. The experiment shows that, for each group of classification algorithms, there are different set of appropriate data imputation methods. Even in each group, a different set of data imputation methods supports a classification algorithm to achieve a good performance. Therefore, the correlation between imputation and learning models can decide the whole performance for classification methods.

Focusing on Rule Induction algorithms, this paper only studies data imputation methods, which provide the best results for Rule Induction algorithms in the Luengo research [11]. This subsection describe five imputation methods used in this paper.

- Case deletion or Ignore Missing (IM). In this method, all instances having a missing value are omitted from the data set. This simplest method is only suitable for data sets with a small percentage of missing values.
- Most Common Attribute Value for Symbolic Attributes, and Average Value for Numerical Attributes (MC) [4]. With this method, for nominal attributes, a missing value is replaced with the most common attribute value, and for numerical values, a missing value is replaced with the average value of the corresponding attribute. This method may be the most popular imputation technique.
- Concept Most Common Attribute Value for Symbolic Attributes, and Concept Average Value for Numerical Attributes (CMC) [4]. Similar as MC, a missing value is replaced by the most repeated one if nominal or the mean

value is numerical, but considering only the instances with the same class as the reference instance. This is an advanced method of MC when considering the class attribute of the imputed data instance.

– Imputation with Fuzzy K-means Clustering (FKMI) [8]. FKMI uses the membership function, which describes the degree to which this data object belongs to a certain cluster, and the values of cluster centroids, to impute a missing value.

– Support Vector Machines Imputation (SVMI) [5]. SVMI applies an SVM regression-based algorithm to fill in missing values.

## 2.2 Rule Induction

CN2 [1,2] is one of the most popular Rule Induction algorithms [14]. CN2, a typical Separate-and-Conquer algorithm, induces the best rule, called "complex" on the current training set, removes covered examples from the current training set, and repeat the process on the reduced training set until no more rules can be induced. To find the best complex, CN2 carries out a pruned general-to-specific beam search. At each stage or the search, CN2 examines the specializations of complexes in the current beam. CN2 evaluate specialized complexes by the rule's entropy (in [2]) or Laplace (in [1]). There are two versions of CN2 [1]: ordered (rules in the rule set are ordered in applying) and unordered (rules in the rule set are unordered in applying). As authors point out, the unordered rule set has much advantage than the ordered one.

The content of the unordered CN2 algorithm are shown in Fig. 1. CN2 induces rules for each class in the training set. For a class, CN2 consequently find the best complex and removes from the current training set all examples in the current class covered by the rule created by the best complex. This process is repeated until CN2 cannot find any best complex for the current class.

CN2-SD [7] is also a beam search Rule Induction algorithm, which adapts the CN2 classification rule learner to subgroup discovery. CN2-SD employs the original CN2 algorithm with the weighted relative accuracy to mine descriptive rules, so that the criterion of CN2-SD is not to maximize the predictive classification of the induced rule set. Using the same criterion with CN2-SD, DoubleBeam-SD [14] uses two separate beams and can combine various heuristics for rule refinement and selection to find rules with high descriptive capability.

Using the same classification criterion with CN2, DoubleBeam-RL [14] uses two separate beams and can combine various heuristics for rule refinement and selection, which widens the search space and allows for finding rules with improved classification capabilities.

Due to the time limit, the paper focus on showing the efficiency of integrating directly processing MVs in the learning process of CN2. The method can be applied on other CN2 versions.

```
procedure CN2unordered(allexamples,classes):
let ruleset={}
for each class in classes:
    generate rules by CN2ForOneClass(allexamples,class)
    add rules to rule set
return ruleset

procedure CN2ForOneClass(examples, class):
let rules={}
repeat
    call FindBestComplex(examples, class) to find bestcond
if bestcond is not null
then add the rule if bestcond then predict class to rules
    & remove from examples all examples in class covered by bestcond
Until bestcond is null
Return rules

procedure FindBestComplex(examples E, class C)
Let STAR be the set containing the empty complex
Let BEST_CPX be nil
While STAR is not empty,
    Specialize all complexes in STAR as follows:
    Let NEWSTAR be the set {x ∧ y|x ∈ STAR, y ∈ SELECTORS}
    Remove all complexes in NEWSTAR that are either in STAR (i.e., the unspecialized ones)
        or null (e.g., big = y ∧ big = n)
    For every complex Cᵢ in NEWSTAR:
        If Cᵢ is statistically significant and better than BEST_CPX by user-defined criteria
            when tested on E,
        Then replace the current value of BEST_CPX by Cᵢ
    Repeat until size of NEWSTAR ≤ user-defined maximum:
        Remove the worst complex from NEWSTAR
    Let STAR be NEWSTAR
Return BEST_CPX
```

**Fig. 1.** The CN2 induction algorithm [1]

## 2.3 Processing Missing Data During Learning Process of Learning Algorithms

There is only a few attempts in processing MVs in ID3 [12]. The approaches dealing with missing values in decision tree induction can be characterized by three groups [6] as follows:

1. Evaluation of a test (in a tree node): This concerns the strategy of how to evaluate different tests when each attribute has a different amount of missing values.
2. Partitioning the training set using a test: This relates to the strategy assigning a case with missing value on an attribute considered in a test.
3. Classifying a new case with unknown value of a tested attribute: This is correspondent to the application of the learned classifier.

Quinlan [13] proposed a method to adopt the ID3 algorithm to process missing values by making changes in evaluating a decision, partitioning data subsets and classifying a new unseen data instance. In comparing the performance several modified versions of ID3, the version with changes in the learning process when processing missing values achieved the best result. In the best version, the Information Gain is reduced by the percentage of missing values in evaluating a decision, a fraction of each data instance with a missing value is assigned to data subsets and when classifying a unseen data instance with a missing value, that data object is considered on all branches of a decision. The experiments of Quinlan's research also shows the versing with modifying the learning process achieves better results than versions using missing-value pre-processing techniques, such as mean replacement or data imputation, the modified version of ID3 achieved the lowest average error.

## 3   Integrating Missing-Value Processing into CN2

In CN2, the four following problems have to be addressed when processing MVs:

1. Generate set SELECTORS. Procedure "FindBestComplex" in CN2 creates NEWSTAR by combining current complexes in the beam with complexes in SELECTORS. An imputed value of a MV can make the CN2 generate unwanted complex in SELECTORS.
2. Evaluation of a complex. Every complex $C_i$ is evaluated by the Laplace measurement. If the training set has several MVs, which are imputed in the preprocessing step, the score of a complex can be incorrectly measured.
3. Remove covered positives instances by the "bestcond" in procedure "CN2ForOneClass". When a new rule is induced and added to the rule set, CN2 removes from "examples" (the current training set) all examples in "class" (the current class) covered by the rule. If an example has a MV, which is imputed in the preprocessing step, it can be accidentally covered by the rule.
4. Classify an unseen instance. The final output of CN2 is a rule set. When classifying an unseen data sample x having an imputed value for a MV, x can be wrongly classified by that imputed value.

The paper introduces CN2MV, an improved version of CN2, with four changes. The main content of CN2MV is similar to CN2 (see Fig. 1) but changes are made in its implementation to address four mentioned problems. CN2MV induces rules from a data set having MVs without data imputation. The four changes are made as follows:

1. Generate set SELECTORS: If any attribute-value pair has a MV, it is not used in generating SELECTORS. For instances, with an example as $(V_1 = A_1, V_2 =?, V_3 = A_3)$, the pair of $(V_2 =?)$ is not used in generating conditions.
2. Evaluation of a complex: When evaluating a complex, a MV can be any value in the corresponding attribute. When checking the covering of rule $(if\ V_1 = A_1\ and\ V_2 = A_2\ then...)$ on example $(V_1 = A_1, V_2 =?, V_3 = A_3)$, the result is true in such cases.
3. Mark covered instances by the "bestcond" in procedure "CN2ForOneClass": When checking whether a data sample is covered by a complex, a MV can be any value in the corresponding attribute (similar approach as "Evaluation of a comple").
4. Classify an unseen instance: Similar approach as in evaluating a complex is used.

In these four changes, the first modification help CN2MV avoid generating complexes from imputed data. The second change improves the complex evaluation when treating MVs as unknown values. Similar approach in the MV treatment are used in the third and four changes. Especially, the fourth change is more natural in treating MVs in unseen data than using DI methods. Each un-seen data in the testing set independently enter the learned classifier, no information for DI methods to estimate the value for MVs. In addition, supervised DI methods, such as CMC or SVMI, cannot be used because the class/concept of a sample is unknown in the testing set.

# 4   Experiment

## 4.1   Data Sets

To evaluate new algorithms, 17 benchmarking data sets are selected from the UCI Machine Learning repository [9]. The characteristics of selected data sets are described in Table 1. These data sets are selected due to the existence of MVs. For data sets without MVs, the modifications proposed in CN2MV have no effect, so that the performances of CN2 and CN2MV are the same.

**Table 1.** Benchmarking data sets used in the experiments

| Data set | Acro. | #Inst. | #Attr. | #Cls | %MV | %Inst. with MV |
|----------|-------|--------|--------|------|-----|----------------|
| Audiology | AUD | 226 | 71 | 24 | 1.98 | 98.23 |
| Autos | AUT | 205 | 26 | 6 | 1.11 | 22.44 |
| Bands | BAN | 540 | 40 | 2 | 4.63 | 48.7 |
| Breast-cancer | BRE | 286 | 10 | 2 | 0.31 | 3.15 |
| Breast-w | BRW | 699 | 10 | 2 | 0.23 | 2.29 |
| Cleveland | CLE | 303 | 14 | 5 | 0.14 | 1.98 |
| Colic | COL | 368 | 23 | 2 | 22.77 | 98.10 |
| Credit-a | CRA | 690 | 16 | 2 | 0.61 | 0.61 |
| Dermatology | DER | 365 | 35 | 6 | 0.06 | 2.19 |
| Heart-c | HRC | 303 | 14 | 5 | 4.73 | 34.09 |
| Hepatitis | HEP | 155 | 20 | 2 | 5.39 | 48.39 |
| Labor | LAB | 57 | 17 | 2 | 33.64 | 98.24 |
| Mammographic | MAM | 961 | 6 | 2 | 2.81 | 13.63 |
| Mushroom | MUS | 8124 | 23 | 2 | 1.33 | 30.53 |
| Primary tumor | PRT | 339 | 18 | 21 | 3.69 | 61.06 |
| Soybean | SOY | 307 | 36 | 19 | 6.44 | 13.36 |
| Vote | VOT | 435 | 17 | 2 | 5.30 | 46.67 |

## 4.2    Settings of Experiments

The CN2MV algorithm is implemented in the Weka framework [15]. Each numeric attributes are discretized by the ten uniform-bin method. Because Weka only has a few Data Imputation methods, 5 mentioned imputation methods are carried out in the KEEL framework [11] on the training sets. The imputed data sets will be imported to Weka to execute the CN2 algorithm.

Table 2 shows the parameters used by applied imputation methods (see Sect. 2.1). These parameters are default values set up in KEEL.

**Table 2.** Method Parameters

| Methods | Parameters |
| --- | --- |
| SVMI | Kernel = RBF, C = 1.0, Epsilon = 0.001, Shrinking = No |
| FKMI | K = 3, Iterations = 100, Error = 100, m = 1.5 |
| CN2 & CN2MV | Max length of complex = 2, Beam size = 5 |

## 4.3    Results

Table 3 shows the error rates of tested CN2 versions in the ten-fold cross-validation. CN2MV achieves the best result on 11 of 17 tested data sets. Specially, on data set Bands, Colic, and Labor, CN2MV has much better results than others from CN2 using data imputation methods in preprocessing MVs.

Table 3 also shows that CN2MV achieves the best average result when comparing with other methods. Method IM-CN2 has the poorest results, especially on data sets with high percentage instances with MVs (Audiology, Bands, Colic, Labor and Primary tumor) because they omits much valuable information from the training set. Method SVMI-CN2 achieves the second best average result but it has one shared best result.

**Table 3.** Average error rates of tested methods

| Data set | CN2MV (%) | IM-CN2 (%) | MC-CN2 (%) | CMC-CN2 (%) | FKMI-CN2 (%) | SVMI-CN2 (%) |
|---|---|---|---|---|---|---|
| AUD | **33.10** | 98.26 | 35.36 | 39.35 | 35.36 | 38.50 |
| AUT | **22.93** | 29.17 | 23.86 | 26.74 | 23.86 | 26.31 |
| BAN | **28.56** | 38.02 | 39.68 | 38.20 | 39.68 | 37.10 |
| BRE | **31.81** | 32.52 | 34.25 | 34.25 | 34.25 | 34.25 |
| BRW | 6.58 | **5.44** | 5.87 | 5.73 | 5.87 | 5.87 |
| CLE | 43.27 | 42.26 | 41.30 | **41.29** | 41.30 | 41.97 |
| COL | **16.52** | 36.95 | 19.27 | 24.73 | 19.27 | 20.35 |
| CRA | **13.33** | 15.07 | 13.91 | 13.91 | 13.91 | 14.49 |
| DER | **6.00** | **6.00** | 6.82 | 6.55 | 6.82 | 6.82 |
| HRC | 22.35 | 22.38 | 21.40 | 22.04 | **21.40** | 23.05 |
| HEP | 18.75 | 18.63 | 18.79 | **14.92** | 18.79 | 16.17 |
| LAB | **17.67** | 64.67 | 37.33 | 33.00 | 37.33 | 24.67 |
| MAM | 18.00 | 18.21 | **17.69** | 18.21 | 17.69 | 18.21 |
| MUS | **0.00** | 16.94 | 0.18 | 0.18 | 0.18 | 0.18 |
| PRT | **54.88** | 59.57 | 56.35 | 59.29 | 56.35 | 56.66 |
| SOY | **17.87** | 27.24 | 18.74 | 19.47 | 18.74 | 18.58 |
| VOT | **4.14** | 5.05 | 4.37 | 4.37 | 4.37 | **4.14** |
| Avg | **19.97** | 30.03 | 22.17 | 22.60 | 22.17 | 21.77 |

## 5 Conclusion

The paper proposed the CN2MV algorithm, which is able to directly process missing values without data imputation in preprocessing. Four main changes has been proposed to efficiently process missing values during the rule inducing process. Testing on 17 benchmarking data sets from the UCI Machine Learning Repository, the modified versions outperformed the original algorithms using data imputation techniques to pre-process missing values.

## References

1. Clark, P., Boswell, R.: Rule induction with CN2: some recent improvements. In: Kodratoff, Y. (ed.) EWSL 1991. LNCS, vol. 482, pp. 151–163. Springer, Heidelberg (1991). https://doi.org/10.1007/BFb0017011
2. Clark, P., Niblett, T.: The CN2 induction algorithm. Mach. Learn. **3**(4), 261–283 (1989)
3. Gheyas, I.A., Smith, L.S.: A neural network-based framework for the reconstruction of incomplete data sets. Neurocomputing **73**(16), 3039–3065 (2010)

4. Grzymala-Busse, J.W., Goodwin, L.K., Grzymala-Busse, W.J., Zheng, X.: Handling missing attribute values in preterm birth data sets. In: Ślęzak, D., Yao, J.T., Peters, J.F., Ziarko, W., Hu, X. (eds.) RSFDGrC 2005. LNCS (LNAI), vol. 3642, pp. 342–351. Springer, Heidelberg (2005). https://doi.org/10.1007/11548706_36
5. Honghai, F., Guoshun, C., Cheng, Y., Bingru, Y., Yumei, C.: A SVM regression based approach to filling in missing values. In: Khosla, R., Howlett, R.J., Jain, L.C. (eds.) KES 2005. LNCS (LNAI), vol. 3683, pp. 581–587. Springer, Heidelberg (2005). https://doi.org/10.1007/11553939_83
6. Latkowski, R.: High computational complexity of the decision tree induction with many missing attribute values. In: Proceedings of Concurrency, Specification and Programming, CS&P 22, pp. 318–325 (2003)
7. Lavrač, N., Kavšek, B., Flach, P., Todorovski, L.: Subgroup discovery with CN2-SD. J. Mach. Learn. Res. 5, 153–188 (2004)
8. Li, D., Deogun, J., Spaulding, W., Shuart, B.: Towards missing data imputation: a study of fuzzy k-means clustering method. In: Tsumoto, S., Słowiński, R., Komorowski, J., Grzymała-Busse, J.W. (eds.) RSCTC 2004. LNCS (LNAI), vol. 3066, pp. 573–579. Springer, Heidelberg (2004). https://doi.org/10.1007/978-3-540-25929-9_70
9. Lichman, M.: UCI machine learning repository (2013). http://archive.ics.uci.edu/ml
10. Little, R.J., Rubin, D.B.: Statistical Analysis with Missing Data. Wiley, Chicester (2002)
11. Luengo, J., García, S., Herrera, F.: On the choice of the best imputation methods for missing values considering three groups of classification methods. Knowl. Inf. Syst. 32(1), 77–108 (2012)
12. Quinlan, J.R.: Induction of decision trees. Mach. Learn. 1(1), 81–106 (1986)
13. Quinlan, J.R.: Unknown attribute values in induction. In: Proceedings of the International Machine Learning Workshop, pp. 164–168 (1989)
14. Valmarska, A., Lavrač, N., Fürnkranz, J., Robnik-Šikonja, M.: Refinement and selection heuristics in subgroup discovery and classification rule learning. Expert Syst. Appl. 81, 147–162 (2017)
15. Witten, I.H., Frank, E., Hall, M.A., Pal, C.J.: Data Mining: Practical Machine Learning Tools and Techniques, 4th edn. Morgan Kaufmann, San Mateo (2016)
16. Wohlrab, L., Fürnkranz, J.: A review and comparison of strategies for handling missing values in separate-and-conquer rule learning. J. Intell. Inf. Syst. 36(1), 73–98 (2011)

# Author Index

Printed in the United States
by Bookmasters

Printed in the United States
By Bookmasters